A Basket Currency for Asia

The failure of the dollar peg to prevent the Asian currency crisis of 1997 to 1998 has highlighted the importance of the exchange rate regime in Asia and provoked much discussion as to what the alternatives are in terms of exchange rate systems.

Bringing together extensive research on Asian basket currencies in one volume, this new text discusses whether a currency basket system is the answer, striking a balance between the theoretical and empirical. With strong policy implications for East Asia, the impressive team of contributors argue that for countries that have close economic relationships with several currency areas, it is well worth considering a currency basket system. The book also pursues the important idea of coordination failure, whereby if each individual country tries to adopt an optimal exchange rate given other neighbouring countries' policies, they may collectively fail to reach a region's optimal exchange rate regime.

A Basket Currency for Asia offers topical and original material that will be an invaluable resource to students and scholars of international finance and Asian economics.

Takatoshi Ito is Professor in the Graduate School of Economics and the Graduate School of Public Policy at the University of Tokyo, Japan.

Routledge Studies in the Growth Economies of Asia

A Basket Currency for Asia

Edited by Takatoshi Ito

Routledge
Taylor & Francis Group

LONDON AND NEW YORK

First published 2007
by Routledge
2 Park Square, Milton Park, Abingdon, Oxon OX14 4RN

Simultaneously published in the USA and Canada
by Routledge
270 Madison Avenue, New York, NY 10016

Routledge is an imprint of the Taylor & Francis Group, an informa business

Typeset in Times New Roman by Keyword Group Ltd
Printed and bound in Great Britain by Biddles Ltd, King's Lynn

British Library Cataloguing in Publication Data
A catalogue record for this book is available from the British Library

Library of Congress Cataloging in Publication Data
A catalogue record for this book has been requested

ISBN 10: 0-415-38376-5 (hbk)
ISBN 10: 0-203-96696-1 (ebk)
ISBN 13: 978-0-415-38376-9 (hbk)
ISBN 13: 978-0-203-96696-9 (ebk)

Contents

List of figures

List of tables

List of contributors

ITO, Takatoshi. Professor, Institute of Economic Research, Hitotsubashi University, Tokyo, Japan.

OGAWA, Eiji. Professor, Department of Commerce and Management, Hitotsubashi University, Tokyo, Japan.

FUKUDA Shin-ichi. Professor, Faculty of Economics, University of Tokyo, Japan.

SASAKI, Yuri Nagataki. Department of Economics, Takachiho University.

KAWASAKI Kentaro. Faculty of Business Administration, Tokyo University.

SHIMIZU, Junko. COE Research Associate, Institute of Economic Research, Hitotsubashi University, Tokyo, Japan.

Preface

Economic integration among the East Asian countries has made remarkable progress in the last decade. Trade and investment among the economies in the region have increased more than those with other regions. However, advances in economic integration has not been without challenges and difficulties. Among others, the Asian currency crisis of 1997–98 set back many of the economies in the region. Economic growth rates declined sharply, into a negative territory for many countries, in 1998, and many banks in the region became insolvent, failed, or significantly weakened for several years.

One of the factors that caused the Asian currency crisis was the *de facto* dollar peg regime that had been adopted by many Asian countries before the crisis. The exchange rate was consciously managed to keep a stable nominal bilateral exchange rate to the US dollar. Several countries, including Thailand, Malaysia, and Korea, were experiencing large capital inflows that more than financed current account deficits. For example, in 1996 Thailand was experiencing current account deficits up to 8 percent of the GDP, while capital inflows were about 10 percent of the GDP, resulting in an increase of foreign reserves by 2 percent of the GDP. Most of capital inflows were short-term, building up currency risk on balance sheets of banks and corporations. When capital flows reversed its direction in 1997, central banks could not prevent the exchange rates from falling without limit. In the second half of 1997, most East Asian currencies, except Chinese yuan and Hong Kong dollar, lost more than half of their value vis-à-vis the US dollar.

The *de facto* dollar peg before the crisis had contributed to building up vulnerabilities to the East Asian economies through two channels, the current account channels and the capital account channels. First, since the exchange rate stability was pursued vis-à-vis the US dollar, the competitiveness of export sectors was subject to fluctuations of non-dollar currencies that are relevant to the country's exports and imports. For example, the devaluation of the Chinese yuan in 1994 weakened sectors that competed against the Chinese products in neighboring countries. Another example is the impact of the yen/dollar fluctuation on exports from East Asian countries. The yen appreciation from 1994 to mid-1995 was one of the factors behind the export boom from some Asian countries, while the yen depreciation from mid-1995 to mid-1997 depressed exports in 1996 to mid-1997.

The decrease in exports subdued the economy and contributed to the weakening confidence of foreign investors. Second, the *de facto* dollar peg made the foreign investors and domestic borrowers almost ignore the currency risk. The foreign investors were attracted to high interest rates of bank deposits and high returns in the securities markets in the emerging markets in Asia, with apparently little risk of exchange rate depreciation. They deposited in banks in local currencies and purchased short-term corporate papers denominated in local currencies. Corporations and banks of the emerging market economies also willingly borrowed from foreign banks in US dollars that carried lower interest rates, while they invested in long-term projects in the local markets. The strategy of borrowing from abroad and investing domestically resulted in currency mismatch on their balance sheets, that is, with respect to assets in the local currency and liabilities in the US dollar.

Due to the Asian currency crisis of 1997 and 1998, many Asian countries were forced to float their currencies. Once floated, most countries maintained the managed float regime even after the crisis was long gone. A conspicuous exception was Malaysia that went back to the dollar peg in September 1998. Politicians and officials in these countries realized that the *de facto* peg was a mistake, but could not agree on what could be an alternative regime. In many policy and academic discussions, some economists have proposed an idea of basket currency as an appropriate regime for East Asian countries. The list of basket currency advocates includes John Williamson, Agnès Bénassy-Quéré, and several Japanese economists, most of whom have been invited as authors in this volume. The key component of the basket currency idea is to use the value of the weighted average of the trading partner's exchange rates as a reference point of the exchange rate policy. Most proposals include a feature to allow a fluctuation band around the reference point. The reference point moves automatically if it is valued against the US dollar. Therefore, Williamson called his proposal a basket, band, and crawl (BBC). Details of the basket band—how many currencies should be included in the band, how wide the band should be, and how hard the band floor or ceiling should be defended when challenged, vary width, commitment to defend the band floor or ceiling—vary from one proposal to another. A major benefit of having a basket is to have some reference point for stability—stability for stable export competitiveness—while risk of fluctuation—a central rate vis-à-vis the US dollar, as well as the basket rate within the band—is realized. Since trading partners include the United States, Japan, and Europe, as well as neighboring countries, the basket proposal is particularly attractive to East Asian countries.

Immediately after the crisis, there were many international conferences and meetings that proposed a new financial architecture in order to increase the stability of international monetary system. The topics discussed in these conferences included the governance of the International Monetary Fund (IMF) and a framework for regional cooperation. One of the important topics that invited an intense discussion, but resulted in no consensus was the question of an appropriate exchange rate regime for East Asian countries. Among the academic economists, a basket system as a desired regime for Asian emerging market economies has gained support. In policy discussions of regional meetings by officials—typically

Ministry of Finance and central bank officials—there has been a keen interest in the basket system. One example is the Discussion Paper jointly prepared by French and Japanese staff presented to the 3rd Asia-Europe Finance Ministers' Meeting (ASEM) held in Kobe in 2001. The paper was cautious on the benefit of the currency board arrangement that was favored by the IMF and US economists as one alternative to the implicit dollar peg. The Japanese–French paper instead emphasized potential benefits of a managed float system, in particular the basket currency regime, backed by consistent and sustainable macroeconomic and structural policies.

After the ASEM meeting, the Ministry of Finance, Japan, commissioned a study on the exchange rate regimes that would be appropriate for the East Asian region. The project became known as the Kobe Research Project. Many of the papers contained in this volume originate its foundation in the Kobe Research Project. After the Kobe Research Project was completed, our research continued in research agenda of each author, with various research supports.

Although theoretical benefits of basket regime were convincing, practical skepticism remained among officials. Once the Governor of the central bank in the region mentioned to me that the basket system is difficult to explain to the public. However, practically several currencies in the region, typically Singaporean dollar, Thai baht, and Korean won, have fluctuated with a feature of basket currencies since 1999. However, the estimated weights on the dollar, the yen, and the euro, have varied across countries and periods of time. However, regional cooperation in the exchange rate policy had remained difficult because China, Hong Kong, and Malaysia had maintained the explicit dollar peg even after the currency crisis. The neighboring countries, such as Thailand, Korea, and Malaysia, adopting the basket regime had to increase the dollar weight because some major trading partners like China and Malaysia had adopted the dollar peg, namely belonging to the dollar zone.

However, a major change occurred in July 2005. Both China and Malaysia announced their abandonment of the dollar peg and moved to a managed float. Moreover, China announced that they would manage the yuan with reference to the basket value. This will probably be regarded as the first step toward a regional basket regime.

If all East Asian countries were to employ a basket regime based on a common basket of currencies, the regional exchange rate system would become extremely solid. China's dollar peg was a major obstacle to such enhanced regional monetary cooperation. With the obstacle removed, East Asian government officials responsible for the exchange rate policy should deepen their discussions on monetary cooperation.

This volume aims at being a comprehensive book of a basket currency proposal, including a reprint of a seminal paper on this subject followed by original contributions to this subject. With this volume, the essential elements of the basket currency proposal in East Asia can be easily understood.

I am personally indebted to many people who encouraged me—sometimes critically as well as affirmatively—to continue research on the basket currency system and to carry out the editorship of this volume. Mr Kuroda, Former Vice Minister for International Affairs, Ministry of Finance (currently, President of Asian Development Bank), has been quite supportive of academic research and interaction between academics and policy makers. I have benefited from discussions with both economists and central bank executives for their wisdom and candid comments on their views on the foreign exchange markets in the past ten years. Just to name a few, Drs John Williamson, Agnès Bénassy-Quéré, and Yunjong Wang; Governor Zeti Akhtar Aziz of Bank Negara, Malaysia; Governor Pridiyathorn Devakula and Bandid Nijathaworn, Deputy Governor of Bank of Thailand; Anwar Nasution, the Former Deputy Governor of Bank Indonesia, Dr Kho Hoe Ee, Assistant Managing Director, Monetary Authority of Singapore; Joseph Yam, Chief Executive, Norman Chan, Former Deputy Chief Executive, and Julia Leung, Executive Director of Hong Kong Monetary Authority; and Li Ruogu, Deputy Governor of People's Bank of China.

Financial supports by Ministry of Education Aid for Science Research on Priority Area, Grant Number 12124203 and JSPS Grants-in-aid for Scientific Research, No. 15203008, for assembling chapters and editing them into this volume are gratefully acknowledged.

Takatoshi Ito
December 2005, Tokyo

1   Introduction

Takatoshi Ito

The Asian currency crisis of 1997–98 has taught many lessons to both scholars and policy makers around the world. One of these lessons concerns the exchange rate regime. East Asian countries chose to fix their currencies to the US dollar, whether explicitly as in Hong Kong's case, or implicitly as in Thailand's. Because East Asian countries have strong trade and investment ties with many other countries, including Japan, European countries, and the United States as well as their own neighboring countries, the *de facto* dollar peg was clearly inappropriate even before the Asian currency crisis. The dollar peg was inextricably tied to a boom-and-bust cycle, as the dollar was at times undervalued and at times overvalued against the yen and European currencies. The export boom and domestic over-investment of 1994–95 was followed by a bust in 1996–97, and this was one of the reasons Thailand fell into difficulties; capital inflows dried up and there was an attack on the baht. After the currency crisis, many Asian countries realized the problems that plagued the dollar peg and did not return to it. Once the worst of the crisis was over, many East Asian countries adopted a managed floating exchange rate regime, with the notable exceptions of Hong Kong, China, and Malaysia. Hong Kong has kept its dollar peg regime under a currency board system, and China has maintained a *de facto* dollar peg. Malaysia officially reverted back to the dollar peg system in September 1998, after using a floating exchange rate regime for a little more than a year.

Another currency crisis could occur if East Asian countries do not improve their exchange rate regimes and instruments for monitoring and controlling capital flows. Even though several years have passed since the Asian currency crisis, the matter of the choice of an exchange rate regime should still be a matter of urgency in East Asian countries. This book includes the proposals and a discussion of what the optimal exchange rate regime for East Asian countries might be. We still observe occasional turmoil in the exchange rate regimes of Latin American countries. New members of the European Union may face exchange-rate vulnerability until they are included in the euro area. Countries that have close economic relationships with several currency areas should consider a currency basket system. This group includes East Asian countries, Latin American countries such as Argentina, and Central European countries. This book provides suggestions that could be insightful for many emerging market countries that have trade and investment relationships with several currency areas.

Many economists and policy makers agree that fixed exchange rates are not appropriate for East Asian countries. So why not just float the currency rates? Emerging market economies tend to fear free floating for various reasons. Uncertainties about future exchange rates discourage domestic investment and inbound foreign direct investment. Policy makers in East Asian countries also fear speculative activity in their currency. These currency markets are small, and concerted actions by foreign-controlled funds can easily generate a potentially disruptive boom-and-bust pattern.

To avoid excessive fluctuations in currency value and export competitiveness, one natural choice would be a currency basket, which could minimize fluctuations in the real effective exchange rates. The reference rate (central rate) could be defined as the weighted average of the values of currencies of countries with which the country has significant trade and investment relationships. Policy makers would have the freedom to choose the currencies in the basket, the weighting of those currencies, and the target band within which they would try to limit movements.

This book is a collection of closely related papers on the theme of the basket currency regime. The papers investigate the kind of exchange rate regime that would be desirable for East Asian countries from several perspectives, including international trade and macroeconomic factors. Since the Asian currency crisis, academic economists and policy makers in Asia have been very interested in exchange rate regimes. Both in academic literature and in policy circles, the notion of a basket currency has been put forward as a sensible alternative to a *de facto* dollar peg or a floating exchange rate.

In fact, some East Asian countries, including Hong Kong, Malaysia (since September 1998), and China, have adopted either an official dollar peg system or a *de facto* dollar peg system even after the Asian currency crisis.[1] The interdependence that exists among East Asian countries may be one reason for the difficulty of choosing the optimal exchange rate regimes. For example, an optimal exchange rate regime for Thailand depends on the exchange rate regime of Singapore, and vice versa. Therefore, it is important to have regional cooperation among East Asian countries. If currency rates are left to the marketplace, East Asian countries may experience a coordination failure.

This book is the first collection of papers ever to focus on the basket currency system. The book is also unique in its balancing of theoretical and empirical work, with strong policy implications for East Asian countries. The book is focused firmly on the situation in Asia, with a number of empirical evidence and original ideas. The papers pursue the important idea of coordination failure—that is, the risk that if each country tries to adopt the exchange rate system best for itself alone, all may collectively fail to reach the exchange rate regime best for the region as a whole. To move from a bad equilibrium (dollar peg) to a good equilibrium (currency basket), regional cooperation is needed.

This book consists of seven chapters. Chapter 2 shows that the *de facto* dollar peg, which was the choice made by several East Asian countries before the Asian currency crisis, was actually a factor that contributed to the crisis. This chapter considers the type of exchange rate system that would be most desirable for East Asian countries from the viewpoint of international trade. A currency basket system would be best for East Asian countries that trade with Japan, Europe, and the United States as well as within the region. However, some East Asian countries have returned to the *de facto* dollar peg system since the currency crisis. Chapter 3 focuses on the impact that Malaysia's official adoption of the dollar peg system in 1998 had on neighboring countries' choice of exchange rate regime. Chapter 4 is a theoretical analysis of the difficulties each country in East Asia might face in choosing an exchange rate system, given the strong economic interdependence among them. Chapter 5 empirically analyzes the possibilities of coordination failure. The analytical results underscore the importance of international coordination in choosing an exchange rate system in East Asia. Chapter 6 considers a common currency basket to solve the problem of coordinating exchange rate systems, by comparing coordinated exchange rates with uncoordinated exchange rates. Chapter 7 considers the advantages and disadvantages of a common currency basket in Asia's bond markets, in terms of liquidity and foreign exchange risks. Chapter 8 investigates the possibility of creating a common currency basket in East Asia according to the Optimal Currency Area theory. It is shown that the ASEAN5 countries (Indonesia, Malaysia, the Philippines, Singapore and Thailand), plus South Korea and China might be able to form a common currency area, and that a common currency basket would be more applicable as an anchor currency than the US dollar if these countries choose this route.

Chapter 2 ('How did the dollar peg fail in Asia?'), which is a seminal work of this literature that first appeared as an article in the *Journal of the Japanese and International Economies*, shows that the *de facto* dollar peg was one cause of the Asian currency crisis of 1997. Monetary authorities in Thailand, for example, had announced as early as 1984 that their country would adopt a currency basket system. Swings in the yen/dollar exchange rate caused trade balances to fluctuate under the *de facto* dollar peg system. The depreciation of the Japanese yen against the US dollar, in particular, harmed the price competitiveness of East Asian nations' export products and slashed their export growth during 1995–1997. This chapter formalizes a theoretical model with a micro-economic foundation, to estimate the optimal weighting of the yen and the dollar in a currency basket to stabilize trade balances for some East Asian countries.

Chapter 3 ('Post-crisis exchange rate regimes in East Asia') considers the factors that affected the values of three ASEAN currencies—the ringgit, the Singapore dollar, and the baht—after the crisis, taking into account the interaction of exchange rate policies among the ASEAN countries. We explore why these East Asian currencies, which exhibited reduced correlation with the US dollar temporarily after the crisis, tended to revert back to *de facto* pegs against the US dollar in the late 1990s. After Malaysia adopted the dollar peg system in September 1998, both the Singapore dollar and the baht resumed their strong correlation with the US dollar and began to revert back to *de facto* dollar pegs. Most of these changes are explained well by the strong links among the ASEAN countries.

Chapter 4 ('On the desirability of a regional basket currency arrangement') is a theoretical consideration of how monetary authorities in East Asian countries face coordination failure in choosing an exchange rate system, focusing on the interdependence of the exchange rate policy. The theoretical model in Chapter 2 is extended to construct a theoretical model of exchange rate policy interaction between two countries, both of which export products to the United States and Japan as well as to neighboring countries. It shows that a country's best choice of exchange rate system (or weights in the basket) is dependent on its neighbor's. The dollar weights in the currency baskets of the two countries are a Nash equilibrium. The two countries may face coordination failure and be stuck with the dollar peg system instead of an optimal currency basket system. The core part of this chapter appeared in the *Journal of the Japanese and International Economies*, but the chapter in this book is an extended version of that article, explaining the theory in more detail.

Chapter 5 ('Economic interdependence and international coordination in East Asia') considers the necessity of coordination in exchange rate policy. The theoretical model developed in Chapter 5 is used to estimate weights for the US dollar in a possible currency basket for some East Asian countries. An empirical analysis is conducted to investigate whether monetary authorities would, in fact, face coordination failure in choosing an exchange rate system for the ASEAN5 countries, China, and Korea. The results of the analysis imply that the ASEAN countries and China are compelled to adopt the dollar peg system because they have an unstable equilibrium or coordination failure.

Chapter 6 ('A case for a coordinated basket for Asian countries') attempts to solve the coordination failure problem demonstrated in Chapters 2, 4, and 5 by considering possible forms of regional coordination for a common currency basket. It shows two ways to calculate the basket currency values for Asian countries, one without coordination and one with coordination. In the post-crisis period, a coordinated solution would have been better than an uncoordinated one, and our study indicates that a coordinated solution would have resulted in a greater appreciation of the regional currencies. Uncoordinated solutions resulted in large currency depreciation for other countries besides Indonesia, precipitated by the very large depreciation in Indonesia's currency. A coordinated solution would have resulted in a more stable exchange rate. In other words, the coordination would have produced more stable exchange-rate dynamics in the post-crisis period.

Chapter 7 ('A common currency basket in bond markets in East Asia') is a discussion of Asian bond markets, and considers the possible advantages and disadvantages of using a common currency basket rather than international currencies for issuing Asian bonds, taking into account liquidity and foreign exchange risks. Chapter 7 focuses on foreign exchange risks to investigate what kind of currency is desirable for bond issuers and investors. In addition, it considers liquidity in Asian bond markets. It concludes that currency-basket-denominated bonds could lessen foreign exchange risks, but might face lower liquidity under current conditions.

Chapter 8 ('Possibilities for the introduction of a currency basket in East Asia, from an OCA standpoint') uses a Generalized Purchasing Power Parity (G-PPP) model to investigate the possibility of creating a common currency basket in East Asia according to the Optimal Currency Area theory. It investigates which East Asian countries might be able to create a common currency area. Its conclusions are that the ASEAN5 countries, South Korea, and China might be able to form a common currency area, and that a common currency basket may be a better anchor currency than the US dollar if these countries form a common currency area.

Note

1 Although China and Malaysia declared their intention to abandon the dollar peg on July 21, 2005, their exchange rates have not fluctuated much between July and December 2005.

2 How did the dollar peg fail in Asia?[1]

Takatoshi Ito, Eiji Ogawa, and Yuri Nagataki Sasaki[2]

1. Introduction

The currency crises in Asia in 1997 highlighted the danger of the fixed exchange rate system. Four ASEAN currencies (the Thai baht, the Malaysian ringgit, the Indonesian rupiah, and the Philippine peso) all depreciated by 30–40 percent in the three months following the baht depreciation of July 2. Thailand asked International Monetary Fund (IMF) for a balance of payment support package in August. The IMF support ($4 billion) was complemented by Japan ($4 billion) and other Asian nations together with the World Bank and Asian Development Bank (ADB). In November, Indonesia asked the IMF, the World Bank, and the ADB to advise them on economic reform together with a support for a potential balance of payment gap. The Indonesian package by IMF, World Bank, and ADB was also complemented by a secondary line of support by Japan, the United States, and the Asian countries. In late November, Korea, after its currency depreciated sharply, asked for the IMF support. Also in November, the sharp decline in the Hong Kong stock market, which was caused by defending the fixed exchange rate based on the currency board, caused a worldwide turmoil. The crisis spread to Korea in November, and the IMF package was hastily put together in the first week of December. The crises in these countries deepened in December 1997 to January 1998, as the value of the Indonesian rupiah depreciated to a level one-sixth of the precrisis level, and other ASEAN currencies and the Korean won depreciated to a level half of the precrisis level.

One of the common factors among these crisis countries was the choice of a de facto dollar peg. Thailand has adopted a basket system, in which the value of the Thai baht is determined as a weighted average of major currencies. However, it was well-known that the US dollar had an overwhelming weight in the basket since 1985. Indonesia had adopted a slide system with a narrow band, where the slide was adjusted for the inflation rate difference between Indonesia and the United States. The Korean won had also maintained a stable value against the US dollar. The Hong Kong dollar has been backed by a currency board arrangement, and nominally pegged to the US dollar at HK $7.7–7.8 per US$, since 1984. Hence, most of these currencies have appreciated in the 'real' exchange rate sense, vis-à-vis the US dollar.

Moreover, these Asian countries in financial turmoil have substantial trade relationships with Japan. As the Japanese yen depreciated against the US dollar from April 1995 to the summer of 1997, and the real 'effective' exchange rates of these countries appreciated. Due to the appreciation, export competitiveness was lost. Thus exports from these countries declined and current account deficits increased in 1996–97. On a practical level, this story makes sense. However, in theory, this needs some examination.

To simplify, consider a case that the nominal exchange rates of (non-Japan) Asian countries are pegged to the US dollar, while Asian products compete with Japanese products in the US and Japanese markets. If the yen depreciates against the US dollar, demands for Asian goods will decline. However, if Asian countries would like to avoid the loss of competitiveness, the export prices (in baht, for example) can be cut instead of the exchange rate depreciation. Therefore, we need a framework in which prices are determined endogenously and adjusted imperfectly to the changes in the exchange rate.

It is easy to see that if Asian goods are perfect substitutes to Japanese and US goods in a one-good, two-country economy, then export prices will change inversely to the exchange rate changes. This can be called a case of perfect pass-through. The exchange rate regime, whether pegged to the dollar or freely floated, is irrelevant when prices are perfectly flexible with perfect competition for exported goods. However, if they compete with the Japanese goods in an oligopolistic market, then the exchange rate fluctuation will not be perfectly offset by the changes in export prices.

Moreover, Asian countries import from Japan parts of the products that are exported to Japan and the United States. The Japanese yen appreciation, therefore, has two different effects, increasing costs of semifinished goods and increasing competitiveness of exports.

In the early 1980s, a number of papers, including Bhandari (1985), Flanders and Helpman (1979), Flanders and Tishler (1981), Lipschitz and Sundararajan (1980), and Turnovsky (1982), studied the optimal currency basket. Based on some open macroeconomic model including export and import functions, these papers explored how variances of balance of payments or some other measures can be minimized when there are shocks to the exchange rates of trading partners. Bhandari (1985) and Turnovsky (1982) considered the question in a general equilibrium macromodel with capital mobility. However, a macroeconomic structure, such as consumption and export functions, is given without a microfoundation in these papers. The optimality is usually defined by minimizing variances of balance of payments or real income.

The present chapter is quite different from those papers in three respects. First, our model has the microfoundation; namely, the oligopolistic exporter maximizes its profits. Competition with exporters of other countries is modeled. Thus, the export price is endogenously determined in response to the exchange rates. Price 'stickiness' in our model is a result of optimizing behavior. Second, imports of parts (semifinished goods) are explicitly modeled. This reflects the cost aspects of the currency changes. Last, optimality in our model is to minimize the fluctuations, in terms of changes in the trade balances, which is equivalent to profits in our model. This criterion is slightly different from criteria adopted in other papers in the literature.

The rest of the chapter is organized as follows. Section 2 will present a theoretical oligopolistic competition model where prices are determined endogenously. Section 3 will use the above model to explore effects of the dollar peg on a trade balance of the ASEAN economy. Section 4 will derive an optimal peg weight to stabilize fluctuations in the trade balance. Section 5 summarizes the theoretical prediction of impacts of exchange rate changes on export volumes and export prices. Section 6 describes stylized facts on the movement of the exchange rates and trade flows. Theoretical predictions are tested in regressions in Section 7. Optimal peg weights are also calculated in this section. Section 8 concludes the chapter.

2.   The models

An ASEAN country is modeled as a one-sector economy where a representative firm assembles parts imported from Japan and the United States into manufactured products.[3] We assume that volumes of parts that the ASEAN firm imports from Japan and the United States are constant shares, ω_m and $1 - \omega_m$, respectively, of the total volumes. The firm is assumed to export its products to the Japanese and US markets. The model is similar to the pricing to market model of Marston (1990).[4]

We set up two competitive situations. The first situation is that each of the Japanese and US markets is modeled as a duopoly where the ASEAN firm competes against the Japanese firm (Model A). The second situation is that each of the Japanese and US markets is modeled as a duopoly one where the ASEAN firm competes against each local firm in the markets (Model B). That is, it competes against the Japanese firm in the Japanese market and against the US firm in the US market. The ASEAN, Japanese, and US firms have identical cost functions. We assume that each of the Japanese and US firms assembles its products with its domestic parts only. Each firm maximizes its profits in terms of its own home currency.

2.1.   Model A

Profits of the ASEAN firm in terms of the home currency π is calculated as

$$\pi = E^{A/Y} P_J^Y f(q_J) + E^{A/\$} P_{US}^\$ g(q_{US}) - E^{A/Y} P_m^Y \omega_m Q$$

$$- E^{A/\$} P_m^\$ (1 - \omega_m) Q - C(Q) \tag{1}$$

where P_J^Y denotes a price of the ASEAN firm's products in the Japanese market in terms of the yen; $P_{US}^\$$ denotes a price of the ASEAN firm's products in the US market in terms of the dollar; P_m^Y denotes a price of parts imported from Japan in terms of the yen; $P_m^\$$ denotes a price of parts imported from the United States in terms of the dollar; Q denotes output of the ASEAN products ($Q = f(q_J) + g(q_{US})$); $f(\bullet)$ denotes a demand function for the ASEAN products in the Japanese market ($f' < 0$); $g(\bullet)$ denotes a demand function for the ASEAN firm's products in the US market ($g' < 0$); $C(\bullet)$ denotes a cost function of the ASEAN firm ($C' > 0$, $C'' \geq 0$); $q_J \equiv P_J^Y / P_J^{Y*}$ denotes a relative price of the ASEAN products relative to the Japanese products in the Japanese market; $q_{US} \equiv P_{US}^\$ / P_{US}^{\$*}$ denotes a relative price of the ASEAN products relative to the Japanese products in the US market; P_J^{Y*} denotes a price of the Japanese products in the Japanese market in terms of the yen; $P_{US}^{\$*}$ denotes a price of the Japanese products in the US market in terms of the dollar; $E^{A/Y}$ denotes an exchange rate of the yen in terms of the ASEAN currency; and $E^{A/\$}$ denotes an exchange rate of the dollar in terms of the ASEAN currency.

From Equation (1), profit-maximizing prices of the ASEAN firm in the Japanese and US markets, respectively, are derived as

$$P_J^Y = \mu_J \left(\omega_m P_m^Y + (1 - \omega_m) \frac{E^{A/\$}}{E^{A/Y}} P_m^\$ + \frac{\overline{C}'}{E^{A/Y}} \right) \tag{2a}$$

$$P_{US}^\$ = \mu_{US} \left(\omega_m \frac{E^{A/Y}}{E^{A/\$}} P_m^Y + (1 - \omega_m) P_m^\$ + \frac{\overline{C}'}{E^{A/\$}} \right) \tag{2b}$$

where $\mu_J \equiv \frac{\varepsilon_J(q_J)}{\varepsilon_J(q_J)-1}$ denotes markups of the ASEAN products in the Japanese market; $\varepsilon_J \equiv -\frac{f'(q_J)q_J}{f(q_J)}$ denotes price elasticity of demand for the ASEAN products in the Japanese market; $\mu_{US} \equiv \frac{\varepsilon_{US}(q_{US})}{\varepsilon_{US}(q_{US})-1}$ denotes markups of the ASEAN products in the US market; and $\varepsilon_{US}(q_{US}) \equiv -\frac{g'(q_{US})q_{US}}{g(q_{US})}$ denotes price elasticity of demand for the ASEAN products in the US market. We assume that $\frac{d\varepsilon_J}{dq_J} > 0$, $\frac{d\mu_J}{dq_J} > 0$, $\frac{d\varepsilon_{US}}{dq_{US}} > 0$, and $\frac{d\mu_{US}}{dq_{US}} > 0$. For simplicity, we also assume that the marginal production costs are constant ($C'(Q) = \overline{C}'$).

We convert Equations (2a) and (2b) into a logarithm form,

$$\log P_J^Y = -\eta_J(\log P_J^Y - \log P_J^{Y*}) + \log \left(\omega_m P_m^Y + (1 - \omega_m) \frac{E^{A/\$}}{E^{A/Y}} P_m^\$ + \frac{\overline{C}'}{E^{A/Y}} \right) \tag{2a'}$$

$$\log P_{US}^\$ = -\eta_{US}(\log P_{US}^\$ - \log P_{US}^{\$*}) + \log \left(\omega_m \frac{E^{A/Y}}{E^{A/\$}} P_m^Y + (1 - \omega_m) P_m^\$ + \frac{\overline{C}'}{E^{A/\$}} \right) \tag{2b'}$$

where $\eta_J \equiv -\frac{\mu'_J q_J}{\mu_J} > 0$ denotes price elasticity of the markups of the ASEAN

products in the Japanese market and $\eta_{US} \equiv -\frac{\mu'_{US} q_{US}}{\mu_{US}} > 0$ denotes price elasticity of the markups of the ASEAN products in the US market.

We derive reaction functions of the ASEAN firm in the Japanese and US markets given the prices of the products made in Japan, respectively.

$$\log P_J^Y = \frac{\eta_J}{1+\eta_J} \log P_J^{Y*} + \frac{1}{1+\eta_J} \log \left(\omega_m P_m^Y + (1-\omega_m) \frac{E^{A/\$}}{E^{A/Y}} P_m^\$ + \frac{\overline{C}'}{E^{A/Y}} \right) \tag{3a}$$

$$\log P_{US}^\$ = \frac{\eta_{US}}{1+\eta_{US}} \log P_{US}^{\$*} + \frac{1}{1+\eta_{US}} \log \left(\omega_m \frac{E^{A/Y}}{E^{A/\$}} P_m^Y + (1-\omega_m) P_m^\$ + \frac{\overline{C}'}{E^{A/\$}} \right) \tag{3b}$$

Profits of the Japanese firm in terms of the yen π^* are calculated as follows:

$$\pi^* = P_J^{Y*} f^*(1/q_J) + \frac{E^{A/\$} P_{US}^{\$*} g^*(1/q_{US})}{E^{A/Y}} - P_m^Y Q^* - C(Q^*) \tag{4}$$

where $Q^* = f^*(1/q_J) + g^*(1/q_{US})$, $f^*(1/q_J)$ denotes a demand function for the Japanese products in the Japanese markets ($f^{*\prime} < 0$) and $g^*(1/q_{US})$ denotes a demand function for the Japanese products in the US markets ($g^{*\prime} < 0$).

Profit-maximizing prices of the Japanese firm in the Japanese and US markets are, respectively, derived as

$$P_J^{Y*} = \mu_J^* \left(P_m^Y + \overline{C}' \right) \tag{5a}$$

$$P_{US}^{\$*} = \mu_{US}^* \left(\frac{E^{A/Y}}{E^{A/\$}} P_m^Y + \frac{E^{A/Y}}{E^{A/\$}} \overline{C}' \right) \tag{5b}$$

where $\mu_J^* \equiv \frac{\varepsilon_J^*(1/q_J)}{\varepsilon_J^*(1/q_J)-1}$ denotes markups of the Japanese products in the Japanese

market; $\varepsilon_J^* \equiv -\frac{f^{*\prime}(1/q_J)}{f^*(1/q_J)q_J}$ denotes price elasticity of demand for the Japanese prod-

ucts in the Japanese market; $\mu_{US}^* \equiv \frac{\varepsilon_{US}^*(1q_{US})}{\varepsilon_{US}^*(1/q_{US})-1}$ denotes markups of the Japanese

products in the US market; and $\varepsilon_{US}^* \equiv -\frac{f^{*\prime}(1/q_{US})}{f^*(1/q_{US})q_{US}}$ denotes price elasticity of

demand for the Japanese products in the US market. We assume that $\frac{d\varepsilon_J^*}{d(1/q_J)} > 0$,

$\frac{d\mu_J^*}{d(1/q_J)} > 0$, $\frac{d\varepsilon_{US}^*}{d(1/q_{US})} > 0$, and $\frac{d\mu_{US}^*}{d(1/q_{US})} > 0$.

We derive reaction functions of the Japanese firm given the prices of the ASEAN products in the Japanese and US market, respectively.

$$\log P_J^{Y*} = \frac{\eta_J^*}{1 + \eta_J^*} \log P_J^Y + \frac{1}{1 + \eta_J^*} \log \left(P_m^Y + \overline{C}' \right) \tag{6a}$$

$$\log P_{US}^{\$*} = \frac{\eta_{US}^*}{1 + \eta_{US}^*} \log P_{US}^\$ + \frac{1}{1 + \eta_{US}^*} \log \left\{ \frac{E^{A/Y}}{E^{A/\$}} \left(P_m^Y + \overline{C}' \right) \right\} \tag{6b}$$

where $\eta_J^* \equiv -\frac{\mu^{*'}}{\mu^* q_J} > 0$ denotes price elasticity of markups of the Japanese products in the Japanese market and $\eta_{US}^* \equiv -\frac{\mu_{US}^{*'}}{\mu_{US}^* q_{US}} > 0$ denotes price elasticity of markups of the Japanese products in the US market.

From Equations (3a) and (6a), we derive equilibrium prices of the ASEAN products and the Japanese products in the Japanese market, respectively:

$$\log P_J^Y = \frac{1 + \eta_J^*}{1 + \eta_J + \eta_J^*} \log \left(\omega_m P_m^Y + (1 - \omega_m) \frac{E^{A/\$}}{E^{A/Y}} P_m^\$ + \frac{\overline{C}'}{E^{A/Y}} \right)$$
$$+ \frac{\eta_J}{1 + \eta_J + \eta_J^*} \log \left(P_m^Y + \overline{C}' \right) \tag{7a}$$

$$\log P_J^{Y*} = \frac{\eta_J^*}{1 + \eta_J + \eta_J^*} \log \left(\omega_m P_m^Y + (1 - \omega_m) \frac{E^{A/\$}}{E^{A/Y}} P_m^\$ + \frac{\overline{C}'}{E^{A/Y}} \right)$$
$$+ \frac{1 + \eta_J}{1 + \eta_J + \eta_J^*} \log \left(P_m^Y + \overline{C}' \right) \tag{7b}$$

From Equations (3b) and (6b), we derive equilibrium prices of the ASEAN products and the Japanese products in the US market, respectively:

$$\log P_{US}^\$ = \log \frac{E^{A/Y}}{E^{A/\$}} + \frac{1 + \eta_{US}^*}{1 + \eta_{US} + \eta_{US}^*} \log \left(\omega_m P_m^Y + (1 - \omega_m) \frac{E^{A/\$}}{E^{A/Y}} P_m^\$ + \frac{\overline{C}'}{E^{A/Y}} \right)$$
$$+ \frac{\eta_{US}}{1 + \eta_{US} + \eta_{US}^*} \log \left(P_m^Y + \overline{C}' \right) \tag{8a}$$

$$\log P_{US}^{\$*} = \log \frac{E^{A/Y}}{E^{A/\$}} + \frac{\eta_{US}^*}{1 + \eta_{US} + \eta_{US}^*} \log \left(\omega_m P_m^Y + (1 - \omega_m) \frac{E^{A/\$}}{E^{A/Y}} P_m^\$ + \frac{\overline{C}'}{E^{A/Y}} \right)$$
$$+ \frac{1 + \eta_{US}}{1 + \eta_{US} + \eta_{US}^*} \log \left(P_m^Y + \overline{C}' \right) \tag{8b}$$

From Equations (7) and (8), we obtain equilibrium relative prices of the ASEAN products relative to the Japanese products in the Japanese and the US markets, respectively:

$$\log q_J = \log P_J^Y - \log P_J^{Y*}$$

$$= \frac{1}{1 + \eta_J + \eta_J^*} \left\{ \log \left(\omega_m P_m^Y + (1 - \omega_m) \frac{E^{A/\$}}{E^{A/Y}} P_m^\$ + \frac{\overline{C}'}{E^{A/Y}} \right) \right.$$

$$\left. - \log \left(P_m^Y + \overline{C}' \right) \right\} \tag{9a}$$

$$\log q_{US} = \log P_{US}^\$ - \log P_{US}^{\$*}$$

$$= \frac{1}{1 + \eta_{US} + \eta_{US}^*} \left\{ \log \left(\omega_m P_m^Y + (1 - \omega_m) \frac{E^{A/\$}}{E^{A/Y}} P_m^\$ + \frac{\overline{C}'}{E^{A/Y}} \right) \right.$$

$$\left. - \log \left(P_m^Y + \overline{C}' \right) \right\} \tag{9b}$$

Equation (9) show that the relative prices q_J and q_{US} depend on both the exchange rate of the yen relative to the ASEAN currency $E^{A/Y}$ and the exchange rate of the dollar relative to the ASEAN currency $E^{A/\$}$. The exchange rate of the yen $E^{A/Y}$ has effects on the relative prices via both the marginal cost of parts imported from the United States and the marginal production cost while the exchange rate of the dollar $E^{A/\$}$ has effects on the relative prices via the marginal cost of parts imported from the United States.

A depreciation of the ASEAN currency against the yen has a negative effect on both of the equilibrium relative prices of the ASEAN products relative to the Japanese products in the Japanese and the US markets. On the other hand, a depreciation of the ASEAN currency against the dollar has a positive effect on both of the equilibrium relative prices.

We specify demand functions for the ASEAN products in the Japanese and the US market from Equation (9a) and (9b) as the price elasticities of demand in the Japanese and US markets are ϵ_J and ϵ_{US}, respectively.

$$\log f = \frac{-\varepsilon_J}{1 + \eta_J + \eta_J^*} \left\{ \log \left(\omega_m P_m^Y + (1 - \omega_m) \frac{E^{A/\$}}{E^{A/Y}} P_m^\$ + \frac{\overline{C}'}{E^{A/Y}} \right) \right.$$

$$\left. - \log \left(P_m^Y + \overline{C}' \right) \right\} \tag{10a}$$

$$\log g = \frac{-\varepsilon_{US}}{1 + \eta_{US} + \eta_{US}^*} \left\{ \log \left(\omega_m P_m^Y + (1 - \omega_m) \frac{E^{A/\$}}{E^{A/Y}} P_m^\$ + \frac{\overline{C}'}{E^{A/Y}} \right) \right.$$

$$\left. - \log \left(P_m^\$ + \overline{C}' \right) \right\} \tag{10b}$$

Equation 10 (a, b) shows that the demands for the ASEAN products in the Japanese market depend on both exchange rates of $E^{A/Y}$ and $E^{A/\$}$. This applies for the US market also. The exchange rate of the yen $E^{A/Y}$ has effects on the demands via both the marginal cost of parts imported from the United States and the marginal production cost, while the exchange rate of the dollar $E^{A/\$}$ has effects on the demands via the marginal cost of parts imported from the United States.

A depreciation of the ASEAN currency against the yen has a positive effect on the demands for the ASEAN products in both the Japanese and the US markets. Thus, the depreciation increases export volume of ASEAN. On the other hand, a depreciation of the ASEAN currency against the dollar has a negative effect on both the demands for the ASEAN products and the export volume.

2.2. Model B

In Model B, the ASEAN firm competes against the Japanese firm in the Japanese market and, on the other hand, against the US firm in the US market. We suppose that the Japanese firm supplies its products only in the Japanese market while the US firm supplies its products only in the US market. The US firm in the theoretical model does not have to be a firm located in the United States in the real world. Goods made in Latin America as well as in the United States can be interpreted as the goods made in the United States in the theoretical model, because many of the Latin American currencies were de facto pegged to the US dollar (especially before the Mexican currency crisis of December 1994).

We formalize the same profit equation of the ASEAN firm as in Model A. However, $q_{US} \equiv P_{US}^\$/P_{US}^{\$*}$ represents the price of the ASEAN products relative to the US products in the United States and $P_{US}^{\$*}$ represents the price of the US products in the US market in terms of the dollar in Model B. Thus, as in Model A, the reaction functions (3a) and (3b) of the ASEAN firm in the Japanese and US markets are derived.

Profits of the Japanese firm in terms of the yen π_J^* are formalized as

$$\pi_J^* = P_J^{Y*} f^*(1/q_J) - P_m^Y f^*(1/q_J) - C(f^*(1/q_J)) \tag{11}$$

where $f^*(1/q_J)$ denotes a demand function for the Japanese products in the Japanese markets ($f^{*'} < 0$).

Profit-maximizing prices of the Japanese firm in the Japanese market are derived as

$$P_J^{Y*} = \mu_J^* \left(P_m^Y + \overline{C}' \right) \tag{12}$$

where $\mu_J^* \equiv \frac{\varepsilon_J^*(1/q_J)}{\varepsilon_J^*(1/q_J)-1}$ denotes markups of the Japanese products in the Japanese market and $\varepsilon_J^* \equiv -\frac{f^{*'}(1/q_J)}{f^*(1/q_J)q_J}$ denotes price elasticity of demand for the Japanese products in the Japanese market. We assume that $\frac{d\varepsilon_J^*}{d(1/q_J)} > 0$ and $\frac{d\mu_J^*}{d(1/q_J)} > 0$.

We derive a reaction function of the Japanese firm given the prices of the ASEAN products in the Japanese market.

$$\log P_J^{Y*} = \frac{\eta_J^*}{1+\eta_J^*} \log P_J^Y + \frac{1}{1+\eta_J^*} \log \left(P_m^Y + \overline{C}' \right) \tag{13}$$

where $\eta_J^* \equiv -\frac{\mu_J^{*'}}{\mu_J^* q_J} > 0$ denotes price elasticity of markups of the Japanese products in the Japanese market.

Profits of the US firm in terms of the dollar π_{US}^* is formalized as

$$\pi_{US}^* = P_{US}^{\$*} g^*(1/q_{US}) - P_m^{\$} g^*(1/q_{US}) - C(g^*(1/q_{US})) \tag{14}$$

where $g^*(1/q_{US})$ denotes a demand function for the US products in the US markets ($g^{*'} < 0$).

Profit-maximizing prices of the US firm in the US market are derived as

$$P_{US}^{\$*} = \mu_{US}^* \left(P_m^{\$} + \overline{C}' \right) \tag{15}$$

where $\mu_{US}^* \equiv \frac{\varepsilon_{US}^*(1/q_{US})}{\varepsilon_{US}^*(1/q_{US})-1}$ denotes markups of the US products in the US market and $\varepsilon_{US}^* \equiv -\frac{f^{*'}(1/q_{US})}{f^*(1/q_{US})q_{US}}$ denotes price elasticity of demand for the US products in the US market. We assume that $\frac{d\varepsilon_{US}^*}{d(1/q_{US})} > 0$ and $\frac{d\mu_{US}^*}{d(1/q_{US})} > 0$.

We derive a reaction function of the US firm given the prices of the ASEAN products in the US market.

$$\log P_{US}^{\$*} = \frac{\eta_{US}^*}{1+\eta_{US}^*} \log P_{US}^{\$} + \frac{1}{1+\eta_{US}^*} \log \left(P_m^{\$} + \overline{C}' \right) \tag{16}$$

$\eta_{US}^* \equiv -\frac{\mu_{US}^{*'}}{\mu_{US}^* q_{US}} > 0$ denotes price elasticity of markups of the US products in the US market.

From Equations (3a) and (13), we derive equilibrium prices of the ASEAN products and Japanese products in the Japanese market, respectively:

$$
\log P_J^Y = \frac{1 + \eta_J^*}{1 + \eta_J + \eta_J^*} \log \left(\omega_m P_m^Y + (1 - \omega_m) \frac{E^{A/\$}}{E^{A/Y}} P_m^\$ + \frac{\overline{C}'}{E^{A/Y}} \right)
$$

$$
+ \frac{\eta_J}{1 + \eta_J + \eta_J^*} \log \left(P_m^Y + \overline{C}' \right) \tag{17a}
$$

$$
\log P_J^{Y*} = \frac{\eta_J^*}{1 + \eta_J + \eta_J^*} \log \left(\omega_m P_m^Y + (1 - \omega_m) \frac{E^{A/\$}}{E^{A/Y}} P_m^\$ + \frac{\overline{C}'}{E^{A/Y}} \right)
$$

$$
+ \frac{1 + \eta_J}{1 + \eta_J + \eta_J^*} \log \left(P_m^Y + \overline{C}' \right) \tag{17b}
$$

From Equations (3b) and (16), we derive equilibrium prices of the ASEAN products and US products in the US market, respectively:

$$
\log P_{US}^\$ = \frac{1 + \eta_{US}^*}{1 + \eta_{US} + \eta_{US}^*} \log \left(\omega_m \frac{E^{A/Y}}{E^{A/\$}} P_m^Y + (1 - \omega_m) P_m^\$ + \frac{\overline{C}'}{E^{A/\$}} \right)
$$

$$
+ \frac{\eta_{US}}{1 + \eta_{US} + \eta_{US}^*} \log \left(P_m^\$ + \overline{C}' \right) \tag{18a}
$$

$$
\log P_{US}^{\$*} = \frac{\eta_{US}^*}{1 + \eta_{US} + \eta_{US}^*} \log \left(\omega_m \frac{E^{A/Y}}{E^{A/\$}} P_m^Y + (1 - \omega_m) P_m^\$ + \frac{\overline{C}'}{E^{A/\$}} \right)
$$

$$
+ \frac{1 + \eta_{US}}{1 + \eta_{US} + \eta_{US}^*} \log \left(P_m^\$ + \overline{C}' \right) \tag{18b}
$$

From Equations (17) and (18), we obtain an equilibrium relative price of the ASEAN products relative to the Japanese products in the Japanese markets and an equilibrium relative price relative to the US products in the US markets, respectively:

$$
\log q_J = \log P_J^Y - \log P_J^{Y*}
$$

$$
= \frac{1}{1 + \eta_J + \eta_J^*} \left\{ \log \left(\omega_m P_m^Y + (1 - \omega_m) \frac{E^{A/\$}}{E^{A/Y}} P_m^\$ + \frac{\overline{C}'}{E^{A/Y}} \right) \right.
$$

$$
\left. - \log \left(P_m^Y + \overline{C}' \right) \right\} \tag{19a}
$$

$$\log q_{US} = \log P_{US}^{\$} - \log P_{US}^{\$*}$$

$$= \frac{1}{1 + \eta_{US} + \eta_{US}^*} \left\{ \log \left(\omega_m \frac{E^{A/Y}}{E^{A/\$}} P_m^Y + (1 - \omega_m) P_m^{\$} + \frac{\overline{C}'}{E^{A/\$}} \right) \right.$$

$$\left. - \log \left(P_m^{\$} + \overline{C}' \right) \right\} \tag{19b}$$

Equations (19) (a and b) show that the relative prices q_J and q_{US} depend on both the exchange rate of the yen relative to the ASEAN currency $E^{A/Y}$ and the exchange rate of the dollar relative to the ASEAN currency $E^{A/\$}$. The exchange rate of the yen $E^{A/Y}$ has negative effects on the relative prices in the Japanese market via both the marginal cost of parts imported from the US and the marginal production cost, while it has positive effects on the relative prices in the US market via the marginal cost of parts imported from Japan. On the other hand, the exchange rate of the dollar $E^{A/\$}$ has positive effects on the relative prices in the Japanese market via the marginal cost of parts imported from the United States, while it has negative effects on the relative prices in the US market via both the marginal cost of parts imported from Japan and the marginal production cost.

A depreciation of the ASEAN currency against the yen has a negative effect on the equilibrium relative prices of the ASEAN products relative to the Japanese products in the Japanese market, while it has a positive effect on the equilibrium relative prices in the US markets. On the other hand, a depreciation of the ASEAN currency against the dollar has a positive effect on the equilibrium relative price in the Japanese market, while it has a negative effect on the equilibrium relative price in the US market.

We specify demand functions for the ASEAN products in the Japanese and the US market from Equation 19 (a and b) as the price elasticities of demand in the Japanese and US markets are ε_J and ε_{US}, respectively.

$$\log f = \frac{-\varepsilon_J}{1 + \eta_J + \eta_J^*} \left\{ \log \left(\omega_m P_m^Y + (1 - \omega_m) \frac{E^{A/\$}}{E^{A/Y}} P_m^{\$} + \frac{\overline{C}'}{E^{A/Y}} \right) \right.$$

$$\left. - \log \left(P_m^Y + \overline{C}' \right) \right\} \tag{20a}$$

$$\log g = \frac{-\varepsilon_{US}}{1 + \eta_{US} + \eta_{US}^*} \left\{ \log \left(\omega_m \frac{E^{A/Y}}{E^{A/\$}} P_m^Y + (1 - \omega_m) P_m^{\$} + \frac{\overline{C}'}{E^{A/\$}} \right) \right.$$

$$\left. - \log \left(P_m^{\$} + \overline{C}' \right) \right\} \tag{20b}$$

Equation (20) shows that both the exchange rates $E^{A/Y}$ and $E^{A/\$}$ have asymmetric effects on the demands for ASEAN products in the Japanese and US markets. As a result, the exchange rates have ambiguous effects on the export volume of ASEAN, which is a sum of both the demands $f + g$.

However, it is clearer how at least the exchange rate of the dollar affects the export volume of ASEAN by supposing an extreme case where the ASEAN firm imported parts from Japan only, that is, $\omega_m = 1$. Demand functions for the ASEAN products in the Japanese and the US market in the case of $\omega_m = 1$ are as follows:

$$\log f = \frac{-\varepsilon_J}{1 + \eta_J + \eta_J^*} \left\{ \log \left(P_m^Y + \frac{\overline{C}'}{E^{A/Y}} \right) - \log \left(P_m^Y + \overline{C}' \right) \right\} \qquad (20a')$$

$$\log g = \frac{-\varepsilon_{US}}{1 + \eta_{US} + \eta_{US}^*} \left\{ \log \left(\frac{E^{A/Y}}{E^{A/\$}} P_m^Y + \frac{\overline{C}'}{E^{A/\$}} \right) - \log \left(P_m^\$ + \overline{C}' \right) \right\} \quad (20b')$$

Equation 20 (a' and b') shows that the exchange rate of the ASEAN currency against the dollar has unambiguous effects on the export volume of the ASEAN $f + g$, while the exchange rate of the ASEAN currency against the yen has much more ambiguous effects on export volume. If the share of parts imported from Japan is higher, it is more likely that the exchange rate against the dollar has unambiguous positive effects on the export volume while the exchange rate against the yen has ambiguous effects.

3.   Effects of the dollar peg on fluctuations in a trade balance

In this section, we explore the effects of the dollar peg on a trade balance of the ASEAN economy.

A trade balance of the ASEAN economy is equal to a total export value or total sales of the ASEAN firm less than the total import value or total costs of imported parts in our model. Therefore, we represent the trade balance in terms of the home currency T,

$$T = E^{A/Y} P_J^Y f(q_J) + E^{A/\$} P_{US}^\$ g(q_{US}) - \omega_m E^{A/Y} P_m^Y Q - (1 - \omega_m) E^{A/\$} P_m^\$ Q$$

$$= \left[\left\{ \omega_x E^{A/Y} P_J^Y + (1 - \omega_x) E^{A/\$} P_{US}^\$ \right\} - \left\{ \omega_m E^{A/Y} P_m^Y + (1 - \omega_m) E^{A/\$} P_m^\$ \right\} \right] Q$$

$$= (P_x^A - P_m^A) Q \qquad (21)$$

where $\omega_x = f/Q$ denotes a share of products exported to Japan in the total export volumes; $P_x^A \equiv \omega_x E^{A/Y} P_J^Y + (1 - \omega_x) E^{A/\$} P_{US}^\$$ denotes the volume-weighted average export price in terms of the home currency; and $P_m^A \equiv \omega_m E^{A/Y} P_m^Y + (1 - \omega_m) E^{A/\$} P_m^\$$ denotes the volume-weighted average import price in terms of the home currency. Equation (21) shows that the trade balance is proportional to a volume-weighted average export price less the volume-weighted average import price because the total export volumes are equal to the total import volumes in our model.

Note that the trade balance is equivalent to nominal GDP in our model. Therefore, we can say that we explore the effects of the dollar peg on nominal GDP in our model.

We derive a relationship between fluctuations in the trade balance and those in the exchange rates in both Model A and B (see Appendix),

$$
\hat{T} = \frac{1}{T}\left[T_J \hat{E}^{A/Y} + T_{US}\hat{E}^{A/\$} + \left\{ \frac{1+\eta_J^* - \varepsilon_J}{1+\eta_J + \eta_J^*}X_J + \frac{1+\eta_{US}^* - \varepsilon_{US}}{1+\eta_{US} + \eta_{US}^*}X_{US} \right\} \right.
$$
$$
\times \left[(1-\omega_m)B_1\hat{E}^{A/\$} - \{(1-\omega_m)B_1 + B_2\}\hat{E}^{A/Y} \right]
$$
$$
+ \left\{ \frac{\varepsilon_J}{1+\eta_J + \eta_J^*}\omega_x + \frac{\varepsilon_{US}}{1+\eta_{US} + \eta_{US}^*}(1-\omega_x) \right\}
$$
$$
\left. \times M \left[(1-\omega_m)B_1\hat{E}^{A/\$} - \{(1-\omega_m)B_1 + B_2\}\hat{E}^{A/Y} \right] \right] \tag{22}
$$

$$
\hat{T} = \frac{1}{T}\left[T_J\hat{E}^{A/Y} + T_{US}\hat{E}^{A/\$} + \frac{1+\eta_J^* - \varepsilon_J}{1+\eta_J + \eta_J^*}X_J \left[(1-\omega_m)B_1\hat{E}^{A/\$} \right. \right.
$$
$$
\left. - \{(1-\omega_m)B_1 + B_2\}\hat{E}^{A/Y} \right] + \frac{1+\eta_{US}^* - \varepsilon_{US}}{1+\eta_{US} + \eta_{US}^*}X_{US}
$$
$$
\times \left[-\{1-(1-\omega_m)B_1\}\hat{E}^{A/\$} + \{1-(1-\omega_m)B_1 - B_2\}\hat{E}^{A/Y} \right]
$$
$$
+ \frac{\varepsilon_J}{1+\eta_J + \eta_J^*}\omega_x M \left[(1-\omega_m)B_1\hat{E}^{A/\$} - \{(1-\omega_m)B_1 + B_2\}\hat{E}^{A/Y} \right]
$$
$$
+ \frac{\varepsilon_{US}}{1+\eta_{US} + \eta_{US}^*}(1-\omega_x)M \left[-\{1-(1-\omega_m)B_1\}\hat{E}^{A/\$} \right.
$$
$$
\left. \left. + \{1-(1-\omega_m)B_1 - B_2\}\hat{E}^{A/Y} \right] \right] \tag{23}
$$

where $T_J \equiv (\omega_x E^{A/Y} P_J^Y - \omega_m E^{A/Y} P_m^Y)Q$ denotes the trade balance with Japan; $T_{US} \equiv \left((1-\omega_x)E^{A/\$}P_{US}^\$ - (1-\omega_m)E^{A/\$}P_m^\$ \right)Q$ denotes the trade balance with the United States; $X_J \equiv \omega_x E^{A/Y}P_J^Y Q$ denotes the value of exports to Japan; $X_{US} \equiv (1-\omega_x)E^{A/\$}P_{US}^\$ Q$ denotes the value of exports to the United States; $M \equiv P_m^A Q$ denotes the total import value, $B_1 \equiv \left(\frac{E^{A/\$}P_m^\$}{E^{A/Y}} \right) \bigg/ TC_A$; $(1-\omega_m)B_1$ denotes the share of marginal cost of parts imported from the United States in the total marginal costs; $B_2 \equiv \left(\frac{\bar{C}'}{E^{A/Y}} \right) \bigg/ TC_A$ denotes the share of marginal production cost in the total marginal costs; $TC_A \equiv \omega_m P_m^Y + (1 - \omega_m)\frac{E^{A/\$} P_m^\$}{E^{A/Y}} + \frac{\bar{C}'}{E^{A/Y}}$ denotes the total marginal costs; and $\hat{x}$ means a rate of change in a variable x.

For simplicity, the price elasticity of demand in the Japanese market is assumed to be equal to that in the US markets ($\varepsilon_J = \varepsilon_{US} = \varepsilon$). When the price elasticities of demand are equal to each other, the price elasticities of markups in both the markets are also equal to each other ($\eta_J = \eta_{US} = \eta$ and $\eta_J^* = \eta_{US}^* = \eta^*$). Therefore, we change Equations (22) and (23) into the following equation,

$$
\hat{T} = \frac{1}{T}\left[\left\{T_J\hat{E}^{A/Y} + T_{US}\hat{E}^{A/\$}\right\} + \frac{1+\eta^*}{1+\eta+\eta^*}X\left\{(1-\omega_m)B_1\hat{E}^{A/\$}\right.\right.
$$

$$
\left. - \left\{(1-\omega_m)B_1 + B_2\right\}\hat{E}^{A/Y}\right\} - \frac{\varepsilon}{1+\eta+\eta^*}
$$

$$
\left. \times T\left\{(1-\omega_m)B_1\hat{E}^{A/\$} - \left\{(1-\omega_m)B_1 + B_2\right\}\hat{E}^{A/Y}\right\}\right] \tag{22'}
$$

$$
\hat{T} = \frac{1}{T}\left[\left\{T_J\hat{E}^{A/Y} + T_{US}\hat{E}^{A/\$}\right\} + \frac{1+\eta^*}{1+\eta+\eta^*}X\left\{(1-\omega_m)B_1\hat{E}^{A/\$}\right.\right.
$$

$$
\left. - \left\{(1-\omega_m)B_1 + B_2\right\}\hat{E}^{A/Y}\right\}
$$

$$
- \frac{\varepsilon}{1+\eta+\eta^*}T\left\{(1-\omega_m)B_1\hat{E}^{A/\$} - \left\{(1-\omega_m)B_1 + B_2\right\}\hat{E}^{A/Y}\right\}
$$

$$
+ \left\{\frac{1+\eta^*}{1+\eta+\eta^*}X_{US} + \frac{\varepsilon}{1+\eta+\eta^*}T_{US}\right\}\left(\hat{E}^{A/Y} - \hat{E}^{A/\$}\right)\right] \tag{23'}
$$

where $X = P_x^A Q$, a total export value.

Equations (22') and (23') show that the effects of the exchange rates on the trade balance have the following transmission channels.

The first channel is a direct effect of the exchange rates on the trade balance as shown in the first curly brace in both the equations. The ASEAN country imports parts from Japan and the United States and exports products to these countries. Thus, the exchange rates have a direct effect via both the export values and the import values.

The second channel is an indirect effect of the exchange rates via the product prices as shown in the second angle bracket of the equations. The exchange rates affect the product prices as shown in Equations (7), (8), (17), and (18). The product prices affect export values. Thus, the price channel is that the exchange rates affect the export volumes.

The third channel is an indirect effect of the exchange rate via the demands for the ASEAN products and, in turn, its outputs as shown in the third curly brace of the equations. The exchange rates affect the product prices, which change the relative prices of the products in the Japanese and the US markets as shown in Equations (9) and (19). The changes in the relative prices affect the demand for the products in both the markets as shown in Equations (10) and (20). The demand for ASEAN products is equivalent to export volumes of the ASEAN economy. On one hand, changes in outputs effect import volumes because the ASEAN economy imports all of the parts from the foreign countries in our model. Thus, this output channel is that the exchange rates affect both the export volumes and the import volumes. The fourth curly brace of Equation (23′) is related to the second and third channels for trade with the United States.

Now we consider the effect of exchanges rate regime on the trade balance of an ASEAN country. The monetary authorities of the ASEAN country are assumed to peg the home currency to the dollar. The dollar peg is equivalent to a case of $\hat{E}^{A/\$} = 0$. Substituting $\hat{E}^{A/\$} = 0$ into Equations (22′) and (23′), we obtain the following equations:

$$\hat{T} = \frac{1}{T}\left[T_J - \frac{1+\eta^*}{1+\eta+\eta^*}X\{(1-\omega_m)B_1 + B_2\}\right.$$

$$\left. + \frac{\varepsilon}{1+\eta+\eta^*}T\{(1-\omega_m)B_1 + B_2\}\right]\hat{E}^{A/Y} \tag{24}$$

$$\hat{T} = \frac{1}{T}\left[T_J - \frac{1+\eta^*}{1+\eta+\eta^*}X\{(1-\omega_m)B_1 + B_2\} + \frac{\varepsilon}{1+\eta+\eta^*}T\right.$$

$$\left. \times \{(1-\omega_m)B_1 + B_2\} + \left\{\frac{1+\eta^*}{1+\eta+\eta^*}X_{US} + \frac{\varepsilon}{1+\eta+\eta^*}T_{US}\right\}\right]\hat{E}^{A/Y} \tag{25}$$

In the case of the dollar peg, changes in the exchange rate of the yen against the ASEAN currency have some effects on the trade balance in our model where the ASEAN firm imports parts for production from Japan and the United States and exports its products to Japan and the United States. The ASEAN products compete against the Japanese firm or the US firm. Changes in the exchange rate of the yen have effects on the trade balance through the above three transmission channels.

For example, a depreciation of the yen ($\hat{E}^{A/Y} < 0$) deteriorates the trade balance via the first direct channel if the ASEAN country has a trade balance surplus with Japan ($T_J > 0$) as shown in the first term in the square bracket of Equations (24) and (25). On the other hand, it improves the trade balance if the ASEAN country has a trade balance deficit with Japan ($T_J < 0$).

Next, a depreciation of the yen against the home currency increases the marginal costs of parts imported from the United States and domestic production of the ASEAN firm relative to those of the Japanese firm. The ASEAN firm is forced to increase its product prices in both the Japanese and the US markets though it imperfectly passes-through the increase in the marginal costs into the product prices because it competes against the Japanese firm in both the markets as shown in Equations (7a), (8a), (17a), and (18a). As a result, the depreciation of the yen improves the trade balance via the price channel as shown in the second term of Equations (24) and (25).

Third, a depreciation of the yen increases the relative prices of the ASEAN products relative to the Japanese products in both the Japanese and the US markets as shown in Equations (9) and (19). In turn, it reduces the demands for the ASEAN products in both the markets as shown in Equations (10) and (20). This results in a contraction in outputs of the ASEAN firm and decreases both the export volumes and the import volumes of parts. Therefore, a depreciation of the yen deteriorates the trade balance surplus ($T > 0$) or improves the trade balance deficit ($T < 0$) via the output channel as shown in the third term of Equations (24) and (25).

4. The optimal weights

The monetary authorities are assumed to choose weights of the yen and the dollar in order to stabilize the fluctuations in the trade balance caused by changes in the exchange rates.[5] In particular, we adopt a criterion of minimizing the squared rate of change in the trade balances. The goal of the monetary authorities is equivalent to stabilizing the fluctuations in profits of exporting firms in our model. Pegging the home currency to a basket of the yen and the dollar implies that the monetary authorities try to keep the exchange rate of the accuracy basket in terms of the home currency unchanged. Therefore, changes in the exchange rate of the currency basket in terms of the home currency is zero,

$$w\hat{E}^{A/\$} + (1 - w)\hat{E}^{A/Y} = 0 \qquad (26)$$

where w is the weight of a dollar in pegging the home currency to the currency basket. If w turns out to be 1 (0, respectively), then this country is in the optimal currency area of the dollar (the yen, respectively).[6]

Note that it is not necessary to take into account a correlation between the exchange rates vis-à-vis the yen and vis-à-vis the dollar, because the optimality is defined to minimize the weighted average (currency basket) of the changes in the exchange rates against the dollar and the yen [that is, the left-hand side of Equation (26)]. The correlation would have been relevant if we were to adopt a criterion that minimizes variance of the currency basket [that is, the variance of the left-hand side of Equation (26)].

For the choice of criteria for 'optimality,' the literature does not have a standard. If the objective of the optimal basket is regarded as a multicountry replacement for the peg to a single currency, then stability of the real effective exchange rate is the criterion. This is a basic stance of Lipschitz and Sundararajan (1980). It is implicit in this choice that if the exchange rate is stable (at around the equilibrium), then the trade balance is stable. One can make it more explicit. The principal role of the exchange rate is to keep the balance of trade or current accounts, so a natural candidate is the trade balance stabilization. This line of thought is followed by Flanders and Helpman (1979) and Flanders and Tishler (1981). However, the exchange rate policy is only one part of overall economic policy that pursues price stabilization and income growth. The balance of payments cannot be a stand-alone objective. Turnovsky (1985) proposes the criterion of stabilizing domestic income, a more general objective of economic policy. For domestic income stabilization, there are policy options other than the currency basket weights. Other policy options should be modeled if a general policy objective is introduced. Bhandari (1985), extending Turnovsky, considered four criteria (or their combination thereof) at the same time, including the real effective exchange rate, in a similar model. It is not clear whether these four criteria can be weighted and combined in one loss function.

Our study is different from the previous papers in the literature. Our model is based on the exporter's maximizing behavior, instead of *ad hoc* macro model. How prices respond to the exchange rate changes is solved in the model. This feature avoids the criticism that the optimal peg literature takes the prices as given. Our model makes it explicit how prices are set by the profit-maximizing firm. The optimality is to minimize the squared rate of change in the trade balance $\hat{T}^2$ subject to Equation (26), where a rate of change in the trade balance $\hat{T}$ is shown in Equation (22') or (23'). The criteria is equivalent to minimizing the variance of the growth rate, provided that the mean growth rate is equal to zero.[7]

In Model A, we obtain optimal weights of pegging the home currency to the dollar w^*;

$$w^* = \frac{T_{US} + \dfrac{1+\eta^*}{1+\eta+\eta^*}X(1-\omega_m)B_1 - \dfrac{\varepsilon}{1+\eta+\eta^*}T(1-\omega_m)B_1}{T - \dfrac{1+\eta^*}{1+\eta+\eta^*}XB_2 + \dfrac{\varepsilon}{1+\eta+\eta^*}TB_2} \qquad (27)$$

where both the denominators and the numerators are assumed to be different from zero. Especially, the optimal peg weights are indeterminate if the numerators are equal to zero.

In Model B, we obtain optimal weights of pegging the home currency to the dollar w^*;

$$w^* = \frac{T_{US} - \dfrac{1+\eta^*}{1+\eta+\eta^*}\{X_{US}-X(1-\omega_m)B_1\} + \dfrac{\varepsilon}{1+\eta+\eta^*}\{T_{US}-T(1-\omega_m)B_1\}}{T - \dfrac{1+\eta^*}{1+\eta+\eta^*}XB_2 + \dfrac{\varepsilon}{1+\eta+\eta^*}TB_2} \qquad (28)$$

Equations (27) and (28) indicate that both the optimal peg weights are related to three factors. The exchange rates made impacts on the trade balance of the ASEAN economy via the above-mentioned three channels: the direct channel, the price channel, and the output channel. Here, we find the three channels in the equations. The first terms in both the denominators and the numerators are related to the direct channel. The second terms are related to the price channel. The third terms are related to the output channel.

We could focus on only a ratio of the trade balance with the United States or Japan to the total trade balances in determining the optimal peg weights if the price and the output channels were ineffective. However, the ASEAN firm sets the product prices in both the Japanese and the US markets by adding the markups to the total marginal costs in terms of the relevant currencies. The exchange rates have effects on the total marginal costs in terms of the relevant currencies. The two components of the total marginal costs for the ASEAN firm—the marginal cost of parts imported from the United States and the production marginal cost—are different from those for the competing Japanese firm. These are expressed in $(1 - \omega_m)B_1$ and B_2 in the equations.

Thus, the optimal peg weights are related with the price elasticities of demand and the cost compositions as well as the trade structures. This makes the difference in choosing an optimality criterion other than the real effective exchange rate, such as Lipschitz and Sundararajan (1980).

5. Theoretical prediction

5.1. Regression forms

In order to prepare for regression, we derive operational regressions from theoretical models in Section 2. Export prices in Model A can be expressed as a function of the exchange rate, say the baht, against the US dollar and the baht against the Japanese yen. (See Appendix for derivation.)

$$\hat{P}_x^A = \alpha_1 \hat{E}^{A/\$} + \alpha_2 \hat{E}^{A/Y} \tag{29}$$

$$\alpha_1 \equiv \frac{1+\eta^*}{1+\eta+\eta^*}(1-\omega_m)B_1 > 0$$

$$\alpha_2 = 1 - \frac{1+\eta^*}{1+\eta+\eta^*}\{(1-\omega_m)B_1 + B_2\} = 1 - \alpha_1 - \frac{1+\eta^*}{1+\eta+\eta^*}B_2 > 0$$

Export prices in Model A can be expressed as a function of the exchange rates against the US dollar and against the Japanese yen. (See Appendix for derivation.)

$$\hat{P}_x^A = \alpha_3 \hat{E}^{A/\$} + \alpha_4 \hat{E}^{A/Y} \tag{30}$$

$$\alpha_3 \equiv \frac{1+\eta^*}{1+\eta+\eta^*}(1-\omega_m)B_1 + \frac{\eta}{1+\eta+\eta^*}(1-\omega_x) > 0$$

$$\alpha_4 = 1 - \frac{1+\eta^*}{1+\eta+\eta^*}\{(1-\omega_m)B_1 + B_2\} - \frac{\eta}{1+\eta+\eta^*}(1-\omega_x)$$

$$= 1 - \alpha_3 - \frac{1+\eta^*}{1+\eta+\eta^*}B_2 > 0$$

Export volume in Model A can be expressed as a function of the exchange rates against the US dollar and against the Japanese yen. (See Appendix for derivation.)

$$\hat{Q} = \beta_1 \hat{E}^{A/\$} + \beta_2 \hat{E}^{A/Y} \tag{31}$$

$$\beta_1 \equiv -\frac{\varepsilon}{1 + \eta + \eta^*}(1 - \omega_m)B_1 < 0$$

$$\beta_2 \equiv \frac{\varepsilon}{1 + \eta + \eta^*}\{(1 - \omega_m)B_1 + B_2\} = -\beta_1 + \frac{\varepsilon}{1 + \eta + \eta^*}B_2 > 0$$

Export volume in Model B can be expressed as a function of the exchange rates against the US dollar and against the Japanese yen. (See Appendix for derivation.)

$$\hat{Q} = \beta_3 \hat{E}^{A/\$} + \beta_4 \hat{E}^{A/Y} \tag{32}$$

$$\beta_3 \equiv -\frac{\varepsilon}{1 + \eta + \eta^*}(1 - \omega_m)B_1 + \frac{\varepsilon}{1 + \eta + \eta^*}(1 - \omega_x)$$

$$\beta_4 \equiv \frac{\varepsilon}{1 + \eta + \eta^*}\{(1 - \omega_m)B_1 + B_2\} - \frac{\varepsilon}{1 + \eta + \eta^*}(1 - \omega_x)$$

$$= -\beta_3 + \frac{\varepsilon}{1 + \eta + \eta^*}B_2$$

5.2.   Sign conditions

Major predictions of the exchange rate changes on the export volumes and prices based on the theoretical model developed in Section 2 can be summarized as follows. Based on Model A (the model where Asian exports compete with Japanese goods in Japan and in the United States), export volume will rise if the baht depreciate against the Japanese yen, but will decline if the baht depreciate against the US dollar. The reason that export volume will decline when the baht depreciate against the US dollar is the hike in costs of imported parts from the United States, while the costs for Japanese producers would not change as they use local parts. If the dollar peg is maintained, then the yen depreciation vis-à-vis the US dollar means the baht appreciates vis-à-vis the yen, while the baht–dollar exchange rate is stable, resulting in a decrease in export volume.

Based on Model B (the model where Asian exports compete in the US market against US-made goods and compete in Japanese markets against Japanese-made goods), the following theoretical prediction is obtained. A depreciation of the baht against the dollar has two effects. The costs of imported parts will rise, so this has a negative effect on export volume. On the other hand, local costs of Thai exporters will become less than for the US producers. This will have positive effects on export volume. Similarly, a depreciation of the baht against the yen has two effects, higher imported parts costs and lower local costs. In the end, sign of the coefficients are not determined.

Table 2.1 Theoretical prediction of sign conditions

Effects on export volume	Model A		Model B	
From	General	Special $(\omega_m = 0)$	General	Special $(\omega_m = 0)$
Baht/dollar hike (depreciation of baht against dollar)	$\beta_1 < 0$	$\beta_1 = 0$	β_3 ?	$\beta_3 > 0$
Baht/yen hike (depreciation of baht against yen)	$\beta_2 > 0$	$\beta_2 > 0$	β_4 ?	β_4 ?

Effects on export prices	Model A		Model B	
From	General	Special $(\omega_m = 0)$	General	Special $(\omega_m = 0)$
Baht/dollar hike (depreciation of baht against dollar)	$\alpha_1 > 0$	$\alpha_1 = 0$	$\alpha_3 > 0$	$\alpha_3 > 0$
Baht/yen hike (depreciation of baht against yen)	$\alpha_2 > 0$	$\alpha_2 > 0$	$\alpha_4 > 0$	$\alpha_4 > 0$

Consider a special case where parts are imported only from Japan ($\omega_m = 1$). In the case of Model A, a baht depreciation against the dollar does not have any effect on export volume, while a baht depreciation against the yen will increase export volume; and in the case of Model B, the baht depreciation against the dollar will increase export volume, while the effect of the baht depreciation against the yen still has an ambiguous sign on export volume.

The effects of the exchange rate changes on the export prices of Thailand are more straightforward. Both in Model A and Model B, a baht depreciation against the dollar results in the hike of export prices. This reflects the increase in costs of the imported parts. However, the increase in the prices is less than the change in the exchange rate, due to competitive pressure in the destination market, thus an imperfect pass-through. The baht depreciation against the yen results in the price hike and also results in the export price increase in Model A and Model B. The discussion is summarized in Table 2.1.

6. The stylized facts and regressions

6.1. *De facto dollar peg*

Many East and Southeast Asian countries had adopted de facto dollar peg regimes until the currency crisis of 1997, some explicitly and others implicitly. Hong Kong has explicitly maintained the currency board, the nominal peg to the dollar. Thailand, before July 1997, adopted a currency basket system with undisclosed currency weights, but it was well-known in the market that the weight of the US dollar in the basket was more than 90 percent. Indonesia adopted the crawling peg against the US dollar, where the rupiah depreciated with a schedule with a narrow band. Malaysia adopted the managed float, but the movement of the ringgit was stable against the US dollar. The movement of the Singaporean dollar and the Korean won was more flexible, compared to other currencies, responding in part to the Japanese yen movement.

The actual weights, which may be quietly adjusted from time to time, can be estimated from actual movements of the exchange rates. Frankel and Wei (1994) estimated the weights of the US dollar, the yen and other currencies in currency baskets of nine Asian currencies. Asian currencies (in terms of the Swiss franc) are regressed on the US dollar (in terms of the Swiss franc) and the Japanese yen (in terms of the Swiss franc), for various subperiods from 1972–92, with weekly data. They showed that the US dollar had an overwhelming weight in all currencies in all periods.

According to Frankel and Wei, the US dollar weight was typically about 95 percent for the Korean won; that is, if the US dollar depreciated by 1 percent vis-à-vis the Swiss franc, the Korean won depreciated 0.95 percent that week. The Hong Kong dollar, Taiwan dollar, Indonesia rupiah, Philippine peso, and Thai baht had a coefficient on the US dollar higher than 90 percent. For the movement of the Singaporean dollar, the weight of the US dollar was about 75 percent, significantly lower than the Korean won. Similarly, the Malaysian ringgit moves with the US dollar by 78 percent. In the case of the Chinese yuan, the coefficient is 0.87. A major part of the Frankel and Wei study is summarized in Table 2.2.

Frankel and Wei (1994) examined whether adding other currencies, DM, Australian dollar, and the New Zealand dollar would change the results. For the Singaporean dollar, when these currencies were added, the coefficients of the US dollar and the Japanese yen were reduced to 0.71 and 0.12, respectively, and the coefficient of DM is 0.14, and that of the NZ dollar 0.02, both being statistically significant. Similarly so for the Malaysian ringgit. (It is also possible that the Singaporean dollar was the genuine basket currency, and the Malaysian ringgit was pegged to the Singaporean dollar.) For other currencies, one cannot reject a hypothesis that coefficients of DM, the Australian dollar, and the NZ dollar were statistically significantly different from zero.

From Frankel and Wei, we may conclude that only the Singaporean dollar and the Malaysian ringgit had a genuine basket system. The former put to the US dollar a weight of 70 percent, and the Japanese yen and the German mark splitting the rest. The weights were similar for the Malaysian ringgit. Other than these currencies, the Asian currencies were de facto pegged to the US dollar, its weight in the basket being about 90 percent or higher.

6.2.   Trade linkage to United States and Japan

One of the reasons for the de facto dollar peg is that a large part of exports is destined for the United States, and the dollar denomination is convenient for avoiding

Table 2.2 The exchange rate basket

Sample period, 1979–1992

LHS	Constant	Dollar	Yen	R2/D.W.
Korean	−0.0007*	0.96**	−0.1	0.82
Won	(0.0003)	(0.02)	(0.03)	1.94
Singaporean	0.0003**	0.75**	0.13**	0.86
Dollar	(0.0002)	(0.01)	(0.02)	2.28
Hong Kong	−0.0007*	0.92**	−0.00	0.76
Dollar	(0.0003)	(0.02)	(0.03)	2.04
Taiwan	0.0005*	0.96**	0.05*	0.88
Dollar	(0.0002)	(0.02)	(0.02)	2.07
Malaysian	−0.0003	0.78**	0.07**	0.79
Ringgit	(0.0003)	(0.02)	(0.02)	2.19
Indonesian	−0.0018*	0.95**	0.16*	0.44
Rupia	(0.0007)	(0.05)	(0.07)	2.04
Philippine	−0.0018**	1.07**	−0.01	0.54
Peso	(0.0006)	(0.04)	(0.06)	2.06
Thai	−0.0004	0.91**	0.05**	0.75
Baht	(0.0003)	(0.02)	(0.03)	2.24
Chinese	−0.0018	0.87**	−0.04	0.54
Yuan	(0.0005)	0.04	(0.05)	2.05

Notes:
SE, in parentheses. **Statistically significant at the 1 percent level; *statistically significant at the 5 percent level.
Source: Frankel and Wei (1994).

fluctuation in export competitiveness. However, Japan is also a major trading partner for Asian countries. In fact, for most Asian economies, Japan and the United States are equally important as export destinations. Many Asian countries import parts and semifinished goods from Japan. As the nominal or real exchange rate vis-à-vis the US dollar has been stabilized by the exchange rate policy, the real effective exchange rate vis-à-vis the Japanese yen fluctuates widely as the Japanese yen fluctuates vis-à-vis the US dollar.

Table 2.3 shows exports and imports of NIEs (except Taipei, China), ASEAN-4 (Thailand, Indonesia, Malaysia, and Philippines), and China, by their destination or origin. Several features stand out. First, Japan is as important as the United States as a trade partner for most Asian countries. The trade linkage to Japan is especially strong for the ASEAN-4.

Table 2.3 NIES Gross Exports and Imports, by country and region
Hong Kong, exports and imports (US$mil. and %)

Exports to	1990	1991	1992	1993	1994	1995	1996
World	**82,160**	**98,577**	**119,512**	**135,248**	**151,395**	**173,754**	**180,745**
US	24.1%	22.7%	23.1%	23.0%	21.9%	21.8%	21.2%
Japan	5.7%	5.4%	5.2%	5.1%	5.6%	6.1%	6.5%
Asia	40.7%	41.9%	43.5%	45.0%	45.6%	46.5%	47.2%
Imports from							
World	**82,474**	**100,255**	**123,430**	**138,658**	**161,777**	**192,777**	**198,560**
US	8.1%	7.6%	7.4%	7.4%	7.1%	7.7%	7.9%
Japan	16.1%	16.4%	17.4%	16.6%	15.6%	14.8%	13.6%
Asia	59.6%	61.1%	60.0%	60.5%	61.5%	61.3%	62.0%

Korea, exports and imports (US$mil. and %)

Exports to	1990	1991	1992	1993	1994	1995	1996
World	**65,016**	**71,870**	**76,632**	**82,236**	**96,013**	**125,058**	**129,835**
US	29.9%	25.9%	23.6%	22.1%	21.4%	19.3%	16.8%
Japan	19.4%	17.2%	15.1%	14.1%	14.1%	13.7%	12.3%
Asia	17.6%	22.6%	28.0%	31.9%	32.2%	35.2%	38.0%
Imports from							
World	**69,844**	**81,525**	**81,775**	**83,800**	**102,348**	**135,119**	**150,212**
US	24.3%	23.2%	22.4%	21.4%	21.1%	22.5%	22.2%
Japan	26.6%	25.9%	23.8%	23.9%	24.8%	24.1%	20.9%
Asia	11.2%	15.9%	17.0%	16.7%	15.9%	16.0%	16.7%

Singapore, exports and imports (US$mil. and %)

Exports to	1990	1991	1992	1993	1994	1995	1996
World	**52,752**	**59,025**	**63,484**	**74,012**	**96,826**	**118,268**	**125,024**
US	21.3%	19.8%	21.1%	20.4%	18.7%	18.2%	18.4%
Japan	8.8%	8.7%	7.6%	7.5%	7.0%	7.8%	8.2%
Asia	42.8%	44.1%	43.3%	46.3%	50.4%	51.4%	51.3%
Imports from							
World	**60,889**	**66,293**	**72,179**	**85,234**	**102,670**	**124,507**	**131,338**
US	16.1%	15.8%	16.4%	16.4%	15.2%	15.0%	16.4%
Japan	20.1%	21.3%	21.1%	21.9%	21.9%	21.1%	18.2%
Asia	32.3%	34.2%	34.3%	36.2%	37.4%	38.1%	37.3%

Source: International Monetary Fund, Direction of Trade Statistics, Year book, 1997.

continued

Table 2.3—Continued

ASEAN exports and imports, by country and region

Thailand, exports and Imports (US$mil. and %)

Exports to	1990	1991	1992	1993	1994	1995	1996
World	**23,070**	**28,428**	**32,472**	**36,775**	**45,130**	**56,459**	**55,789**
US	22.7%	21.3%	22.5%	21.8%	21.1%	17.9%	18.0%
Japan	17.2%	18.1%	17.5%	17.1%	17.1%	16.8%	16.8%
Asia	22.1%	22.8%	24.0%	28.8%	34.8%	36.0%	36.8%
Imports from							
World	**33,379**	**37,591**	**40,686**	**45,922**	**54,459**	**70,776**	**73,484**
US	10.8%	10.6%	11.7%	11.7%	11.8%	12.0%	12.6%
Japan	30.4%	29.4%	29.3%	30.4%	30.2%	30.6%	27.8%
Asia	28.0%	30.0%	28.8%	26.8%	28.9%	26.6%	28.2%

Indonesia, exports and imports (US$mil. and %)

Exports to	1990	1991	1992	1993	1994	1995	1996
World	**25,675**	**29,142**	**33,967**	**36,823**	**40,054**	**45,417**	**49,814**
US	13.1%	12.0%	13.0%	14.2%	15.4%	14.3%	16.0%
Japan	42.5%	36.9%	31.7%	30.3%	28.6%	27.2%	27.8%
Asia	25.1%	29.2%	31.1%	30.6%	28.0%	31.2%	25.4%
Imports from							
World	**21,837**	**25,869**	**27,280**	**28,328**	**31,985**	**40,629**	**42,292**
US	11.5%	13.1%	14.0%	11.5%	10.7%	11.3%	10.3%
Japan	25.0%	24.5%	22.0%	22.1%	25.8%	24.3%	23.6%
Asia	24.8%	26.0%	26.2%	27.2%	26.0%	27.0%	27.7%

Malaysia, exports and imports (US$mil. and %)

Exports to	1990	1991	1992	1993	1994	1995	1996
World	**29,416**	**34,349**	**40,713**	**47,122**	**58,756**	**74,037**	**78,246**
US	15.9%	16.9%	18.7%	20.3%	21.2%	20.7%	18.2%
Japan	15.3%	15.9%	13.3%	13.0%	11.9%	12.4%	13.4%
Asia	44.6%	44.4%	44.6%	43.9%	44.2%	43.6%	46.8%
Imports from							
World	**29,258**	**36,648**	**39,926**	**45,657**	**59,581**	**77,751**	**78,422**
US	16.9%	15.4%	15.9%	16.9%	16.6%	16.3%	15.5%
Japan	24.1%	26.1%	26.0%	27.5%	26.7%	27.2%	24.5%
Asia	32.0%	33.8%	35.4%	34.3%	32.6%	31.8%	34.6%

Philippines, exports and imports (US$mil. and %)

Exports to	1990	1991	1992	1993	1994	1995	1996
World	**8,068**	**8,767**	**9,752**	**11,089**	**13,304**	**17,502**	**20,417**
US	38.5%	35.9%	39.4%	39.2%	38.9%	35.5%	34.1%
Japan	20.1%	20.2%	17.9%	16.3%	15.2%	15.7%	18.0%
Asia	18.1%	18.8%	16.8%	21.0%	22.9%	25.6%	25.9%
Imports from							
World	**13,041**	**12,786**	**15,449**	**18,754**	**22,546**	**28,337**	**34,122**
US	19.5%	20.4%	17.0%	18.8%	18.5%	18.4%	18.3%
Japan	18.4%	19.7%	20.0%	21.4%	24.2%	22.2%	20.3%
Asia	28.2%	30.1%	26.8%	27.5%	30.2%	29.4%	27.8%

Source: International Monetary Fund, Direction of Trade Statistics Year book, 1997.

Second, Japan tends to be more important as an import origin than as an export destination. Except for Indonesia and India, the import share from Japan is higher than the export share. The export share of Japan is lower than the export share of the United States for all countries in the table, except for Indonesia and China. The import share of Japan is higher than that of the United States for all countries except for Korea (in 1996 only).

Third, the Asian developing countries collectively are also an important trading partner. For Hong Kong, Malaysia, and Singapore, about one half of their exports go to Asian developing countries. For Thailand and the Philippines, the share going to Asian developing countries has increased market from 1990 to 1996, reflecting the trade linkage is now stronger among the ASEAN-4.

6.3.   *Real exchange rates and export volume*

In order to make observations on the relationship between the exchange rate movement and export performance, the real exchange rate of Country A (say, Thailand) vis-à-vis the Japanese yen, say the baht/yen real exchange rate, or RER(A/Y), is calculated using the baht/yen nominal exchange rate, or (A/Y), and the CPI of Country A, CPIA, and the CPI of Japan, or CPIJ. Therefore, RER(A/Y) = (A/Y)*(CPIJ)/(CPIA). The real exchange rate vis-à-vis the US dollar, RER(A/D), is similarly defined, RER(A/D) = (A/D)*(CPIU)/(CPIA), where CPIU is the CPI of the United States.

In Figures 2.1–2.7, the real exchange rates, RER(A/Y) and RER(A/D), are plotted against the export volume, in bars, for each of NIEs (except Hong Kong)

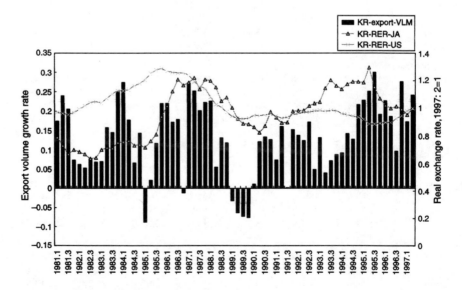

Figure 2.1 Korea—real exchange rate and export volume.

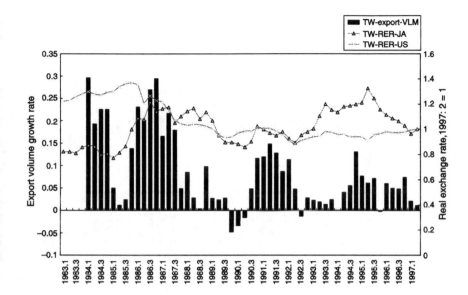

Figure 2.2 Taiwan—real exchange rate and export volume.

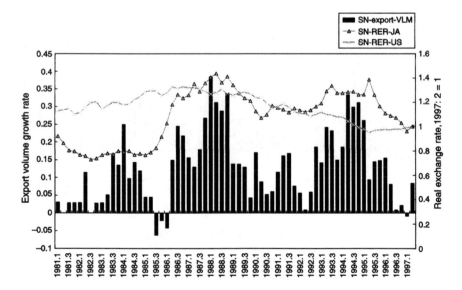

Figure 2.3 Singapore—real exchange rate *vs*. US and export volume.

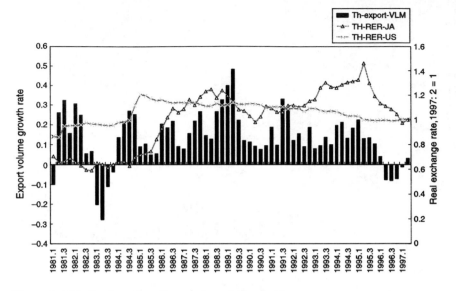

Figure 2.4 Thailand—real exchange rate and export volume.

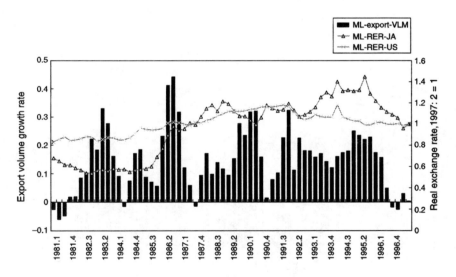

Figure 2.5 Malaysia—real exchange rate and export volume.

and the four ASEAN countries, with quarterly frequency from 1981:1 to 1997:2. The levels of the real exchange rates are measured with normalization where the last observation equals one. The export volume is measured as the changes over the preceding four quarters.

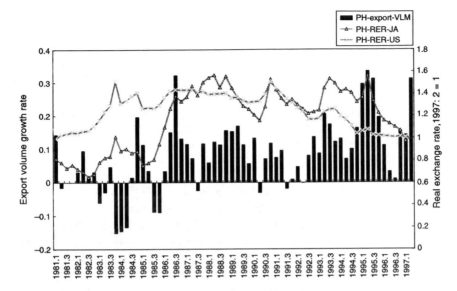

Figure 2.6 Philippines—real exchange rate and export volume.

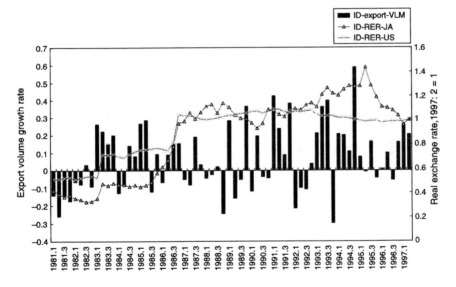

Figure 2.7 Indonesia—real exchange rate and export volume.

In general, the real exchange rate vis-à-vis the US dollar, RER(A/D), is stable, reflecting the dollar peg policy. However, it is also evident that occasional devaluation (vis-à-vis the US dollar) took place, such as Thailand in 1984, and Indonesia in 1983 and 1986. The degree of stability varies from country to country. As the RER-US movement is not volatile, its correlation with export volume is not apparent. The trend real appreciation of their currencies vis-à-vis the US dollar mainly reflects the inflation differential. The real exchange rate vis-à-vis the US dollar, RER(A/D), for Thailand and Indonesia has been remarkably stable since the mid-1980s.

The real exchange rate vis-à-vis the yen, RER(A/Y), fluctuates as the yen/dollar rate fluctuates. In some countries, strong correlation between RER(A/Y) and export volume is observed. In all countries, the yen appreciation (or depreciation of an Asian currency vis-à-vis yen) episodes of 1985–87 and 1992–95 are accompanied by a surge in export volume growth rates. Also, in many countries, the yen depreciation (or appreciation of an Asian currency vis-à-vis the yen) of 1989–90 affected export volume adversely.

For Malaysia, the correlation between the RER(A/Y) and export volume was weak in the 1980s but became stronger in the 1990s, because its export structure became much more industrial (especially, electronics) in the 1990s. The Indonesian export movement does not seem to be correlated with its RER. This is because oil and other mineral resources have a large share in the Indonesian trade structure, and their export performances, which may not be directly related to RER, have a large impact on the Indonesian growth of exports. It is more important to look at the non-oil-and-gas exports, in order to see the impact of the exchange rate.

Therefore, it is reasonable to conclude that the exchange rate movement vis-à-vis Japan and its effects on the export industry is important, and this is a result of the policy that de facto fixed their exchange rate to the US dollar.

In each figure, the spike of RER(A/Y) in the second quarter of 1995 is very prominent. This reflects a sharp yen appreciation at the time and the Asian currencies' de facto dollar peg. The yen had an appreciation trend in the first half of the 1990s and climaxed at 80 yen/dollar in April 1995. The yen reversed its movement and depreciated to the 100 level in the following five months, and further depreciated to 120 level in the following two years. The yen appreciation in the first half of the 1990s helped exports from most Asian countries. The subsequent yen depreciation significantly dampened exports from these countries, especially from Thailand.

7.   Regression analysis

7.1.   Pass-through equation

This section investigates quantitatively theoretical prediction of the model (Section 5), with some prior knowledge of general movements of exports from stylized facts (Section 6). First, the pass-through equation, the response of export price to the changes in the exchange rate, will be estimated. The innovative feature of our model is that there are two exchange rates in the model. The ASEAN firm is expected to respond to both the baht/yen exchange rate and the baht/dollar exchange rate. Consider the effects of the baht/yen exchange rate change and the baht/dollar exchange rate, in order. Second, the volume of exports will be regressed on the bilateral real exchange rates of the baht/yen and baht/dollar, and the real income growth of Japan and the United States. The coefficients of the exchange rates will capture the price elasticities of the demand for the ASEAN goods, and the coefficients of the income variables will capture the income elasticities of the ASEAN goods.

Pass-through equation: The change in the real export price in local currency is regressed on the changes in the real exchange rates against the dollar and the yen.

$$D(\text{Real export price in local currency}(t)) = \gamma_0 + \gamma_1 D(\text{RER}(A/D)(t))$$

$$+ \gamma_2 D(RER(A/Y)(t)) + e(t)$$

where $D(x(t))$ is the growth rate of x, namely $(x(t) - x(t-1))/x(t-1)$; export prices are divided by the respective CPI; coefficients γ_1 and γ_2 represent the pass-through coefficients, or sensitivities, of the real export price to the changes in the real exchange rate vis-à-vis the dollar and vis-à-vis the yen, respectively. When the export price trend is different from CPI, then it is captured in the constant term. For example, when the Balassa–Samuelson effect is present, that is, productivity growth is significantly different in nontradable and tradable sectors, the nontradable prices are likely to increase faster than the tradable prices. If the pass-through coefficient is unity, then the changes in the export price fully reflect the exchange rate changes; that is, 1 percent depreciation vis-à-vis the dollar will increase the export price in local currency by 1 percent so that the export price in the dollar remains the same (a full pass-through). However, this would put the exporters in the less competitive positions against the Japanese exporters in the Japanese market, and, in case of Model A, in the US market as well.

Monthly data are collected either from IFS or national sources. The change was taken against the same month of the previous year. The moving average process in the error terms is dealt with by using the Newey–West method. The sample period is from 1981–1996, except as noted. Table 2.4 summarizes the regression results. In general, the degree of export price adjustment varies from one country to another.

In Thailand, where the sample period starts in 1986 to avoid the exchange rate regime change of 1984, the sensitivity of the export prices to the dollar is small and insignificant, while the sensitivity with respect to the yen is about 0.14 and barely significant (at 10 percent).[8] The constant term is insignificant (no Balassa–Samuelson effect).

In Indonesia, where the sample period starts in 1988 to avoid the exchange rate regime in 1986, sensitivities with respect to the dollar and the yen are both statistically insignificant.

The Korean case presents an interesting picture. Korean export prices respond to the dollar and the yen in a similar magnitude of sensitivity, 0.12 and 0.13, respectively, but only the yen is statistically significant. The constant term is also significant, with a negative coefficient, suggesting that the prices of the nontradables (contained in CPI) are increasing more than the export prices (tradables).

Table 2.4 Pass-through equations

$D(\text{Export Price in l.c.}(t)) = \gamma_0 + \gamma_1 D((A/D)(t)) + \gamma_2 D((A/Y)(t)) + e(t)$

where $D(*)$ is the difference over the same month of year $t - 1$. The 'Robusterrors' option (RATS) is used to correct for autocorrelation in error terms.

Thailand
Period: 1986:01–1996:05
Data source of export price: IFS

With constant

	Coef.	t-value	Signif.
Constant	−0.01	−0.53	0.598
Dollar Ex.	0.03	0.06	0.954
Yen Ex.	0.14	1.68	0.092

R-bar-sq.: 0.086

Without constant

	Coef.	t-value	Signif.
Dollar Ex.	0.28	0.76	0.447
Yen Ex.	0.14	1.62	0.106

R-bar-sq.: 0.080

Indonesia
Period: 1988:1–1996:12
Data source of export price: Biropusat Statiskik

With constant

	Coef.	t-value	Signif.
Constant	−0.02	−1.38	0.167
Dollar Ex.	−0.62	−1.28	0.200
Yen Ex.	0.08	1.21	0.228

R-bar-sq.: 0.145

Without constant

	Coef.	t-value	Signif.
Dollar Ex.	−0.48	−0.99	0.323
Yen Ex.	0.09	0.91	0.362

R-bar-sq.: 0.038

Korea
Period: 1981:1–1996:12
Data source of export price: Bank of Korea

With constant

	Coef.	t-value	Signif.
Constant	−0.03	−4.47	0.000
Dollar Ex.	0.12	1.35	0.176
Yen Ex.	0.13	5.93	0.000

R-bar-sq.: 0.386

Without constant

	Coef.	t-value	Signif.
Dollar Ex.	0.16	2.20	0.028
Yen Ex.	0.10	2.03	0.042

R-bar-sq.: −0.184

continued

Table 2.4—Continued
Taiwan
Period: 1985:12–1988:12, 1990:9–1996:12
Data source of export price: The Central Bank of China

With constant

	Coef.	t-value	Signif.
Constant	0.02	1.13	0.257
Dollar Ex.	0.49	3.40	0.001
Yen Ex.	−0.06	−1.18	0.239

R-bar-sq.: 0.314

Without constant

	Coef.	t-value	Signif.
Dollar Ex.	0.39	2.86	0.004
Yen Ex.	−0.02	−0.48	0.630

R-bar-sq.: 0.258

Singapore
Period: 1981:1–1996:12
Data source of export price: IFS

With constant

	Coef.	t-value	Signif.
Constant	−0.03	−3.57	0.000
Dollar Ex.	−0.82	−5.38	0.000
Yen Ex.	−0.07	−0.93	0.350

R-bar-sq.: 0.318

Without constant

	Coef.	t-value	Signif.
Dollar Ex.	−0.68	−3.68	0.000
Yen Ex.	−0.09	−0.89	0.375

R-bar-sq.: 0.111

Philippines
Period: 1981:1–1991:12
Data source of export price: IFS

With constant

	Coef.	t-value	Signif.
Constant	−0.16	−3.96	0.000
Dollar Ex.	−0.20	−0.51	0.608
Yen Ex.	0.41	1.89	0.059

R-bar-sq.: 0.142

Without constant

	Coef.	t-value	Signif.
Dollar Ex.	−0.67	−1.19	0.233
Yen Ex.	0.34	0.91	0.364

R-bar-sq.: −0.715

The Taiwan case is rather different from the above countries, in that the sensitivity of export prices with respect to the dollar movement is large, 0.49. About half of the dollar fluctuation is absorbed by the export price changes. The sensitivity with respect to the yen is small and insignificant.

Singapore presents a puzzling case in that the sensitivity with respect to the dollar is negative, large, and significant. A small Balassa–Samuelson effect is detected.

In the case of the Philippines, the sensitivity with respect to the yen is large (0.41) and mildly significant (at 6 percent). A strong Balassa–Samuelson effect is detected. Note that the Balassa–Samuelson effect is a proposition on the relative magnitude of the two sectors. A large negative constant term is consistent with a case where nontradables are extremely unproductive and experienced high inflation, while tradables are not.

7.2.   Volume equation

The export volume is regressed on the real exchange rate changes against the US dollar and the Japanese yen, and real GDP growth rates of the United States and Japan. The latter terms represent export demand increase due to income increases in the United States and Japan.

$$D(\text{Export volume } (t)) = \omega_1 D(RER(A/D)(t)) + \omega_2 D(RER(A/Y)(t))$$
$$+ \omega_3 D(USGDP(t)) + \omega_4 D(JAGDP(t)) + e(t)$$

where $D(\cdot)$ is the growth rate operator, $RER(\cdot)$ is the real exchange rate using CPI, and USGDP and JAGDP denote real GDP of the United States and Japan, respectively. Data are quarterly, due to the availability of GDP data. All variables are measured as the change over the preceding year (four quarters). The moving average process in the error terms are dealt with by the Newey–West method.

Table 2.5 summarizes the results of this regression. There is no general observation. In all countries but Taiwan, the export volume has an increasing trend (a positive constant in the above regression with export volume increase on the left-hand-side variable).

Table 2.5 Export volume

$$D(\text{Export volume } (t)) = \omega_1 D(RER(A/D)(t)) + \omega_2 D(RER(A/Y)(t)) + \omega_3 D(USGDP(t))$$
$$+ \omega_4 D(JAGDP(t)) + e(t)$$

where $D(*)$ is the difference over the four quarters. The 'Robusterrors' option (RATS) is used to correct for autocorrelation in error terms.

Thailand
Period: 1986:Q1–1996:Q4
Data source of export volume: IFS

	Coef.	*t-value*	*Signif.*
Constant	0.14	3.17	0.002
Dollar Ex.	2.42	1.45	0.148
Yen Ex.	0.34	1.87	0.061
US-RGDP	0.43	0.36	0.718
JP-RGDP	0.91	1.29	0.195

R-bar-sq.: 0.126

continued

Table 2.5—Continued
Indonesia
Period: 1988:Q1–1996:Q4
Data source of export volume: IFS

	Coef.	t-value	Signif.
Constant	0.19	4.38	0.000
Dollar Ex.	−0.08	−0.06	0.950
Yen Ex.	0.10	0.48	0.632
US-RGDP	−2.76	−1.64	0.100
JP-RGDP	−1.68	−1.80	0.071

R-bar-sq.: −0.048

Korea
Period: 1981:Q1–1996:Q4
Data source of export volume: IFS

	Coef.	t-value	Signif.
Constant	0.10	2.96	0.003
Dollar Ex.	−0.03	−0.10	0.921
Yen Ex.	0.17	1.72	0.085
US-RGDP	1.13	3.41	0.001
JP-RGDP	−0.22	−0.29	0.773

R-bar-sq.: 0.114

Taiwan
Period: 1985:Q1–1996:Q4
Data source of export volume: IFS

	Coef.	t-value	Signif.
Constant	0.01	0.15	0.880
Dollar Ex.	−0.25	−1.14	0.253
Yen Ex.	0.35	4.64	0.000
US-RGDP	1.27	1.19	0.233
JP-RGDP	1.00	1.32	0.188

R-bar-sq.: 0.304

continued

Table 2.5—Continued
Singapore
Period: 1981:Q1–1996:Q4
Data source of export volume: IFS

	Coef.	t-value	Signif.
Constant	0.08	1.99	0.047
Dollar Ex.	−0.89	−2.62	0.009
Yen Ex.	0.16	1.54	0.124
US-RGDP	1.47	3.22	0.001
JP-RGDP	0.17	0.14	0.885

R-bar-sq.: 0.209

Philippines
Period: 1981:Q1–1996:Q4
Data source of export volume: IFS

	Coef.	t-value	Signif.
Constant	0.13	3.53	0.000
Dollar Ex.	−0.67	−2.83	0.005
Yen Ex.	0.27	3.26	0.001
US-RGDP	−1.00	−1.81	0.071
JP-RGDP	−0.97	−1.17	0.242

R-bar-sq.: 0.253

For Thai export volume, the baht/yen rate is the only significant (at 10 percent) variable. The elasticity of the export volume with respect to the yen movement is estimated as 0.34. Recall that the Thai graph in stylized facts section gave a general impression that the yen movement and the export volume are correlated. This regression confirmed that observation. Although insignificant, the coefficient of the dollar movement is positive, suggesting that, for Thailand, Model B (Thai products compete with the US products in the United States) is more consistent than Model A (Thai products compete with Japanese products in the United States).

For Indonesian exports, the coefficient of the rupiah/dollar rate is negative, suggesting that Model A is applicable, but neither the rupiah/yen nor the rupiah/dollar exchange rate is statistically significant. The Japanese growth is mildly significant. This may reflect the fact that Japan is a number one destination of Indonesian exports.

Korean exports are explained by the won/yen real exchange rate (significance at 10 percent) and US economic growth (significance at 1 percent). This result is consistent with theoretical predictions. The Korean exports are found to be negatively affected by the won/US dollar and Japanese growth rates, but the coefficients are statistically insignificant. Recalling the theoretical prediction (Table 2.1), this may mean that Korean exports face a situation similar to Model A (competing with Japanese exports in both Japanese and US markets, while importing parts from Japan).

Unlike Korea and Singapore, Taiwan exports are most significantly affected by the NTdollar/yen rate. The yen depreciation of 10 percent will decrease the export volume by 3.5 percent. Other factors are insignificant.

Singaporean export volumes are explained by the Singapore dollar/US dollar exchange rate, with negative coefficient, and the US growth. The Singaporean case, being consistent with Model A, indicates that Singaporean exports have an industrial structure and technological levels similar to Japanese exports and that they are competing in the United States.

Philippine exports are shown to be very sensitive with both exchange rates. The peso/dollar rate has a negative coefficient, suggesting that Model A is more applicable to the Philippines case. On the contrary, the export volumes from the Philippines increase with the yen devaluation. However, a puzzling feature is that the Philippine export volume declines when the US economic growth rate increases.

In sum, export volume regressions present a reasonable result, with only a few puzzling coefficients. For Thailand, Model B applies, and for other countries, Model A seems to apply, but t-statistics of the exchange rate vis-à-vis the US dollar are low, except for the Singapore and the Philippines, so that the result may not be reliable.

7.3. Optimal currency weight

At the end of the theory section, a formula for the optimal currency basket weight was proposed, Equation (27) for Model A and Equation (28) for Model B. The optimal dollar peg weight in Model A (Equation 27) can be rewritten by using coefficients α_1, α_2, β_1, β_2 of regression Equations (29)–(32).

$$w^* = \frac{T_{US} + \alpha_1 X + \beta_1 T}{T + (\alpha_1 + \alpha_2 - 1)X + (\beta_1 + \beta_2)T} \tag{33}$$

The optimal dollar peg weight in Model B (Equation 28) can be rewritten by using coefficients α_3, α_4, β_3, β_4 of regression Equations (29)–(32). For simplicity, we assume that that ω_x and ω_m are nearly equal to each other.

$$w^* = \frac{-M_{US} + \alpha_3 X + \beta_3 T}{T + (\alpha_3 + \alpha_4 - 1)X + (\beta_3 + \beta_4)T} \tag{34}$$

where M_{US} denotes a value of imports from the United States.

Now with regression results in the preceding subsections, and bilateral trade balance shown in Table 2.3, we can calculate the optimal weights according to Equation (33) for Model A and Equation (34) for Model B. Table 2.6 shows the optimal weights for each country, for Model A [with a constant term in price Equation (A-1), and without a constant term (A-2)] and Model B [with a constant term in price Equation (B-1), and without a constant term (B-2)].

Table 2.6 Optimal weight

| | Actual weight | | Optimal weight | | | | | | | |
| | | | Model A-1 | | Model A-2 | | Model B-1 | | Model B-2 | |
	US$ (%)	Yen (%)	US$ (%)	Yen (%)	US$ (%)	Yen (%)	US$ (%)	Yen (%)	US$ (%)	Yen (%)
Thai Baht	91	5	42.9	57.1	4.3	95.7	61.3	38.7	35.3	64.7
Indonesian Rupia	95	16	40.5	59.5	47.7	52.3	71.2	28.8	77.9	22.1
Korean Won	96	−10	10.5	89.5	10.9	89.1	47.4	52.6	45.7	54.3
Taiwan Dollar	96	5	−92.7	192.7	−73.7	173.7	−5.3	105.3	7.3	92.7
Singaporean Dollar	75	13	22.6	77.4	12.4	87.6	57.4	42.6	51.0	49.0
Philippine Peso	107	−1	−2.9	102.9	27.6	72.4	67.3	32.7	72.8	27.2

Notes:
Model A-1 uses the coefficients estimated in the case of price equations (Model A) with constant in Table 2.4 and the coefficients estimated in the volume equations in Table 2.5.
Model A-2 uses those in price equations (Model A) without constant in Table 2.4 and those in the volume equations in Table 2.5.
Model B-1 uses those in the price equations (Model B) with constant in Table 2.4 and those in the volume equations in Table 2.5.
Model B-2 uses those in the price equations (Model B) without constant in Table 2.4 and those in the volume equations in Table 2.5.

In calculating the export to and import from the world in equations (27) and (28), only the sum of those with Japan and the US are used.

For Actual Weight, see Table 2.2.

In general, the estimates fall between 0 and 1, except three subcases of Taiwan and one subcase of the Philippines. According to our estimates, in all countries, the yen weight should be much higher than the actual weight estimated by Frankel and Wei, cited in Table 2.2. Unfortunately, estimates are sensitive to the choice of model (A-1, A-2, B-1, or B-2) for each country. Estimates naturally vary across countries. As we interpreted results of volume regressions, we may tentatively choose Model B for Thailand and Model A for all other cases. For Thailand, the optimal yen weight is estimated anywhere between 39 percent (Model B-1) and 65 percent (Model B-2). For Indonesia, the yen optimal weight is between 52 percent (Model A-1) and 60 percent (Model A-2). For Korea, both A-1 and A-2 models indicate that the optimal yen weight is 89 percent. Taiwan shows a puzzling case in which the optimal yen weight is more than 100 percent. We suspect that coefficients in either price and volume equations are somehow wrongly estimated for the Taiwan case, and we do not take the Taiwan result seriously.[9] The optimal weight of the yen for the Singaporean dollar is between 77 percent (Model A-1) and 88 percent (Model A-2). The case of Model A-1 for the Philippines is puzzling in that the weight of the yen exceeds 100 percent. Again, we do not take this case seriously. However, in the case of A-2, the optimal yen weight is calculated as 72 percent.

In sum, the optimal weight of the yen is highest in Korea and Singapore. Since these countries are often thought to have industrial structure and associated technological levels similar to Japan, their exports directly compete with Japanese products in Japan and the United States. Therefore, the results of the high optimal yen weights in the two countries look reasonable.

Of course, we are aware that many of the coefficients in the price and volume equations which are used in calculating the optimal weights have low *t*-statistics. The robustness of our results with respect to theoretical model specification and variables in the regressions are not as ideal as we desire. However, the result shows an important avenue for further research on the optimal currency weight in Asia.

8. Conclusion

In this chapter, we have constructed a theoretical model in which the Asian firm maximizes its profit, competing with the Japanese and the US firms in their markets. The duopoly model is used to determine export prices and volumes in response to the exchange rate fluctuations vis-à-vis the Japanese yen and the US dollar. Then, the optimal basket weight that would minimize the fluctuation of the growth rate of trade balance was derived. These are the novel features of our model.

The export price equation and export volume equation are estimated for several Asian countries for the sample period from 1981 to 1996. The results are generally reasonable. The optimal currency weights for the yen and the US dollar are derived and compared with actual weights that have been adopted before the currency crisis of 1997. For all countries in the sample, it is shown that the optimal weight of the yen is significantly higher than the actual weight.

So, how did the dollar peg fail in Asia? In this chapter, the basket peg is called 'optimal' when it minimizes variation of profits which equals net exports to the Japanese and US markets, each of which is a duopoly market competing against the Japanese goods or the US goods. In the optimal peg of the typical Asian country, say Thailand, the weight of the yen was higher than the actual weight. In fact, the actual weight of the US dollar always exceeds the dollar's optimal weight, and the actual weight of the Japanese yen is always less than the optimal weight. Under the optimal peg, the currency, baht, would have appreciated (vis-à-vis the US dollar) when the yen appreciated, so that the boom would have been less; and the currency would have depreciated when the yen depreciated, so that weakening in exports would have been mitigated. Under the dollar peg, which the Asian countries had adopted, an amplified boom and bust of exports created irreversible redundancy in real estates and other industries. Thus the sharp decline in exports convinced investors and speculators that the dollar peg would be unsustainable.

It would be interesting to extend our model so that multiple Asian countries are included. In such a model, Asian exporters compete with other (non-Japan)

Asian exporters, as well as with Japanese and US producers, in the world market. The cross exchange rates (e.g., the baht/rupiah rate) would become relevant in such a model, and the optimal currency basket include those cross rates. Then, we can investigate issues such as competitive devaluation, contagion of a currency crisis, a benchmark basket, and the optimal weights of the benchmark basket. However, these topics are left for future research.

Appendix

(a) Model A

We use Equations (7a) and (8a) to derive rates of changes in the prices of the ASEAN products in the Japanese and US markets in Model A, respectively.

$$
\hat{P}_J^Y = \frac{1 + \eta_J^*}{1 + \eta_J + \eta_J^*} \left\{ (1 - \omega_m) \frac{E^{A/\$} P_m^\$}{E^{A/Y}} (\hat{E}^{A/\$} - \hat{E}^{A/Y}) - \frac{\overline{C}'}{\frac{E^{A/Y}}{TC_A}} \hat{E}^{A/Y} \right\}
$$

$$
= \frac{1 + \eta_J^*}{1 + \eta_J + \eta_J^*} \left\{ (1 - \omega_m) B_1 (\hat{E}^{A/\$} - \hat{E}^{A/Y}) - B_2 \hat{E}^{A/Y} \right\}
$$

$$
= \frac{1 + \eta_J^*}{1 + \eta_J + \eta_J^*} (1 - \omega_m) B_1 \hat{E}^{A/\$} - \frac{1 + \eta_J^*}{1 + \eta_J + \eta_J^*} \left\{ (1 - \omega_m) B_1 + B_2 \right\} \hat{E}^{A/Y}
$$

$$
\tag{A1}
$$

$$
\hat{P}_{US}^\$ = \hat{E}^{A/Y} - \hat{E}^{A/\$} + \frac{1 + \eta_{US}^*}{1 + \eta_{US} + \eta_{US}^*} \left\{ (1 - \omega_m) \frac{E^{A/\$} P_m^\$}{E^{A/Y}} (\hat{E}^{A/\$} - \hat{E}^{A/Y}) \right.
$$

$$
\left. - \frac{\overline{C}'}{\frac{E^{A/Y}}{TC_A}} \hat{E}^{A/Y} \right\}
$$

$$
= \hat{E}^{A/Y} - \hat{E}^{A/\$} + \frac{1 + \eta_{US}^*}{1 + \eta_{US} + \eta_{US}^*} \left\{ (1 - \omega_m) B_1 (\hat{E}^{A/\$} - \hat{E}^{A/Y}) - B_2 \hat{E}^{A/Y} \right\}
$$

$$
= \left\{ \frac{1 + \eta_{US}^*}{1 + \eta_{US} + \eta_{US}^*} (1 - \omega_m) B_1 - 1 \right\} \hat{E}^{A/\$}
$$

$$
+ \left\{ 1 - \frac{1 + \eta_{US}^*}{1 + \eta_{US} + \eta_{US}^*} \left\{ (1 - \omega_m) B_1 + B_2 \right\} \right\} \hat{E}^{A/Y}
$$

$$
\tag{A2}
$$

$$\hat{P}_x^A = \frac{X_J}{X}\left(\hat{P}_J^Y + \hat{E}^{A/Y}\right) + \frac{X_{US}}{X}\left(\hat{P}_{US}^\$ + \hat{E}^{A/\$}\right)$$

$$= \left[\frac{1+\eta^*}{1+\eta+\eta^*}(1-\omega_m)B_1\right]\hat{E}^{A/\$} + \left[1 - \frac{1+\eta^*}{1+\eta+\eta^*}\{(1-\omega_m)B_1 + B_2\}\right]\hat{E}^{A/Y} \tag{A3}$$

We use Equations (10a) and (10b) to derive rates of changes in the outputs exported to the Japanese and US markets, respectively:

$$\hat{f} = \frac{-\varepsilon_J}{1+\eta_J+\eta_J^*}\left\{\frac{(1-\omega_m)\dfrac{E^{A/\$}P_m^\$}{E^{A/Y}}}{TC_A}\hat{E}^{A/\$} - \frac{(1-\omega_m)\dfrac{E^{A/\$}P_m^\$}{E^{A/Y}} + \dfrac{\overline{C'}}{E^{A/Y}}}{TC_A}\hat{E}^{A/Y}\right\}$$

$$= \frac{-\varepsilon_J}{1+\eta_J+\eta_J^*}\left[(1-\omega_m)B_1\hat{E}^{A/\$} - \{(1-\omega_m)B_1 + B_2\}\hat{E}^{A/Y}\right] \tag{A4}$$

$$\hat{g} = \frac{-\varepsilon_{US}}{1+\eta_{US}+\eta_{US}^*}\left\{\frac{(1-\omega_m)\dfrac{E^{A/\$}P_m^Y}{E^{A/Y}}}{TC_A}\hat{E}^{A/\$} - \frac{(1-\omega_m)\dfrac{E^{A/\$}P_m^Y}{E^{A/Y}} + \dfrac{\overline{C'}}{E^{A/Y}}}{TC_A}\hat{E}^{A/Y}\right\}$$

$$= \frac{-\varepsilon_{US}}{1+\eta_{US}+\eta_{US}^*}\left[(1-\omega_m)B_1\hat{E}^{A/\$} - \{(1-\omega_m)B_1 + B_2\}\hat{E}^{A/Y}\right] \tag{A5}$$

From Equations (A3) and (A4), we derive the rate of changes in the total outputs of the ASEAN firm:

$$\hat{Q}_A = \omega_x\hat{f} + (1-\omega_x)\hat{g}$$

$$= \frac{-\varepsilon_J}{1+\eta_J+\eta_J^*}\omega_x\left[(1-\omega_m)B_1\hat{E}^{A/\$} - \{(1-\omega_m)B_1 + B_2\}\hat{E}^{A/Y}\right]$$

$$+ \frac{-\varepsilon_{US}}{1+\eta_{US}+\eta_{US}^*}(1-\omega_x)\left[(1-\omega_m)B_1\hat{E}^{A/\$} - \{(1-\omega_m)B_1 + B_2\}\hat{E}^{A/Y}\right]$$

$$= -\left\{\frac{\varepsilon_J}{1+\eta_J+\eta_J^*}\omega_x + \frac{\varepsilon_{US}}{1+\eta_{US}+\eta_{US}^*}(1-\omega_x)\right\}$$

$$\times \left[(1-\omega_m)B_1\hat{E}^{A/\$} - \{(1-\omega_m)B_1 + B_2\}\hat{E}^{A/Y}\right] \tag{A6}$$

From Equation (21), we obtain the rate of changes in the trade balance of the ASEAN economy:

$$\hat{T} = \left\{ \frac{E^{A/Y}P_J^Y f}{T} - \frac{E^{A/Y}P_m^Y \omega_m Q_A}{T} \right\} \hat{E}^{A/Y} + \left\{ \frac{E^{A/\$}P_{US}^\$ g}{T} - \frac{E^{A/\$}P_m^\$(1-\omega_m)Q_A}{T} \right\} \hat{E}^{A/\$}$$

$$+ \frac{E^{A/Y}P_J^Y f}{T}(\hat{P}_J^Y + \hat{f}) + \frac{E^{A/\$}P_{US}^\$ g}{T}(\hat{P}_{US}^\$ + \hat{g})$$

$$- \frac{E^{A/Y}P_m^Y \omega_m Q_A + E^{A/\$}P_m^\$(1-\omega_m)Q_A}{T}\hat{Q}_A$$

$$\hat{T} = \left\{ \frac{f}{Q_A} \frac{E^{A/Y}P_J^Y Q_A}{T} - \frac{E^{A/Y}P_m^Y \omega_m Q_A}{T} \right\} \hat{E}^{A/Y} + \left\{ \frac{g}{Q_A} \frac{E^{A/\$}P_{US}^\$ Q_A}{T} \right.$$

$$\left. - \frac{E^{A/\$}P_m^\$(1-\omega_m)Q_A}{T} \right\} \hat{E}^{A/\$} + \frac{f}{Q_A} \frac{E^{A/Y}P_J^Y Q_A}{T}(\hat{P}_J^Y + \hat{f})$$

$$+ \frac{g}{Q_A} \frac{E^{A/\$}P_{US}^\$ Q_A}{T}(\hat{P}_{US}^\$ + \hat{g}) - \frac{E^{A/Y}P_m^Y \omega_m Q_A + E^{A/\$}P_m^\$(1-\omega_m)Q_A}{T}\hat{Q}_A$$

$$\hat{T} = \frac{Q_A}{T} \left[\left\{ \omega_x E^{A/Y}P_J^Y - \omega_m E^{A/Y}P_m^Y \right\} \hat{E}^{A/Y} + \left\{ (1-\omega_x)E^{A/\$}P_{US}^\$ \right. \right.$$

$$-(1-\omega_m)E^{A/\$}P_m^\$ \Big\} \hat{E}^{A/\$} + \omega_x E^{A/Y}P_J^Y(\hat{P}_J^Y + \hat{f})$$

$$+ (1-\omega_x)E^{A/\$}P_{US}^\$(\hat{P}_{US}^\$ + \hat{g}) - \left\{ \omega_m E^{A/Y}P_m^Y + (1-\omega_m)E^{A/\$}P_m^\$ \right\} \hat{Q}_A \Bigg]$$

$$\text{(A7)}$$

Substituting Equations (A1)–(A5) into Equation (A6), we obtain Equation (22).

(b) Model B

We use Equations (17a) and (18a) to derive rates of changes in the prices of the ASEAN products in the Japanese and US markets in Model B, respectively.

$$\hat{P}_J^Y = \frac{1+\eta_J^*}{1+\eta_J+\eta_J^*} \left\{ (1-\omega_m)\frac{E^{A/\$}P_m^\$}{E^{A/Y}}(\hat{E}^{A/\$} - \hat{E}^{A/Y}) - \frac{\overline{C}'}{E^{A/Y}}\hat{E}^{A/Y} \right\}$$

$$= \frac{1+\eta_J^*}{1+\eta_J+\eta_J^*} \left\{ (1-\omega_m)B_1(\hat{E}^{A/\$} - \hat{E}^{A/Y}) - B_2\hat{E}^{A/Y} \right\}$$

$$= \frac{1+\eta_J^*}{1+\eta_J+\eta_J^*} \left[(1-\omega_m)B_1\hat{E}^{A/\$} - \{(1-\omega_m)B_1 + B_2\}\hat{E}^{A/Y} \right]$$

$$= \frac{1+\eta_J^*}{1+\eta_J+\eta_J^*}(1-\omega_m)B_1\hat{E}^{A/\$} - \frac{1+\eta_J^*}{1+\eta_J+\eta_J^*}\{(1-\omega_m)B_1+B_2\}\hat{E}^{A/Y}$$

$$(A1')$$

$$\hat{P}_{US}^{\$} = \frac{1+\eta_{US}^*}{1+\eta_{US}+\eta_{US}^*}\left\{\hat{E}^{A/Y} - \hat{E}^{A/\$} + \frac{(1-\omega_m)\frac{E^{A/\$}P_m^{\$}}{E^{A/Y}}}{TC_A}(\hat{E}^{A/\$} - \hat{E}^{A/Y})\right.$$

$$\left. - \frac{\frac{\overline{C}'}{E^{A/Y}}}{TC_A}\hat{E}^{A/Y}\right\}$$

$$= \frac{1+\eta_{US}^*}{1+\eta_{US}+\eta_{US}^*}\left\{\hat{E}^{A/Y} - \hat{E}^{A/\$} + (1-\omega_m)B_1(\hat{E}^{A/\$} - \hat{E}^{A/Y})\right.$$

$$\left. - B_2\hat{E}^{A/Y}\right\}$$

$$= \frac{1+\eta_{US}^*}{1+\eta_{US}+\eta_{US}^*}\left[-\{1-(1-\omega_m)B_1\}\hat{E}^{A/\$}\right.$$

$$\left. + \{1-(1-\omega_m)B_1-B_2\}\hat{E}^{A/Y}\right]$$

$$= -\frac{1+\eta_{US}^*}{1+\eta_{US}+\eta_{US}^*}\{1-(1-\omega_m)B_1\}\hat{E}^{A/\$}$$

$$+ \frac{1+\eta_{US}^*}{1+\eta_{US}+\eta_{US}^*}\{1-(1-\omega_m)B_1-B_2\}\hat{E}^{A/Y} \qquad (A2')$$

$$\hat{P}_x^A = \frac{X_J}{X}\left(\hat{P}_J^Y + \hat{E}^{A/Y}\right) + \frac{X_{US}}{X}\left(\hat{P}_{US}^{\$} + \hat{E}^{A/\$}\right)$$

$$= \left[\frac{1+\eta^*}{1+\eta+\eta^*}(1-\omega_m)B_1 + \frac{\eta}{1+\eta+\eta^*}\frac{X_{US}}{X}\right]\hat{E}^{A/\$}$$

$$+ \left[1 - \frac{1+\eta^*}{1+\eta+\eta^*}\{(1-\omega_m)B_1+B_2\} - \frac{\eta}{1+\eta+\eta^*}\frac{X_{US}}{X}\right]\hat{E}^{A/Y} \quad (A3')$$

We use Equations (20a) and (20b) to derive rates of changes in the outputs exported to the Japanese and US markets, respectively:

$$\hat{f} = \frac{-\varepsilon_J}{1+\eta_J+\eta_J^*}\left\{\frac{(1-\omega_m)\frac{E^{A/\$}P_m^{\$}}{E^{A/Y}}}{TC_A}\hat{E}^{A/\$} - \frac{(1-\omega_m)\frac{E^{A/\$}P_m^{\$}}{E^{A/Y}} + \frac{\overline{C}'}{E^{A/Y}}}{TC_A}\hat{E}^{A/Y}\right\}$$

$$= \frac{-\varepsilon_J}{1 + \eta_J + \eta_J^*} \left[(1 - \omega_m)B_1 \hat{E}^{A/\$} - \{(1 - \omega_m)B_1 + B_2\} \hat{E}^{A/Y} \right] \qquad (A4')$$

$$\hat{g} = \frac{-\varepsilon_{US}}{1 + \eta_{US} + \eta_{US}^*} \left\{ \left(\frac{(1 - \omega_m)\dfrac{E^{A/\$} P_m^Y}{E^{A/Y}}}{TC_A} - 1 \right) \hat{E}^{A/\$} \right.$$

$$\left. + \left(1 - \frac{(1 - \omega_m)\dfrac{E^{A/\$} P_m^Y}{E^{A/Y}} + \dfrac{\overline{C}'}{E^{A/Y}}}{TC_A} \right) \hat{E}^{A/Y} \right\}$$

$$= \frac{-\varepsilon_{US}}{1 + \eta_{US} + \eta_{US}^*} \left[-\{1 - (1 - \omega_m)B_1\} \hat{E}^{A/\$} + \{1 - (1 - \omega_m)B_1 - B_2\} \hat{E}^{A/Y} \right]$$

$$(A5')$$

From Equations (A3′) and (A4′), we derive the rate of changes in the total outputs of the ASEAN firm:

$$\hat{Q}_A = \omega_x \hat{f} + (1 - \omega_x)\hat{g}$$

$$= \frac{-\varepsilon_J}{1 + \eta_J + \eta_J^*} \omega_x \left[(1 - \omega_m)B_1 \hat{E}^{A/\$} - \{(1 - \omega_m)B_1 + B_2\} \hat{E}^{A/Y} \right]$$

$$+ \frac{-\varepsilon_{US}}{1 + \eta_{US} + \eta_{US}^*} (1 - \omega_x) \left[-\{1 - (1 - \omega_m)B_1\} \hat{E}^{A/\$} \right.$$

$$\left. + \{1 - (1 - \omega_m)B_1 - B_2\} \hat{E}^{A/Y} \right]$$

$$= \left[\frac{\varepsilon_{US}}{1 + \eta_{US} + \eta_{US}^*} (1 - \omega_x) - \left\{ \frac{\varepsilon_J}{1 + \eta_J + \eta_J^*} \omega_x \right. \right.$$

$$\left. \left. + \frac{\varepsilon_{US}}{1 + \eta_{US} + \eta_{US}^*} (1 - \omega_x) \right\} (1 - \omega_m)B_1 \right] \hat{E}^{A/\$}$$

$$+ \left[\frac{-\varepsilon_{US}}{1 + \eta_{US} + \eta_{US}^*} (1 - \omega_x) + \left\{ \frac{\varepsilon_J}{1 + \eta_J + \eta_J^*} \omega_x \right. \right.$$

$$\left. \left. + \frac{\varepsilon_{US}}{1 + \eta_{US} + \eta_{US}^*} (1 - \omega_x) \right\} \{(1 - \omega_m)B_1 + B_2\} \right] \hat{E}^{A/Y} \qquad (A6')$$

Substituting Equations (A1′), (A2′), (A3′), (A4′), and (A5′) into Equation (A6′), we obtain Equation (22′).

Notes

1 This chapter was originally published in the *Journal of the Japanese and International Economies* (vol. 12, no. 4, pp. 256–304). It is reprinted here with permission of Elsevier (then Academic Press).
2 Affiliations of the authors at the time of original publication were Faculty of Commerce, Hitotsubashi University; Institute of Economic Research, Hitotsubashi University, and Department of Economics, Takachiho University, respectively. The authors are grateful to Professors Shinji Takagi, Masahiro Kawai, and Shinichi Fukuda, and other participants of the conference.
3 Ohno (1989) examined pass-through effects of exchange rates on export pricing behavior in manufacturing after taking account of prices of raw materials.
4 Krugman (1987) and Knetter (1989, 1993) analyzed the pricing to market questions.
5 Flanders and Helpman (1979), Lipschitz and Sundararajan (1980), and Flanders and Tishler (1981) emphasized only the real side of the economy in modeling the basket peg issue. On the other hand, Turnovsky (1982) and Bhandari (1985) used a general equilibrium macromodel which include capital mobility.
6 The standard references of optimal currency areas include Kenen (1969), Mundell (1961), and McKinnon (1963).
7 In the literature, minimizing the variance of the level of trade balance is used, while minimizing the growth rate of the trade balance is our objective function. The difference is that in our case, when the level is deviated from the mean, staying at the new level (growth rate is zero) is not penalized in the objective function, while it is penalized in the objective function of the literature. We consider that a particular level cannot be determined as the long run optimum in our model, because the firm is maximizing profits, which is the trade balance in our model.
8 The magnitude of the coefficient and *t*-statistics are only slightly different when the sample period is extended back to 1981.
9 The optimal weights of all cases of Taiwan and some cases of the Philippines seem counterintuitive. The price and volume equations may be misspecified so that our estimates may not be 100 percent accurate. We tested the robustness of the optimal peg estimates for Taiwan and the Philippines. Instead of point estimates, those with plus or minus one standard deviation were used to check what variables may be responsible for the result. To our surprise, no reason was uncovered by this simulation exercise.

References

Bhandari, J. S. (1985). Experiments with the optimal currency composite. *Southern Economic Journal*, **51**(3), 711–30.

Flanders, M. J. and Helpman, E. (1979). An optimal exchange rate peg in a world of general floating. *The Review of Economic Studies*, July, 533–42.

Flanders, M. J. and Tishler, A. (1981). The role of elasticity optimism in choosing an optimal currency basket with applications to Israel. *Journal of International Economics*, 11, 395–406.

Frankel, J. A. and Wei, S.-J. (1994). Yen bloc or dollar bloc? exchange rate policies of the East Asian economies. In T. Ito, and A. O. Krueger, eds., *Macroeconomic Linkage: Savings, Exchange Rates, and Capital Flows*. University of Chicago Press.

International Monetary Fund, Direction of Trade Statistics Yearbook, 1997.

Kenen, P. B. (1969). The theory of optimal currency area: an eclectic view. In R. Mundell and A. K. Swoboda, eds., *Monetary Problems of the International Economy*. University of Chicago Press.

Knetter, M. M. (1989). Price discrimination by US and German exporters. *American Economic Review*, **79**(1), 198–210.

Knetter, M. M. (1993). International comparisons of pricing-to-market behavior. *American Economic Review*, **83**(3), 473–86.

Krugman, P. (1987). Pricing to market when the exchange rate changes. In S. W. Arndt and J. D. Richardson, eds., *Real-Financial Linkages among Open Economies*. Cambridge: MIT Press.

Lipschitz, L. and Sundararajan, V. (1980). The optimal basket in a world of generalized floating. *IMF Staff Papers*, **27**(1), 80–100.

McKinnon, R. (1963). Optimum currency area. *American Economic Review*, **53** (September), 717–25.

Marston, R. C. (1990). Pricing to market in Japanese manufacturing. *Journal of International Economics*, **29**(3/4), 217–36.

Mundell, R. A. (1961). A theory of optimum currency areas. *American Economic Review*, **51**(September), 657–65.

Ohno, K. (1989). Export pricing behavior in manufacturing: a US-Japan comparison. *IMF Staff Papers*, **36**(3), 550–79.

Turnovsky, S. J. (1982). A determination of the optimal currency basket. *Journal of International Economics*, **12**, 333–354.

3 Post-crisis exchange rate regimes in East Asia[1]

Shin-ichi Fukuda[2]

1. Introduction

More than five years after the onset of the Asian crisis, the characteristics of the exchange rate regimes of East Asian economies remain a topic of considerable discussion. In the pre-crisis period, it was fairly evident that currencies of most East Asian economies maintained de facto pegs to the US dollar. Among the East Asian economies, Hong Kong was the only East Asian economy that adopted the fixed exchange rate regime backed by a currency board arrangement. It was, however, well-known that currencies in the other East Asian economies had maintained highly stable values against the US dollar since the mid-1980s [see, for example, Frankel and Wei (1994), Kwan (1995), Goldberg and Klein (1997), and McKinnon (2001)].[3]

For example, Table 3.1 reports the estimated weights of the US dollar and the Japanese yen in the pre-crisis East Asian currencies by Frankel-Wei and Kwan. From the table, we can easily see that the weights of the US dollar were close to one and those of the Japanese yen were negligible for the Korean won, the Indonesian rupiah, the Philippine peso, and the Thai baht. The weights of US dollar were smaller than 0.9 and those of the Japanese yen were not negligible for the Singapore dollar and the Malaysian ringgit. However, even for these currencies, the weights of US dollar was dominant. The results were almost stable from the 1980s to the early 1990s.[4]

The de facto pegs to the US dollar sometimes destabilized the real 'effective' exchange rates of these currencies in the pre-crisis period. In particular, as the Japanese yen depreciated against the US dollar from April 1995 to the summer of 1997, the appreciation of the real 'effective' exchange rates reduced the export competitiveness and increased current account deficits in the East Asian economies [see, for example, Corsetti *et al.* (1999) and Ito *et al.* (1998)]. Several economists have, thus, proposed the desirability of intermediate exchange rate regimes in East Asia that might stabilize their effective exchange rates [see, for example, Bénassy-Quéré (1999), Williamson (1999, 2000), Rajan (2002)].[5] The post-crisis experience in East Asia, however, taught us that the road to the intermediate exchange rate regimes in the region is still pretty hard.[6]

Table 3.1 The weights of the US dollar and the Japanese yen in the pre-crisis period

Currencies	Frankel and Wei (1994)		Kwan (1995)			
	Weekly data		Monthly data		Weekly data	
	1979.1–1992.5		1991.1–1995.5		1995.1–1995.8	
	US$	Yen	US$	Yen	US$	Yen
Korean won	0.96	−0.01	0.94	0.06	0.84	0.17
Singapore dollar	0.75	0.13	0.69	0.1	0.74	0.18
Malaysian ringgit	0.78	0.07	0.84	0.04	0.87	0.16
Indonesian rupia	0.95	0.16	0.99	0	0.97	0.01
Philippine peso	1.07	−0.01	1.15	−0.24	1.07	0.02
Thai baht	0.91	0.05	0.82	0.1	0.86	0.09

In the post-crisis period, Hong Kong kept its currency board arrangement and the Chinese yuan virtually maintained its peg to the US dollar. After experiencing some transitional regime, Malaysia started pegging to the US dollar on September 1, 1998. In contrast, Thailand, Indonesia, and Korea as well as the Philippines and Taiwan have adopted managed float since the crisis. After going through steep devaluations and high volatility in 1997–98, their currencies have mostly stabilized over the past couple of years. Hernández and Montiel (2001) have suggested that they are now allowed to float more at low frequencies than before 1997–98. Some other observers, however, have argued that the so-called floating exchange regimes of the countries are not really floating when we look at high-frequency day-to-day observations (Kawai and Akiyama, 2000; McKinnon, 2001; McKinnon and Schnabl, 2002). In particular, using a regression framework from Fankel and Wei (1994), they have interpreted that the East Asian currencies are reverting back to de facto pegs against the US dollar.[7]

Table 3.2 reports the top 5 trade partners and their trade shares for Malaysia, Singapore, and Thailand from 1997 to 2003. The United States of America has been the biggest trade partner for Malaysia, and one of the two biggest partners for Singapore and Thailand. However, its trade share is far from dominant; Japan and the other East Asian countries have had significant trade shares for the three countries. The result suggests that the large trade weight of the United States provides no satisfactory explanation on why the East Asian currencies had very high correlations with the US dollar.

The purpose of this chapter is to investigate why the East Asian currencies, which temporarily reduced correlations with the US dollar after the crisis, had a tendency to revert back to de facto pegs against the US dollar in the late 1990s. During the crisis, several East Asian economies shifted their exchange rate regimes from de facto US dollar pegs to managed float. However, except for Malaysia, the East Asian economies had no institutional switch of exchange rate regimes in the

Table 3.2 Trade weights by Country in Malaysia, Singapore, and Thailand

		1st	2nd	3rd	4th	5th
(1) Malaysia						
1997		USA	Japan	Singapore	Taiwan	Korea
	Among all	17.60%	17.32%	16.65%	4.59%	4.17%
	Among top 5	29.17%	28.70%	27.60%	7.61%	6.92%
1998		USA	Singapore	Japan	Taiwan	Korea
	Among all	20.74%	15.44%	14.56%	4.55%	3.82%
	Among top 5	35.09%	26.12%	24.63%	7.69%	6.46%
1999		USA	Japan	Singapore	Taiwan	Korea
	Among all	19.96%	15.64%	15.42%	4.90%	3.93%
	Among top 5	33.35%	26.14%	25.77%	8.18%	6.57%
2000		USA	Japan	Singapore	Taiwan	Korea
	Among all	18.76%	16.70%	16.53%	4.62%	3.82%
	Among top 5	31.04%	27.63%	27.35%	7.65%	6.33%
2001		USA	Japan	Singapore	China	Taiwan
	Among all	18.36%	16.08%	14.98%	4.72%	4.62%
	Among top 5	31.24%	27.37%	25.50%	8.03%	7.85%
2002		USA	Singapore	Japan	China	Taiwan
	Among all	18.47%	14.75%	14.29%	6.60%	4.60%
	Among top 5	31.46%	25.13%	24.34%	11.24%	7.83%
2003		USA	Singapore	Japan	China	Hong Kong
	Among all	17.79%	14.03%	13.59%	7.52%	4.82%
	Among top 5	30.81%	24.30%	23.53%	13.02%	8.34%
(2) Singapore						
1997		USA	Malaysia	Japan	Hong Kong	Thailand
	Among all	17.64%	16.22%	12.46%	6.18%	4.89%
	Among top 5	30.74%	28.26%	21.71%	10.77%	8.51%
1998		USA	Malaysia	Japan	Hong Kong	Thailand
	Among all	19.22%	15.33%	11.46%	5.70%	4.28%
	Among top 5	34.32%	27.38%	20.47%	10.19%	7.65%
1999		USA	Malaysia	Japan	Hong Kong	Thailand
	Among all	18.19%	16.07%	11.97%	5.31%	4.56%
	Among top 5	32.43%	28.65%	21.33%	9.47%	8.12%
2000		Malaysia	USA	Japan	Hong Kong	China
	Among all	17.57%	16.20%	12.32%	5.27%	5.21%
	Among top 5	31.06%	28.64%	21.79%	9.31%	9.20%
2001		Malaysia	USA	Japan	China	Hong Kong
	Among all	17.34%	15.95%	10.70%	5.72%	5.27%
	Among top 5	28.70%	26.40%	17.71%	9.47%	8.72%

continued

Table 3.2—Continued

		1st	2nd	3rd	4th	5th
2002		Malaysia	USA	Japan	China	Hong Kong
	Among all	17.81%	14.78%	9.73%	6.51%	5.93%
	Among top 5	30.72%	25.49%	16.78%	11.23%	10.22%
2003		Malaysia	USA	Japan	China	Hong Kong
	Among all	16.30%	14.18%	9.22%	7.79%	6.44%
	Among top 5	29.44%	25.61%	16.66%	14.08%	11.63%

(3) Thailand

		1st	2nd	3rd	4th	5th
1997		Japan	U.S.A.	Singapore	Malaysia	Taiwan
	Among all	20.69%	16.47%	7.94%	4.57%	3.68%
	Among top 5	38.78%	30.88%	14.88%	8.57%	6.89%
1998		U.S.A.	Japan	Singapore	Taiwan	Malaysia
	Among all	18.68%	18.08%	7.26%	4.08%	4.08%
	Among top 5	35.80%	34.66%	13.91%	7.82%	7.81%
1999		Japan	U.S.A.	Singapore	Malaysia	Taiwan
	Among all	18.85%	17.56%	7.40%	4.26%	4.05%
	Among top 5	36.17%	33.69%	14.20%	8.17%	7.77%
2000		Japan	U.S.A.	Singapore	China	Malaysia
	Among all	19.47%	16.81%	7.19%	4.72%	4.70%
	Among top 5	36.80%	36.80%	13.60%	8.93%	8.89%
2001		Japan	U.S.A.	Singapore	China	Malaysia
	Among all	18.75%	16.08%	6.40%	5.17%	4.56%
	Among top 5	36.80%	31.55%	12.56%	10.14%	8.95%
2002		Japan	U.S.A.	China	Singapore	Malaysia
	Among all	18.64%	14.76%	6.35%	6.33%	4.85%
	Among top 5	36.60%	28.98%	12.47%	12.43%	9.52%
2003		Japan	U.S.A.	China	Singapore	Malaysia
	Among all	19.00%	13.36%	7.53%	5.85%	5.39%
	Among top 5	37.16%	26.13%	14.73%	11.44%	10.54%

Sources. IMF, *Direction of Trade Statistics*, Various Issues.

post-crisis period. It is thus far from clear why the East Asian currencies reverted back to de facto pegs against the US dollar in the late 1990s.

Based on high-frequency day-to-day observations, we examine how and when three ASEAN currencies, the Malaysia ringgit, the Singapore dollar, and the Thai baht, changed their correlations with the US dollar and the Japanese yen in the post-crisis period. Before September 1, 1998, these currencies increased correlations with the Japanese yen in the post-crisis period. In particular, the increased correlations were larger than theoretical correlations based on the trade weights. However, after Malaysia adopted the fixed exchange rate, both the Singapore dollar and the Thai baht increased correlations with the US dollar drastically and began reverting back to de facto pegs against the US dollar.

One possible factor that may explain the structural change is a change of macroeconomic correlations that could alter the correlations of East Asian exchange rates with the US dollar and the Japanese yen. Throughout the late 1990s, the US economy was booming, while the Japanese economy experienced a long stagnation. Since East Asian economies had started a sharp recovery from the crisis around the middle of 1998, macroeconomic fundamentals in the East Asian economies thus had a strong positive correlation with those of Japan in the first half of 1998 but with those of the United States after the latter half of 1998. To the extent that macroeconomic fundamentals affect exchange rates, the change of macroeconomic correlations may explain part of exchange rate movements in the East Asian economies in the late 1990s. However, since the change of macroeconomic correlations was gradual, it cannot explain why several ASEAN currencies had drastic structural changes for a short period. We thus need an alternative answer to explain why the East Asian currencies reverted back to de facto pegs against the US dollar for a short period.

The main conclusion of this chapter is that a regime switch in Malaysian had an enormously large impact on the exchange rates of the other ASEAN countries in the post-crisis period. A policy change in one country generally has an impact on the exchange rate in the other country when their economic linkage is tight. It is thus highly possible that the regime switch in Malaysian on September 1, 1998 had a strong impact on the exchange rates in its neighboring countries and that the affected exchange rates had other impacts on the exchange rates in other neighboring countries. Our empirical studies support this view and suggest that the exchange rate linkage was very important to see why the post-crisis ASEAN countries had a tendency to revert back to de facto pegs against the US dollar.

The chapter proceeds as follows. Section 2 considers the theoretical determinants of exchange rates under a currency basket regime in East Asia. After reviewing the post-crisis exchange regimes in Malaysia in Section 3, Sections 4 and 5 investigate how the regime switch in Malaysia had a large impact on the post-crisis exchange regimes in Singapore and Thailand respectively. Section 6 explores how robust our results are when allowing some structural changes in the yen–dollar exchange rate in the late 1990s. Section 7 examines the impacts of the Malaysian regime switch on the post-crisis exchange regimes in Korea and the Philippines. Section 8 summarizes our main results and refers to their implications.

2. The trade weighted currency basket regime

In order to analyze the interdependence of exchange rates in East Asian economies, this section theoretically considers the determinants of exchange rates under a currency basket regime. For analytical simplicity, we suppose that the Singapore dollar is determined by a basket of the US dollar, the Japanese yen, and the Malaysian ringgit. All the exchange rates are denominated by a common numéraire currency such as the Swiss franc. Denoting the nominal exchange rates of the US dollar, the Japanese yen, the Singapore dollar, and the Malaysian ringgit by USD_t, JPY_t, SD_t, and MR_t, respectively, the growth rate of Singapore dollar is thus written as

$$\Delta SD_t = a1 * \Delta USD_t + a2 * \Delta JPY_t + a3 * \Delta MR_t + \varepsilon_t, \tag{1}$$

where ΔE_t is the growth rate of an exchange rate E_t, and ε_t is a disturbance term.

If the growth rate of the Malaysian ringgit (ΔMR_t) is determined by

$$\Delta MR_t = b1 * \Delta USD_t + b2 * \Delta JPY_t + b3 * \Delta SD_t + \eta_t, \tag{2}$$

where η_t is a disturbance term, Equations (1) and (2) therefore lead to

$$\Delta SD_t = \frac{a1 + a3 * b1}{1 - a3 * b3} \Delta USD_t + \frac{a2 + a3 * b2}{1 - a3 * b3} \Delta JPY_t + \upsilon_t \tag{3}$$

$$\Delta MR_t = \frac{b1 + a1 * b3}{1 - a3 * b3} \Delta USD_t + \frac{b2 + a2 * b3}{1 - a3 * b3} \Delta JPY_t + \zeta_t \tag{4}$$

where $\upsilon_t \equiv (\varepsilon_t + a3 * \eta_t)/(1 - a3 * b3)$ and $\zeta_t \equiv (b3 * \varepsilon_t + \eta_t)/(1 - a3 * b3)$.

To the extent that ε_t and η_t are independent of ΔUSD_t and ΔJPY_t, Equation (3) indicates that the manner in which the Singapore dollar is correlated with the US dollar and with the Japanese yen depends not only the basket weights of the Singapore dollar in (1), but also on the basket weights of the Malaysian ringgit in (2). Thus, even if Singapore keeps its basket weights constant, the regime switch of the Malaysian exchange rate policy can have a significant impact on the Singapore dollar, particularly when $a3$ is large.

For example, suppose that the basket weights of the Singapore dollar are based on trade weights among five major trade partners. Then, noting that the Hong Kong dollar is fixed to the US dollar, Singapore's trade weights in 1997 imply the basket weights $a1 = 0.4152$, $a2 = 0.2171$, and $a3 = 0.2826$. Therefore, if the weights of the Malaysian ringgit are also based on the trade weights among five major trade partners in 1997, that is, $b1 = 0.2917$, $b2 = 0.2870$, and $b3 = 0.2760$, then Equations (3) and (4) lead to theoretical correlations. Table 3.3-(1) summarizes the calculated theoretical correlations among the exchange rates before Malaysia adopted the fixed exchange rate.[8] It indicates that both the Malaysian ringgit and the Singapore dollar have a slightly larger correlation with the US dollar than with the Japanese yen. The weights of the Japanese yen, however, amount to more than 0.3 in both currencies, which are much larger than the estimated weights in the pre-crisis period.

In contrast, when the Malaysian ringgit is fixed to the US dollar, it holds that $\Delta MR_t = \Delta USD_t$, that is, $b1 = 1$, and $b2 = b3 = 0$. Substituting the trade weights in 1997, 1998, and 1999 into Equations (3) and (4) respectively, we can obtain Table 3.3-(2). The table summarizes theoretical correlations of the

Table 3.3 Theoretical weights of the exchange rates based on
trade weights—Malaysia and Singapore

(1) Theoretical weights before August 31, 1998

	Malaysian ringgit	*Singapore dollar*
US dollar	0.441	0.540
Japanese yen	0.376	0.323

(2) Theoretical weights after September 1, 1998 — The case of
the Singapore dollar

	Case 1	*Case 2*	*Case 3*
US dollar	0.698	0.719	0.706
Japanese yen	0.217	0.205	0.213

Notes:
1) The theoretical weights in (1) were calculated based on trade weights
   in 1997.
2) After September 1, 1998, the theoretical weights in cases 1, 2, and 3
   were calculated based on the trade weights in 1997, 98, and 99,
   respectively.

Singapore dollar with the US dollar and the Japanese yen after Malaysia adopted
the fixed exchange rate.

Comparing the theoretical correlations in Table 3.3-(2) with those in
Table 3.3-(1), we find that the weight of the US dollar rose from 0.540 to about 0.7,
while the weight of the Japanese yen declined from 0.323 to about 0.2. This implies
that the switch of the Malaysian exchange rate regime had significant impacts on the
theoretical correlations of the Singapore dollar. It is noteworthy that these changes
occurred even if Singapore did not switch its exchange rate regime. Instead, these
changes are attributable to the high degree of interdependence of the Singapore
dollar and the Malaysian ringgit.

3.   The post-crisis exchange rate regimes in Malaysia

On September 1, 1998, the Malaysian government shifted its exchange rate regime
from managed float to the fixed exchange rate. The regime shift was the only
drastic regime switch in the post-crisis East Asian economies. However, before
shifting the fixed exchange rate regime, Malaysia adopted managed float after
the crisis. The purpose of this section is to estimate the extent of correlations the
post-crisis Malaysian ringgit had with the US dollar and the Japanese yen before
September 1, 1998.

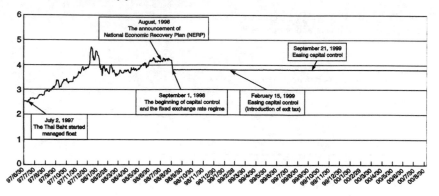

Figure 3.1 Movements of the Malaysian ringgit after the crisis (ringgit/$).

After the Thai crisis in July 1997, Malaysia experienced serious devaluation of its currency. During the crisis, the market value of the Malaysian ringgit dropped to half of the pre-crisis level until January 1998. It was towards the end of January 1998 that the Malaysian ringgit almost stabilized (Figure 3.1). After the Malaysian ringgit stabilized, the Malaysian government began to explore a new economic policy, including the stabilization policy of real effective exchange rates of the ringgit. For example, the National Economic Action Council (NEAC), which was established by Prime Minister Mahathir in December 1997, announced the National Economic Recovery Plan (NERP) in August 1998. The plan stressed the importance of stabilizing the real 'effective' exchange rates and proposed the adoption of a trade weighted basket system as a desirable exchange rate regime. The plan is based on the idea that the de facto pegs to the US dollar sometimes destabilize the real 'effective' exchange rates.

In order to investigate the determinants of the ringgit during this period, we use the method of Frankel-Wei to estimate the weights of the US dollar and the Japanese yen in the Malaysian ringgit before September 1, 1998. In this approach, an independent currency is chosen as an arbitrary numéraire for measuring the exchange variation. The goal here is to estimate the weight a currency assigns to another currency on a given frequency. The regression model, where the local currency's value against the independent currency is regressed against the major world currencies, is

$$\Delta MR_t = \text{constant term} + \alpha 1 * \Delta USD_t + \alpha 2 * \Delta JPY_t + \alpha 3 * \Delta DM_t, \quad (5)$$

where ΔE_t is the growth rate of an exchange rate E_t.

The data of each currency's exchange rate is the daily data at 11 a.m. in the Tokyo market. Using the Swiss franc as a numéraire, we estimated Equation (5) by the ordinary least square method with and without ΔDM_t. Table 3.4 reports the estimation results for three alternative sample periods: (i) from the beginning of January 1998 to the end of August 1998, (ii) from the beginning of March 1998 to

Table 3.4 The correlations of the Malaysia ringgit with the US dollar and the Japanese yen

Sample period	US dollar	Yen	D. Mark	adj. R^2	D.W.
Jan. 1998 to Aug. 1998	0.1997 (0.844)	0.9090 (5.480)		0.1896	1.863
	0.0479 (0.185)	0.8920 (5.380)	0.8226 (1.422)	0.1947	1.853
April 1998 to Aug. 1998	0.5244 (2.504)	0.6332 (5.125)		0.3044	2.426
	0.4255 (1.814)	0.6258 (5.051)	0.4093 (0.939)	0.3036	2.401
July 1998 to Aug. 1998	0.3353 (2.355)	0.5077 (4.599)		0.5562	2.619
	0.2889 (1.641)	0.5201 (4.532)	0.1447 (0.456)	0.5472	2.579

Note:
t-values are in parentheses.

the end of August 1998, (iii) from the beginning of July 1998 to the end of August 1998. The results clearly show that regardless of the choice of ΔDM_t and the sample period, the Japanese yen had kept much larger weights than the US dollar during this post-crisis period.

The estimated weight of the yen was largest for the sample period from January 1998 to August 1998. For this period, the estimated weight of the yen was close to 0.9, while the estimated weight of the US dollar was positive but not statistically significant. The adjusted R^2, however, was less than 0.2, implying that the yen and the US dollar explain only small part of the ringgit's fluctuations during this period.

In contrast, the adjusted R^2 rose up to 0.55 for the sample period from July 1998 to August 1998. This implies that during this period, the yen and the US dollar came to explain a significant part of the ringgit's fluctuations. For this sample period, the estimated weight of the yen was approximately equal to 0.5, while the estimated weight of the US dollar was approximately equal to 0.3. Compared with the other sample period, the estimated weight of the yen was modest for this period. However, even for this modest period, the estimated weight of the yen was larger than the theoretical weight in Table 3.3-(1), while that of the US dollar was much smaller than the theoretical weight in Table 3.3-(1). This suggests that the Malaysian ringgit had a temporal but drastic increase in the weight of the yen before adapting to the fixed exchange rate in the post-crisis period.

4.   Determinants of the Singapore dollar after the crisis

Compared with the other ASEAN countries, Singapore experienced a relatively modest devaluation of its currency during the crisis. Singapore thus kept the exchange regime of a basket system before and after the crisis. In the pre-crisis period, the US dollar had a dominant weight in the currency basket of the Singapore dollar, although the weight of the Japanese yen was also significantly positive. The estimated weight of the US dollar in the pre-crisis period was much larger than the theoretical weight calculated by the trade weights. However, in the post-crisis period, the other ASEAN countries shifted their exchange rate regimes from de facto US dollar pegs to managed float. It is thus possible that there were some structural changes in the basket weights of the Singapore dollar in the post-crisis period.

The purpose of this section is to investigate how the Singapore dollar changed the weights of the US dollar and the Japanese yen in the post-crisis period. The particular interest of the analysis is to investigate how the regime shifts of the Malaysia ringgit affected the weights of the US dollar and the Japanese yen in the post-crisis Singapore dollar. As we have shown in the last section, the Malaysian ringgit had a temporary but drastic increase in the weight of the Japanese yen in 1998 before adopting the fixed exchange rate on September 1, 1998. Since Malaysia is the second largest trade partner for Singapore, it is highly possible that the changes of the Malaysian exchange rate policy had strong impacts on the movements on the Singapore dollar.

In order to investigate the determinants of the Singapore dollar, we estimate

$$\Delta SD_t = \text{constant term} + \beta 1 * \Delta USD_t + \beta 2 * \Delta JPY_t + \beta 3 * \Delta DM_t, \quad (6)$$

by the ordinary least square. The exchange rates, for which the Swiss franc is used as a numéraire, are the daily data at 11 a.m. in the Tokyo market. The sample periods of estimations are: (i) from the beginning of January 1998 to the end of August 1998, (ii) from the beginning of March 1998 to the end of August 1998, (iii) from the beginning of July 1998 to the end of August 1998, (iv) from the beginning of September 1998 to the end of October 1998, (v) from the beginning of September 1998 to the end of December 1998, and (vi) from the beginning of September 1998 to the end of December 1999. The first three sample periods are those before September 1, 1998, while the latter three sample periods are those after September 1, 1998. Comparing the estimation results for two types of sample periods, we can examine the strong impact of the Malaysian regime swift on September 1, 1998 on the determinants of the Singapore dollar.

Table 3.5 summarizes the estimation results with and without ΔDM_t in an explanatory variable. For the sample periods before September 1, 1998, we can easily see that the Japanese yen had larger weights than the US dollar. That is, the coefficient of the US dollar was approximately equal to 0.4, while that of the Japanese yen took the values from 0.6 to 0.65. The estimation results are highly stable throughout the sample periods. The results indicate that corresponding to

Table 3.5 The correlations of the Singapore dollar with the US dollar and the yen—the estimations before and after September 1, 1998.

(a) The estimations before September 1, 1998

Sample period	US dollar	Yen	D. Mark	adj. R^2	D.W.
Jan. 1998 to Aug. 1998	0.4102 (4.255)	0.6547 (9.685)		0.5045	2.302
	0.3620 (3.424)	0.6492 (9.586)	0.2610 (1.105)	0.5052	2.311
April 1998 to Aug. 1998	0.4426 (4.109)	0.6221 (9.790)		0.6049	2.330
	0.3943 (3.268)	0.6185 (9.704)	0.1996 (0.8905)	0.6041	2.344
July 1998 to Aug. 1998	0.3893 (3.822)	0.6220 (7.875)		0.7849	2.212
	0.4398 (3.503)	0.6085 (7.438)	−0.1577 (−0.697)	0.7820	2.252

(b) The estimations after September 1, 1998

Sample period	US dollar	Yen	D. Mark	adj. R^2	D.W.
Sep. 1998 to Oct. 1998	0.7959 (7.567)	0.1444 (2.422)		0.6086	2.457
	0.6692 (4.988)	0.1997 (2.873)	0.4610 (1.486)	0.6204	2.411
Sep. 1998 to Dec. 1998	0.7161 (10.857)	0.1619 (3.671)		0.6314	2.198
	0.5973 (6.816)	0.2036 (4.244)	0.4248 (2.012)	0.6451	2.183
Sep. 1998 to Dec. 1999	0.7825 (26.992)	0.1553 (7.537)		0.7755	2.115
	0.7368 (21.741)	0.1658 (7.953)	0.2316 (2.546)	0.7792	2.117

Note:
t-values are in parentheses.

the regime shifts of the other ASEAN countries, Singapore increased the weight of the Japanese yen in its currency basket after the crisis.

However, the estimation results for the sample periods after September 1, 1998 show that such an increase in the weight was only temporary. That is, after September 1, 1998, the coefficient of the US dollar took the values from 0.6 to 0.8, while the coefficient of the Japanese yen declined less than 0.2. The coefficients are almost equivalent to those in the pre-crisis period that were reported in Table 3.1. The results imply that the weights in the currency basket returned to the pre-crisis levels after Malaysia adopted the fixed exchange rate.

The implication seems to be supported more strongly when we compare the estimates from July 1998 to August 1998 with those from September 1998 to October 1998. The comparison of the estimates with two short sample periods shows how drastic a change happened around September 1, 1998. That is, the coefficient of the US dollar was only 0.4 from July to August. But it rose up to about 0.7 from September to October, which is not so different from any other estimates after September 1, 1998. Conversely, the coefficient of the Japanese yen was 0.6 from July to August, but it dropped below 0.2 from September to October.

It is noteworthy that the estimated weight of the yen (the US dollar) was larger (smaller) than the theoretical weight in Table 3.3-(1) before September 1, 1998, while that of the yen (the US dollar) was much smaller (larger) than the theoretical weight in Table 3.3-(2) after September 1, 1998. The estimated weight of the yen (the US dollar) was larger (smaller) before September 1, 1998 partly because the Malaysian ringgit put higher weight on the yen than its theoretical level. However, even if we calculate the theoretical correlations of the Singapore dollar based on the estimated correlations of the ringgit in Table 3.4, we can still see that the estimated weight of the yen (the US dollar) was larger (smaller) than the theoretical weight.

For example, Table 3.6 reports the theoretical weights in the Singapore dollar based on the estimated weights in the ringgit from the beginning of January 1998

Table 3.6 Theoretical weights of the Singapore dollar—correlations based on the estimates in Malaysia

(1) Theoretical weights based on the estimates from January 1998 to August 1998

	Case 1	*Case 2*
US dollar	0.47	0.50
Yen	0.48	0.45

(2) Theoretical weights based on the estimates from July 1998 to August 1998

	Case 1	*Case 2*
US dollar	0.51	0.54
Yen	0.37	0.35

Note:
The theoretical weights in cases 1 and 2 were calculated based on the trade weights in 1997 and 1998, respectively.

to the end of August 1998 and from the beginning of July 1998 to the end of August 1998. In both periods, the theoretical weights were calculated based on the trade weights in 1997 and 1998. The calculated weights show that the US dollar still has a larger weight than the Japanese yen in three cases and that the US dollar has marginally smaller weight than the Japanese yen in one case. In all cases, the estimated weight of the yen (the US dollar) in Table 3.5 was larger (smaller) than its theoretical weight. This implies that a regime switch in Malaysia had an enormously large impact on the Singapore dollar in the post-crisis period.

5. Determinants of Thai baht after the crisis

5.1. The analytical motivation

After the speculative attack in July 2, 1997, Thailand started adopting managed float. Under the managed float, the Thai baht first experienced serious devaluation and its market value had dropped to half of the pre-crisis level until January 1998. After the end of January 1998, the Thai baht, however, stabilized gradually.

The purpose of this section is to estimate the extent of correlations the Thai baht had with the US dollar and the Japanese yen after January 1998. In the analysis, we assume that the Thai baht is determined by the weighted average of major currencies. Strictly speaking, this may not be an appropriate assumption because Thailand did not adopt an explicit currency basket. However, even under managed floats, the exchange rate tends to be affected by the exchange rates of major trade partners. This assumption may thus hold as an approximation.

Before estimating the actual correlations, we first calculate the theoretical weights in the Thai baht. Suppose that the Thai baht is determined by the weighted average of the US dollar, the Japanese yen, the Singapore dollar, and the Malaysian ringitt. Then, the growth rate of the Thai baht (ΔTB_t) can be written as

$$\Delta TB_t = c1 * \Delta USD_t + c2 * \Delta JPY_t + c3 * \Delta SD_t + c4 * \Delta MR_t + \mu_t. \quad (7)$$

Substituting Equations (3) and (4) into Equation (7), we obtain

$$\Delta TB_t = (c1 + c3 * d1 + c4 * e1) * \Delta USD_t$$
$$+ (c2 + c3 * d2 + c4 * e2) * \Delta JPY_t + \lambda_t \quad (8)$$

where $d_1 = \dfrac{b1 + a1 * b3}{1 - a3 * b3}, d_2 = \dfrac{b2 + a2 * b3}{1 - a3 * b3}, e_1 = \dfrac{b1 + a1 * b3}{1 - a3 * b3}, e_2 = \dfrac{b2 + a2 * b3}{1 - a3 * b3},$

and $\lambda_t = \mu_t + c3 * \upsilon_t + c4 * \zeta_t$.

To the extent that ΔSD_t and ΔMR_t are independent of μ_t, it is natural to assume that the disturbance term λ_t is independent of ΔUSD_t and ΔJPY_t.[9] Under this assumption, we can thus obtain the theoretical weights of the US dollar and

Table 3.7 Theoretical weights of the exchange rates based on trade weights—the case of Thailand

(1) Theoretical weights before August 31, 1998

US dollar	0.43
Yen	0.47

(2) Theoretical weights after September 1, 1998

	Case 1	*Case 2*	*Case 3*
US dollar	0.50	0.54	0.53
Yen	0.42	0.38	0.38

Notes:
1) The theoretical weights in (1) were calculated based on trade weights in 1997.
2) After September 1, 1998, the theoretical weights in cases 1, 2, and 3 were calculated based on the trade weights in 1997, 98, and 99, respectively.

the Japanese yen in the Thai baht. Table 3.7-(1) reports the calculated theoretical weights before Malaysia shifted to the fixed exchange rate regime based on the trade weights among five major trade partners in 1997. It shows that the Japanese yen had a slightly higher theoretical weight than the US dollar before Malaysia shifted to the fixed exchange rate regime.

Table 3.7-(2) reports the calculated theoretical weights after Malaysia shifted to the fixed exchange rate regime, that is, when $b1 = 1$, and $b2 = b3 = 0$. The weights are calculated for three alternative cases based on the trade weights among five major trade partners in 1997, 1998, and 1999, respectively. In all cases, the weight of the Japanese yen became smaller than that of the US dollar. The decline of the weight of the yen was more conspicuous when we used the trade weights in 1998 and 1999.

5.2.   The estimations of the actual weights

We next estimate the actual weights in the Thai baht after the crisis. As in the previous sections, we estimate

$$\Delta TB_t = \text{constant term} + \gamma 1 * \Delta USD_t + \gamma 2 * \Delta JPY_t + \gamma 3 * \Delta DM_t, \quad (9)$$

by the ordinary least square. The exchange rates, for which the Swiss franc is used as a numéraire, are the daily data at 11 a.m. in the Tokyo market. As in the previous section, the sample periods of estimations are: (i) from the beginning of January 1998 to the end of August 1998, (ii) from the beginning of March 1998 to the end of August 1998, (iii) from the beginning of July 1998 to the end of August 1998, (iv) from the beginning of September 1998 to the end of

October 1998, (v) from the beginning of September 1998 to the end of December 1998, and (vi) from the beginning of September 1998 to the end of December 1999. Comparing the estimation results for two types of sample periods, we can examine how strong the impact of the Malaysian regime shift on September 1, 1998 was on the determinants of the Thai baht.

Table 3.8 summarizes the estimation results with and without ΔDM_t in an explanatory variable. For the sample period from January 1998 to August 1998 or from March 1998 to August 1998, we can see that the Japanese yen had larger

Table 3.8 The correlations of the Thai baht with the US dollar and the yen—the estimations before and after September 1, 1998.

(a) The estimations before September 1, 1998

Sample period	US dollar	Yen	D. Mark	adj. R^2	D.W.
Jan. 1998 to Aug. 1998	0.1602 (0.664)	0.7460 (4.408)		0.1279	2.246
	0.0328 (0.124)	0.7317 (4.318)	0.6907 (1.168)	0.1298	2.257
April 1998 to Aug. 1998	0.3715 (1.660)	0.6966 (5.278)		0.2780	2.489
	0.2243 (0.899)	0.6855 (5.202)	0.6089 (1.314)	0.2831	2.495
July 1998 to Aug. 1998	0.5775 (3.385)	0.3615 (2.732)		0.4824	1.974
	0.5403 (2.556)	0.3714 (2.697)	0.1163 (0.305)	0.4704	1.995

(b) The estimations after September 1st 1998

Sample period	US dollar	it Yen	D. Mark	adj. R^2	D.W.
Sep. 1998 to Oct. 1998	0.9314 (7.074)	0.0833 (1.116)		0.5520	1.890
	0.9715 (5.633)	0.0658 (0.736)	−0.1459 (−0.366)	0.5418	1.863
Sep. 1998 to Dec. 1998	0.8406 (8.510)	0.0871 (1.319)		0.4814	1.912
	0.8181 (6.081)	0.0950 (1.290)	0.0807 (0.249)	0.4752	1.926
Sep. 1998 to Dec. 1999	0.8187 (15.680)	0.1408 (3.794)		0.5277	2.077
	0.7858 (12.767)	0.1483 (3.919)	0.1669 (1.010)	0.5277	2.091

Note:
t-values are in parentheses.

weights than the US dollar. In those cases, the coefficient of the Japanese yen was approximately equal to 0.7, while that of the US dollar was not statistically significant. The estimated weight of the yen (the US dollar) was much larger (smaller) than the theoretical weight in Table 3.7-(1). The results indicate that the Thai baht drastically increased the weight of the Japanese yen after the crisis.

In contrast, for the sample period from July 1998 to August 1998, we can see that the weight of the Japanese yen became slightly smaller than that of the US dollar. In particular, the estimated weight of the yen (the US dollar) became smaller (larger) than the theoretical weight in Table 3.7-(1). The results indicate that in case of Thailand, the weight of the Japanese yen declined and the weight of the US dollar had risen even before September 1, 1998.

However, the changes of the weights were more drastic after September 1, 1998. That is, for the sample period from September 1998 to October 1998, the coefficient of the US dollar rose up to more than 0.9, while the coefficient of the Japanese yen declined less than 0.1. The coefficients are almost equivalent to those in the pre-crisis period that were reported in Table 3.1. The results imply that the weights in the currency basket returned to the pre-crisis levels after Malaysian adopted the fixed exchange rate.

6. Asymmetric impacts of the yen/dollar rate on east Asian exchange rates

In the previous sections, we have shown that both the Singapore dollar and the Thai baht placed quite different weights on the yen and the US dollar before and after September 1, 1998. The adoption of the fixed exchange rate by the Malaysian government was the only big institutional regime shift around September 1, 1998. The results thus suggest that the regime shift of the Malaysian exchange rate had a strong impact on the determinants of the Singapore dollar and the Thai baht in the post-crisis period.

However, it is to be noted that, in 1998, the Japanese yen/US dollar exchange rate had a big structural break. Figure 3.2 depicts the movements of the yen/dollar exchange rates from January 1994 to December 2001. It shows that the yen steadily depreciated against the US dollar and that the rate of depreciation was accelerated after November 1997. The trend of depreciation continued until the end of July 1998. However, after August 1998, the yen, in turn, started appreciating against the US dollar and the appreciation continued until the end of December 1999. This indicates that if the Singapore dollar and the Thai baht had had asymmetric responses to appreciation and depreciation of the yen/dollar exchange rates, they could have had different correlations with the US dollar and the Japanese yen before and after August 1998.

The purpose of this section is to investigate whether the Singapore dollar and the Thai baht showed different responses to appreciation and depreciation of the Japanese yen in the post-crisis period. We first investigate the existence of asymmetric responses by estimating the following equations:

$$\Delta SD_t = \text{constant} + \beta_1 * \Delta USD_t + \beta_2 * \Delta JPY_t + \beta_{12} * D * \Delta USD_t$$

$$+ \beta_{22} * D * \Delta JPY_t + \beta_3 * \Delta DM_t, \tag{10}$$

$$\Delta TB_t = \text{constant} + \gamma_1 * \Delta USD_t + \gamma_2 * \Delta JPY_t + \gamma_{12} * D * \Delta USD_t$$

$$+ \gamma_{22} * D * \Delta JPY_t + \gamma_3 * \Delta DM_t, \tag{11}$$

where D_t is a dummy variable which takes a value of one when the Japanese yen depreciated against the US dollar, but takes zero otherwise.

The sample period of estimations is from September 1998 to December 1999 when the Japanese yen had a tendency to appreciate against the US dollar. Table 3.9 summarizes the estimation results with and without ΔDM_t. In all cases, variables without the dummy had similar estimated coefficients to those in Tables 3.5 and 3.8. In contrast, the US dollar multiplied by the dummy variable had a negative sign and the Japanese yen multiplied by the dummy variable had a positive sign. This implies that the Singapore dollar and the Thai baht had smaller responses to the US dollar and larger responses to the Japanese yen when the yen depreciates against the US dollar. The estimated coefficients of the US dollar with the dummy variable took values around −0.3 and were marginally significant. The estimated coefficients of Japanese yen with the dummy variable were, however, very small and were far from significant.

We next estimated Equations (6) and (9) for the sample period from January 2000 to December 2001. We chose this sample period because the yen/dollar exchange rates had a tendency to depreciate throughout the period. If the asymmetric responses to the yen/dollar exchange rates were important, the

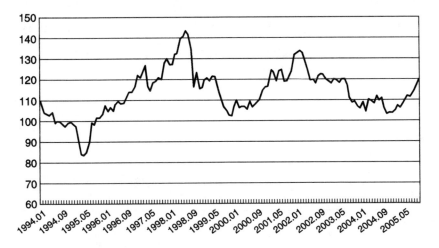

Figure 3.2 Movements of the yen/the US dollar exchange rate (Yen/$).

Table 3.9 The correlations with the US dollar and the yen—the estimations allowing asymmetric responses

(a) The case of Singapore

Sample period	US dollar	Yen	dummy dollar	dummy Yen	D. Mark	adj. R^2	D.W.
Sep. 1998 to Dec. 1999	0.8232	0.1525	−0.3208	0.037		0.6581	2.336
	(9.560)	(2.504)	(−1.861)	(0.291)			
	0.7003	0.2026	−0.2790	0.003	0.3969	0.6517	2.288
	(6.510)	(3.087)	(−1.630)	(0.026)	(1.874)		

(b) The case of Thailand

Sample period	US dollar	Yen	dummy dollar	dummy Yen	D. Mark	adj. R^2	D.W.
Sep. 1998 to Dec. 1999	0.9556	0.0466	−0.3527	0.1288		0.4801	1.960
	(7.303)	(0.504)	(−1.348)	(0.670)			
	0.9480	0.0496	−0.3501	0.1267	0.0244	0.4734	1.970
	(5.677)	(0.487)	(−1.318)	(0.648)	(0.074)		

Note:
t-values are in parentheses.

Table 3.10 The correlations with the US dollar and the yen

(a) The case of Singapore

Sample period	US dollar	Yen	D. Mark	adj. R^2	D.W.
Jan. 2000 to Dec. 2001	0.7966	0.2252		0.8827	2.091
	(24.658)	(7.832)			
	0.7856	0.2309	0.0728	0.8828	2.122
	(23.291)	(7.912)	(1.123)		

(b) The case of Thailand

Sample period	US dollar	Yen	D. Mark	adj. R^2	D.W.
Jan. 2000 to Dec. 2001	0.7688	0.2886		0.8174	2.400
	(17.785)	(7.498)			
	0.7667	0.2896	0.0135	0.8166	2.400
	(16.945)	(7.398)	(0.156)		

Note:
t-values are in parentheses.

estimated correlations would be similar to those for the post-crisis period before September 1998. Table 3.10 reports the estimation results with and without ΔDM_t as an explanatory variable. In the case of Singapore, the estimated coefficients are significantly different from those for the post-crisis period before September 1998. Instead, the estimated coefficients are almost similar to those after September 1998 that were reported in Table 3.5. Even in the case of Thailand, the estimated coefficients are significantly different from those for the post-crisis period before September 1998. However, in the case of Thai baht, the US dollar had smaller coefficients and the Japanese yen had large coefficients than the other estimates after September 1998 that were reported in Table 3.8. This implies that the Thai baht had smaller responses to the US dollar and larger to the Japanese yen from January 2000 to December 2001when the yen depreciates against the US dollar.

The above overall results show some marginal evidence that the Singapore dollar and the Thai baht had smaller correlations with the US dollar and larger correlations with the yen when the yen depreciates against the US dollar. The results are, however, not so definitive and do not explain why large structural changes were observed before and after September 1, 1998.

7. The post-crisis exchange rates in Korea and the Philippines

Concerning the impacts on the exchange rates, Korea and the Philippines also experienced serious devaluations of their currencies during the East Asian crisis. The arrival of the Korean won crisis was late and it was November 1997 when the currency showed a sharp devaluation. In contrast, the Philippine peso had already experienced frequent exchange rate depreciation before the East Asian crisis. However, both the Korean won and the Philippine peso reduced their market values to half of the pre-crisis levels until January 1998. Like the other East Asian currencies, it was after the end of January 1998 when these currencies almost stabilized.

The purpose of this section is to examine what impacts the Malaysian regime switch had on the Korean won and the Philippine peso. Concerning economic interdependence, Malaysia has had smaller links with Korea and the Philippines than with Singapore and Thailand. For example, when we look at the trade linkage, we can easily see that the dominant trade partners have been the United States and Japan for Korea and the Philippines. This indicates that intra-regional linkages with the other East Asian countries, particularly with Malaysia have been less important for Korea and the Philippines. It is thus far from clear what impacts the Malaysian regime switch had on the Korean won and the Philippine peso.

Table 3.11 The correlations of the Korean won with the US dollar and the yen—the estimations before and after September 1, 1998.

(a) The estimations before September 1, 1998

Sample period	US dollar	Yen	D. Mark	adj. R^2	D.W.
Jan. 1998 to Aug. 1998	0.8352 (3.184)	0.3778 (2.054)		0.1126	2.021
	0.6675 (2.326)	0.3590 (1.953)	0.9093 (1.418)	0.1181	2.031
July 1998 to Aug. 1998	1.1521 (3.252)	0.3143 (1.144)		0.3293	1.480
	1.1480 (2.612)	0.3154 (1.102)	0.013 (0.016)	0.3121	1.479

(b) The estimations after September 1, 1998

Sample period	US dollar	Yen	D. Mark	adj. R^2	D.W.
Sep. 1998 to Oct. 1998	0.9612 (6.263)	0.2463 (2.832)		0.5379	1.708
	0.7442 (3.844)	0.3411 (3.400)	0.7896 (1.764)	0.5617	1.541
Sep. 1998 to Dec. 1998	1.0369 (9.511)	0.2411 (3.309)		0.5687	1.888
	1.0061 (6.777)	0.2519 (3.100)	0.1101 (0.308)	0.5637	1.876

Note:
t-values are in parentheses.

As in the previous sections, we estimate the following equations:

$$\Delta KW_t = \text{constant} + \beta_1 * \Delta USD_t + \beta_2 * \Delta JPY_t + \beta_3 * \Delta DM_t, \qquad (12)$$

$$\Delta PP_t = \text{constant} + \gamma_1 * \Delta USD_t + \gamma_2 * \Delta JPY_t + \gamma_3 * \Delta DM_t, \qquad (13)$$

where ΔKW_t and ΔPP_t denote the growth rates of the Korean won and the Philippine peso denominated by the Swiss franc, respectively.

The sample period of estimations is from the beginning of January 1998 to December 1998. To examine the impacts of the Malaysian regime switch, we split the sample before and after September 1, 1998. Tables 3.11 and 3.12 summarize the estimation results for Korea and the Philippines respectively. The tables report the results both with and without ΔDM_t. Throughout the periods, the US dollar had larger weights than the Japanese yen. However, in most of the estimates, the coefficient of the Japanese yen was greater than 0.2 and statistically significant. This indicates that both Korea and the Philippines

Table 3.12 The correlations of the Philippine peso with the US dollar and the yen—the estimations before and after September 1, 1998.

(a) The estimations before September 1, 1998

Sample period	US dollar	Yen	D. Mark	adj. R^2	D.W.
Jan. 1998 to Aug. 1998	0.8462 (4.557)	0.5463 (4.195)		0.2693	2.286
	0.9077 (4.447)	0.5532 (4.231)	−0.3337 (−0.732)	0.2672	2.276
July 1998 to Aug. 1998	0.7133 (3.883)	0.2505 (1.758)		0.4498	1.853
	0.9609 (4.423)	0.1844 (1.303)	−0.7726 (−1.973)	0.4870	1.734

(b) The estimations after September 1, 1998

Sample period	US dollar	Yen	D. Mark	adj. R^2	D.W.
Sep. 1998 to Oct. 1998	1.0556 (9.382)	0.1880 (2.949)		0.7065	2.200
	1.3021 (9.751)	0.0804 (1.161)	−0.8970 (−2.905)	0.7535	2.194
Sep. 1998 to Dec. 1998	0.9402 (8.477)	0.2471 (3.334)		0.5194	2.283
	1.0053 (6.670)	0.2243 (2.718)	−0.2326 (−0.640)	0.5158	2.281

Note:
t-values are in parentheses.

have increased the weight of the Japanese yen in its currency basket after the crisis.

Comparing the coefficients before and after September 1, 1998, the coefficient of the US dollar becomes close to one and that of the Japanese yen drops down after September 1, 1998. This suggests that the currencies had some moderate reversions to de facto pegs against the US dollar. However, comparing the estimates from July 1998 to August 1998 with those from September 1998 to October 1998, we can see no such structural change in the Korean won. In the case of the Philippine peso, we can see some structural change. The change is, however, less drastic than what we observed for the Singapore dollar and the Thai baht during the same period. This implies that, in the case of the Korean won and the Philippine peso, the moderate reversions to de facto pegs against the US dollar are not attributable to the Malaysian regime shift on September 1, 1998.

8.   Concluding remarks

In this chapter, we investigated the determinants of three ASEAN currencies, the Malaysian ringgit, the Singapore dollar, and the Thai baht after the crisis. In particular, we examined how these three ASEAN currencies had correlations with the US dollar and the Japanese yen in the post-crisis period. We found that before September 1, 1998, these currencies increased correlations with the Japanese yen in the post-crisis period. In particular, the increased correlations were larger than the theoretical correlations that were calculated based on the trade weights. The increased correlations with the Japanese yen were, however, temporary in the post-crisis period. We found that after Malaysian adopted the fixed exchange rate, both the Singapore dollar and the Thai baht increased correlation with the US dollar drastically and began reverting back to de facto pegs against the US dollar.

One possible answer to explain the structural change is a change in macroeconomic correlations that altered correlations of East Asian exchange rates with the US dollar and the Japanese yen. Since East Asian economies had started a sharp recovery from the crisis around the middle of 1998, macroeconomic fundamentals in the East Asian economies may have a positive correlation with those of Japan in the first half of 1998 but with those of the United States during the latter half of 1998. Our regression results also showed that a part of the change was attributable to the structural change of the yen–dollar exchange rate.

Our main results, however, suggested that the structural change was explained well by the strong linkage among the ASEAN countries and that a regime switch in Malaysia had an enormously large impact on the exchange rates of the other ASEAN countries in the post-crisis period. This implies the importance of regional cooperation among the East Asian countries. Without regional cooperation, the East Asian countries might come to adopt the exchange rate regime that does not necessarily contribute to economic stability in the region.

In the present period, several East Asian economies adopt different types of exchange rate regimes; Hong Kong kept its currency board arrangement and the Chinese yuan virtually maintained its peg to the US dollar. After experiencing some transitional regime, Malaysia started pegging to the US dollar on September 1, 1998. In contrast, Thailand, Indonesia, and Korea as well as the Philippines and Taiwan have adopted managed float since the crisis. The so-called floating exchange regimes of these countries are not really floating. The de facto pegs to the US dollar may destabilize the real 'effective' exchange rates of these currencies. To avoid another crisis in East Asia, it is importantly to reconsider urgently what the desirable exchange rate regime in East Asia should be from the view point of regional cooperation.

Notes

1 An earlier version of this chapter was presented at the Ministry of Finance in Japan, ESRI of the Cabinet Office in Japan, the European Central Bank, and Taiwan National

University. I would like to thank Masahiro Kawai, William Branson, Chelsea Lin, and other seminar participants for their helpful comments.

2 Correspondence: Shin-ichi FUKUDA, Faculty of Economics, University of Tokyo, Hongo Bunkyo-ku Tokyo 113, Japan. E-mail: sfukuda@e.u-tokyo.ac.jp, Fax: 81-3-5841-5521.

3 Takagi (1996) is an exceptional study that found some significant correlations between the East Asian currencies and the Japanese yen during this period.

4 The US dollar had also been dominant in various international transactions in East Asia. See, for example, Ito (1993), Fukuda (1995) and Kawai (1996).

5 The bipolar or two-corner solution view of exchange rates states that intermediate policy regimes between hard pegs and floating are not sustainable. Fischer (2001), however, argued that the proponents of the bipolar view have probably exaggerated their point.

6 Bayoumi *et al.* (2000, 2001) showed that on economic criteria, ASEAN appears less suited for a regional currency arrangement than Europe before the Maastricht Treaty, although the difference is not large.

7 Calvo and Reinhart (2002), and Reinhart and Rogoff (2003) found that many emerging market countries that say they allow their exchange rate to float mostly do not.

8 The values of a1 and b1 are calculated by the sum of the trade weights to the USA and those to Hong Kong.

9 Strictly speaking, this is not an appropriate assumption because Thailand is the fifth largest trade partner for Singapore. However, since the trade weight is 8 percent, the bias caused by this assumption will be small.

References

Bayoumi, T., Eichengreen, B. and Mauro, P. (2000). On regional monetary arrangements for ASEAN. *Journal of the Japanese and International Economies*, **14**(2), 121–48.

Bayoumi, T., Eichengreen, B. and Mauro, P. (2001). The suitability of ASEAN for a regional currency arrangement. *The World Economy*, **24**(7), 933–54.

Bénassy-Quéré, A. (1999). Optimal pegs for Asian currencies. *Journal of the Japanese and International Economies*, **13**(1), 44–60.

Calvo, G. and Reinhart, C. (2002). Fear of floating. *Quarterly Journal of Economics*, **117**(2), 379–408.

Corsetti, G., Pesenti, P. and Roubini, N. (1999). What caused the asian currency and financial crisis? *Japan and the World Economy*, **11**(3), 305–73.

Fischer, S. (2001). Exchange rate regimes: is the bipolar view correct? *Journal of Economic Perspectives*, **15**(2), 3–24.

Frankel, J. A. and Wei, S.-J. (1994). Yen bloc or dollar bloc: exchange rate policies of the East Asian economies. In T. Ito and A. O. Krueger, eds., *Macroeconomic Linkage*, Chicago: University of Chicago Press.

Fukuda, S. (1995). The structural determinants of invoice currencies in Japan: the case of foreign trades with East Asian countries. In T. Ito and A. O. Krueger, eds., *Financial Deregulation and Integration in East Asia*, Chicago: University of Chicago Press.

Goldberg, L. and Klein, M. (1997). Foreign direct investment, trade and real exchange rate linkages in Southeast Asia and Latin America. NBER Working Paper #6344.

Hernández, L. and Montiel, P. (2001). Post-crisis exchange rate policy in five Asian countries: filling in the "Hollow Middle"? IMF Working Paper 01/170.

Ito, T. (1993). The yen and the international monetary system. In C. F. Bergsten and M. Noland, eds., *Pacific Dynamism and International Monetary System*, Washington DC: Institute of International Economics.

Ito, T., Ogawa, E. and Sasaki, Y. N. (1998). How did the dollar peg fail in Asia? *Journal of the Japanese and International Economies*, **12**(4), 256–304.

Kawai, M. (1996). The Japanese yen as an international currency: performance and prospects. In R. Sato and H. Hori, eds., *Organization, Performance, and Equity: Perspectives on the Japanese Economy*, Kluwer Academic Publishers: Boston, 334–87.

Kawai, M. and Akiyama, S. (2000). Implications of the currency crisis for exchange rate arrangements in emerging East Asia. Mimeo, World Bank.

Kwan, C. (1995). *Economics of the Yen Block (in Japanese)*, Nihon Keizai Shimbun Sya.

McKinnon, R. I. (2001). After the crisis, the East Asian dollar standard resurrected: an interpretation of high-frequency exchange rate pegging. In J. Stiglitz and Y. Shahid, eds., *Rethinking the East Asian Miracle*, New York: Oxford University Press, 197–244.

McKinnon, R. I. and Schnabl, G. (2002). Synchronized business cycles in East Asia: fluctuations in the yen/dollar exchange rate and china's stabilizing role. IMES Discussion Paper No.2002-E-13, Bank of Japan.

Rajan, R. S. (2002). Exchange rate policy options for post-crisis Southeast Asia: is there a case for currency baskets? *The World Economy*, **25**(1), 137–63.

Reinhart, C. M. and Rogoff, K. S. (2003). The modern history of exchange rate arrangements: a reinterpretation. *The Quarterly Journal of Economics*, **119**(1), 1–48.

Takagi, S. (1996). The yen and its East Asian neighbors, 1980–95: cooperation or competition? NBER Working Paper #5720.

Williamson, J. (1999). The case for a common basket peg for East Asian currencies. In S. Collignon, J. Pisani-Ferry, and Y. C. Park, eds., *Exchange Rate Policies in Emerging Asian Countries*, London and New York: Routledge, 327–343.

Williamson, J. (2000). *Exchange Rate Regimes for Emerging Markets: Reviving the Intermediate Option*, Washington, DC: Institute for International Economics.

4 On the desirability of a regional basket currency arrangement[1]

Eiji Ogawa and Takatoshi Ito

1. Introduction

One of the lessons of the Asian Currency Crises is the danger of the *de facto* dollar peg adopted by Asian economies that had extensive trade and investment relationships with countries other than the United States.[2] When the yen appreciated vis-à-vis the US dollar, the Asian economies enjoyed a boom, or a bubble in some cases, due to increased exports. But when the yen depreciated, these same Asian economies tended to experience a recession, or a burst bubble. The experience of the Asian boom and bust in the 1990s, along with the yen–dollar exchange rate fluctuation, is a stark reminder of risk of the fixed exchange rate regime.

An obvious solution for this problem would be to increase the flexibility of the exchange rate. If the baht had appreciated during the yen appreciation phase of 1993–95, the extent of overheating in Thailand might have been limited; if the baht had depreciated along with the yen in 1996–97, then the decline in exports might have been mitigated. This kind of exchange rate flexibility can be achieved through a flexible exchange rate regime that keeps the real effective exchange rate relatively stable.

An obvious insight here is that an emerging market economy that exports to both the United States and Japan is well advised to consider managed exchange rate regimes, to avoid excessive volatility of the real effective exchange rate.[3] The questions to be considered include how to determine a reference rate as an appropriate real effective exchange rate and how much fluctuation is excessive.

The optimal exchange rate regime is defined as one that minimizes the fluctuation of trade balances[4] when the yen–dollar exchange rate fluctuates. Ito *et al.* (1998) proposed how to calculate the optimal weights in cases where an emerging market economy exports only to Japan and the United States. These optimal weights were calibrated with some assumptions regarding demand elasticities and export shares. Ogawa and Ito (2000) extend the Ito *et al.* (1998) model to include a neighboring emerging market as well as Japan and the United States. A typical Asian economy exports about one-third to the United States and one-third to Japan, and the rest to countries in the Asian region (and EU). Therefore, to simplify, we consider the case that Country A exports to the United States, Japan, and Country B (and that Country B exports to the United States, Japan, and Country A). Therefore, the real effective exchange rate calculation includes the currency of the neighboring country.

This chapter considers how the optimal weights may depend on what weights the neighboring country adopts. In an extreme case, if Country A adopts a dollar peg, Country B should also adopt a dollar peg, and vice versa. That is to say, the dollar peg is a Nash equilibrium. However, if Country A is using a currency basket which mirrors the export shares, adjusted for demand elasticities, then Country B should adopt a (similar) currency basket; and if Country B is using a currency basket, then Country A should adopt a currency basket. This trade-weighted currency basket is also a Nash equilibrium.

Although this chapter is motivated by the recent Asian experiences, the application is not limited to Asia. Results obtained in this chapter are relevant to any developing countries with a trading structure with export destinations including different currency areas.

Which of the Nash equilibria is chosen depends on inertia as well as rational calculation. If countries can coordinate, then they should choose the Nash equilibrium that would be best for all. This process of choosing the optimal Nash equilibrium can be regarded as a regional currency arrangement. Coordination failure could occur if a country has some obstacles to coordination stemming from political or social obstacles against breaking inertia. What this chapter shows is that a coordinated managed float by the two countries would increase stability in trade balance fluctuations.

The rest of the chapter is organized as follows. Section 2 explains our micro-foundation framework where domestic firms import parts from the United States and Japan, and compete in US and Japanese product markets with firms from the neighboring country. We assume that the Marshall–Lerner condition is satisfied throughout the chapter, meaning that depreciation of the local currency will increase the net trade surpluses. Section 3 examines what the Marshall–Lerner condition implies in our oligopoly model with imported parts. It also examines in what situations the Marshall–Lerner condition is satisfied in the model. In Section 4, monetary authorities' exchange rate policies are introduced into a two-country model with the micro-foundation framework. It is assumed that the monetary authorities of Country A (hereafter, Country A) and Country B (hereafter, Country B) conduct their exchange rate policies to stabilize trade balances in a situation of mutual interdependence. We derive reaction functions of the countries for their optimal exchange rate policies. We use the model to analyze the interdependence between their exchange rate policies. In Section 5, we show cases of stable equilibrium and of unstable equilibrium. In Section 6, we show possibilities of multiple equilibra and coordination failure in the stable equilibrium case. We point out that it is difficult for the two countries to conduct optimal exchange rate regimes without coordination if they try to shift directly from the current dollar peg system to an optimal exchange rate regime. In Section 7, we conclude our analysis.

2. Model

2.1. Settings

Our earlier work, Ito *et al.* (1998), considered the question of choosing optimal weights in the basket currency system for a country that exports goods to the United States and Japan. We constructed a model of an Asian country as a one-sector economy where a representative firm assembles manufactured products using parts imported from Japan and the United States. The representative firm in one Asian country was assumed to compete with Japanese firms and/or US firms in the Japanese and US markets. We extend our earlier model to include another neighbor country in the model in order to analyze interactions of exchange rate policies among Asian countries.

We assume that a representative firm in Country A imports parts from the United States and Japan and exports its products to markets in the United States, Japan, and Country B as well as selling in the domestic market.[5] Also, a representative firm in Country B imports parts from the United States and Japan and supplies its products to markets in the United States, Japan, and Country A as well as a domestic market. We assume that prices of parts from the United States and Japan are denominated in the currency of their country of origin.[6]

Asian countries export goods and services mainly to Japan, the United States, and neighboring Asian countries. For example, one-fourth of Thailand's exports go to Japan, one-fifth to NIES (Korea, Singapore, Hong Kong, and Taiwan) and ASEAN-4 countries (Thailand, Philippines, Indonesia, and Malaysia), and one-seventh to the United States. These three categories account for more than 60 percent of Thailand's exports. Similarly, 22 percent of Malaysia's exports go to the United States, 34 percent to Japan, and 17 percent to Asian countries. The sum of these three categories reaches 72 percent. The structure is similar in Indonesia and the Philippines. Table 4.1 shows export shares for Japan, the United States, Asian countries, and four European countries (Germany, France, UK, and Italy). This shows that the assumptions of the model are realistic.

The markets in countries A and B are each supposed to be duopoly markets where firms from Country A and B compete with one another. Markets in the United States and Japan are under monopolistic competition. Firms from Country A and Country B compete with many domestic firms in both the US and Japanese markets. They supply their products in the US and Japanese monopolistically competitive markets given average prices of their domestic products made in the United States and Japan. For simplicity, we assume that prices of products made in the US and Japan are kept unchanged (exogenous to this model). Moreover, we assume that all firms in Countries A and B have identical cost functions. Each firm maximizes its profits in terms of its own home currency.

Table 4.1 Export shares by destination

Exports from	To Japan	To US	To NIEs4+ASEAN4	To EU
Korea	19.5	19.8	10.8	9.0
Singapore	17.6	16.9	32.0	10.5
Indonesia	23.4	11.3	32.8	15.1
Thailand	25.7	13.8	21.5	9.6
Malaysia	22.0	16.8	34.1	10.4
Philippines	20.5	17.5	24.7	10.4
China	20.4	11.5	35.3	9.7

Notes:
All data are from 1997, except Indonesia exports to Taiwan, and Philippines exports to Taiwan, 1996.
EU4=Germany, France, UK, Italy.
ASEAN4=Indonesia, Thailand, Malaysia, Philippines.
NIEs4=Korea, Taiwan, Hong Kong, Singapore.

Source: Economic Planning Agency, Asian Economies 1999.

Profits of each firm in Countries A and B in terms of the home currency A and B (π_i ($i = A, B$)) are calculated as

$$\pi_i = P_i^i d_i(q_i) + E^{i/Y} P_J^i f_i(q_J^i) + E^{i/\$} P_{US}^i g_i(q_{US}^i) + E^{i/j} P_j^i h_i(q_j)$$

$$- \left(E^{i/y} P_m^Y \omega_m^J - E^{i/\$} P_m^\$ \omega_m^{US} \right) Q_i - C(Q_i) \qquad (1)$$

for $i = A, B$ and $j = B, A$, where P_i^i denotes the prices of Country i firm's products in the domestic market in terms of the home currency ($i = A, B$); P_j^i, the price of Country i firm's products in the Country j market in terms of Country j currency ($i = A, B$, and $j = J$ (Japan); US (the United States), B, A); P_m^i, the price of parts imported from Country i in terms of Country i currency ($i = J, US$); $Q_i,(Q_i = d_i(q_i) + f_i(q_J^i) + g_i(q_{US}^i) + h_i(q_j))$ outputs of Country A firm's products ($i = A, B$ and $j = B, A$); d_i, the demand function for Country i firm's products in the domestic market; f_i, the demand function for Country i firm's products in the Japanese market; g_i, the demand function for Country i firm's products in the US market; h_i, the demand function for Country i firm's products in the neighbor country's market; $C(\ )$, the cost function ($C' < 0$, for simplicity we assume that $C'' = 0$); $q_i^j \equiv P_i^j/P_i$, the relative price of Country j firm's products relative to Country i in the Country i market ($i = J, US$ and $j = B, A$); q_i, the relative price of Country i firm's products relative to the neighbor country's product in the Country i market; P_i, the price of Country i products in Country i market in terms of Country i currency ($i = J, US$); $E^{j/i}$, the exchange rate of currency i in terms of Country j currency ($i = \$, B$ and $j = A, B$); and ω_m^i, the share of parts imported from country i ($i = J, US$), $\omega_m^J + \omega_m^{US} = 1$.

From the first-order conditions of Equation (1), the profit-maximizing prices of the Country i firm in the Japanese, US, Country A and B markets, respectively, are derived as

$$P_J^i = \mu_J^i \frac{C_i}{E^{i/y}} \tag{2}$$

$$P_{US}^i = \mu_{US}^i \frac{C_i}{E^{i/\$}} \tag{3}$$

$$P_i^i = \mu_i^i C_i \tag{4}$$

$$P_j^i = \mu_j^i \frac{C_i}{E^{i/j}} \tag{5}$$

$$C_i \equiv \omega_m^J E^{i/y} P_m^J + \omega_m^{US} E^{i/\$} P_m^{US} + C'(Q_i) \tag{6}$$

for $i = A, B$ and $j = B, A$, where $\mu_i^j \equiv \varepsilon_i^j(q_i^j)/\{\varepsilon_i^j(q_i^j) - 1\}$ denotes markups of the Country A firm's products in the Country i market ($i = J$, US, A, B and $j = A, B$), and ε_i^j denotes price elasticity of demand for the Country j firm's product in the Country i market ($i=J$, US, A, B and $j = A, B$). We assume that $\varepsilon_i^j > 1$.

We convert Equations (2) to (5) into logarithm form and derive the reaction functions of Country A firm in Japanese, US, and Country A and B markets given the prices of the products made in Japan, the United States, and Country B, respectively.

$$\log P_J^i = \frac{\eta_J^i}{1 + \eta_J^i} \log P_J + \frac{1}{1 + \eta_J^i} \left(\log C_i - \log E^{i/Y} \right) \tag{7}$$

$$\log P_{US}^i = \frac{\eta_{US}^i}{1 + \eta_{US}^i} \log P_{US} + \frac{1}{1 + \eta_{US}^i} \left(\log C_i - \log E^{i/\$} \right) \tag{8}$$

$$\log P_i^i = \frac{\eta_i^i}{1 + \eta_i^i} \log P_i^j + \frac{1}{1 + \eta_i^i} \log C_i \tag{9}$$

$$\log P_j^i = \frac{\eta_j^i}{1 + \eta_j^i} \log P_j^j + \frac{1}{1 + \eta_j^i} \left(\log C_i - \log E^{i/j} \right) \tag{10}$$

for $i = A, B$ and $j = B, A$, where $\eta_i^j \equiv \mu_i^{j'} q_i^j / \mu_i^j$ denotes price elasticity of the markups of the Country j firm's products in the Country i market for $i=J$, US, A, B and $j = A, B$.

For simplicity, we assume that price elasticities of demand for the Country A and B firms' products are equal to each other in each of the Country A and B markets. That is, $\varepsilon_A^B = \varepsilon_A^A = \varepsilon_A$ and $\varepsilon_B^A = \varepsilon_B^B = \varepsilon_B$. Thus, price elasiticities of the markups of Country A and B firms' products are equal to each other in each of the Country A and B markets. That is, $\eta_A^B = \eta_A^A = \eta_A$ and $\eta_B^A = \eta_B^B = \eta_B$.

From Equation (9), we obtain equilibrium prices for Country A and B firms' products in the duopoly market of countries A and B, respectively:

$$\log P_i^i = \frac{1 + \eta_i}{1 + 2\eta_i} \log C_i + \frac{\eta_i}{1 + 2\eta_i} \left(\log C_j + \log E^{i/j} \right) \tag{11}$$

$$\log P_i^j = \frac{\eta_i}{1 + 2\eta_i} \log C_i + \frac{1 + \eta_i}{1 + 2\eta_i} \left(\log C_j + \log E^{i/j} \right) \tag{12}$$

for $i = A, B$ and $j = A, B$.

Equations (11) and (12) show that the equilibrium prices of Country A and B firms' products depend not only on the marginal total costs of Country A and B products but also on the exchange rate of currency A vis-à-vis currency B.

2.2.   Relative prices and demand functions

From Equations (7) and (8), we obtain equilibrium relative prices of Country A and B firms' products relative to the Japanese and the US domestic products in the Japanese and US markets, respectively.

$$\log q_J^i = \varphi_J^i \left(\log C_i - \log E^{i/Y} - \log P_J \right) \tag{13}$$

$$\log q_{US}^i = \varphi_{US}^i \left(\log C_i - \log E^{i/\$} - \log P_{US} \right) \tag{14}$$

where $\varphi_j^i \equiv \frac{1}{1 + \eta_j^i}$ for $i = A, B$ and $j = J, US$.

Moreover, from Equations (11) and (12), we obtain equilibrium relative prices of Country A products relative to Country B products in each of the Country A and B markets, respectively.

$$\log q_i = \varphi_i \left(\log C_i - \log C_j + \log E^{i/j} \right) \tag{15}$$

where $\varphi_i \equiv \frac{1}{1 + 2\eta_i}$ for $i = A, B$.

Equation (15) shows that the equilibrium relative prices depend on the marginal total costs and the exchange rate of currency A vis-à-vis currency B.

We specify demand functions for Country A and B firms' products exported to Japan, the United States, Country A, and Country B from Equations (13) to (15):

$$\log d_i = \varepsilon_i \varphi_i \left(\log C_j - \log C_i + \log E^{i/j} \right) \tag{16}$$

$$\log f_i = \varepsilon_j^i \varphi_J^i \left(\log P_J + \log E^{i/Y} - \log C_i \right) \tag{17}$$

$$\log g_i = \varepsilon_{US}^i \varphi_{US}^i \left(\log P_{US} + \log E^{i/\$} - \log C_i \right) \tag{18}$$

$$\log h_i = \varepsilon_i \varphi_i \left(\log C_j - \log C_i + \log E^{i/j} \right) \tag{19}$$

for $i = A$, B and $j = B$, A. The equations show that demand depends on exchange rates as well as on the marginal total costs, the Japanese and US prices.

3. Effects of exchange rates on trade balances

In the next section, we introduce into our model the exchange rate policies of the monetary authorities of the two countries under the Marshall–Lerner condition, to analyze interdependence and coordination failure between exchange rate policies. In this section, we examine what the Marshall–Lerner condition implies in the model where domestic firms import parts from Japan and the United States, and in what situation the Marshall–Lerner condition is satisfied in the model.

First, we analyze the effects of changes in exchange rates on the trade balances of countries A and B. In the model, trade balances are equal to total exports (to Japan and the United States) less the sum of total costs of imported parts (from Japan and the United States) and imports from the neighbor country. Therefore, the dollar-denominated trade balances for countries A and B are shown as:

$$T_i = E^{i/Y} P_J^i f_i + E^{i/\$} P_{US}^i g_i + E^{i/\$} E^{\$/j} P_j^i h_i - E^{i/Y} P_m^J \omega_m^J Q_i - E^{i/\$} P_m^{US} \omega_m^{US} Q_i - P_i^j h_j \tag{20}$$

for $i = A$, B and $j = B$, A.

From Equation (20) we derive a relationship between changes in the trade balances and changes in the exchange rates.

$$\hat{T}_i = \left\{ \left(\tau_i^{ExJ} - \tau_i^{ImJ} \right) \hat{E}^{i/Y} + \left(\tau_i^{ExUS} - \tau_i^{ImJ} - \tau_i^{ImUS} \right) \hat{E}^{i/\$} - \tau_i^{Exj} \hat{E}^{j/\$} \right\}$$

$$+ \left\{ \tau_i^{ExJ} \hat{P}_J^i + \tau_i^{ExUS} \hat{P}_{US}^i + \tau_i^{Exj} \hat{P}_j^i - \tau_i^{Imj} \hat{P}_i^j \right\} \tag{21}$$

$$+ \left\{ \tau_i^{ExJ} \hat{f}_i + \tau_i^{ExUS} \hat{g}_i + \tau_i^{Exj} \hat{h}_i - \tau_i^{ImJUS} \hat{Q}_i - \tau_i^{Imj} \hat{h}_j \right\}$$

where $\tau_i^{ExJ} \equiv E^{i/Y} P_J^i f_i / T_i$, $\tau_i^{ExUS} \equiv E^{i/\$} P_{US}^i g_i / T_i$, $\tau_i^{Exj} \equiv E^{i/\$} E^{\$/j} P_j^i h_i / T_i$, $\tau_i^{ImJ} \equiv E^{i/Y} P_m^J \omega_m^J Q_i / T_i$, $\tau_i^{ImUS} \equiv E^{i/\$} P_m^{US} \omega_m^{US} Q_i / T_i$, $\tau_i^{Imj} \equiv P_i^j h_j / T_i$, $\tau_i^{ImJUS} \equiv (E^{i/Y} P_m^J \omega_m^J + E^{i/\$} P_m^{US} \omega_m^{US}) Q_i / T_i$, for $i = A$, B and $j = A$, B, and $\hat{x}$ represents the rate of change in variable. It is assumed, as mentioned earlier, that prices of products made in Japan and the United States remain unchanged.

The first line of Equation (21) represents the direct price effect of exchange rates on trade balances. The second line of Equation (21) represents the indirect effect of exchange rates via PTM (pricing to market) behaviors of Country A and B firms. The third line of Equation (21) represents an indirect effect of exchange rates on trade balances via trade volumes. For the Marshall–Lerner condition, it is necessary that the volume effect [third line of Equation (21)] dominates the *sum* of the direct price effect [first line of Equation (21)] and the PTM effect [second line of Equation (21)]. We consider whether the Marshall–Lerner condition is always satisfied in our model if the volume effect dominates the sum of the direct price effect and the PTM effect. For simplicity, we examine whether depreciation of the local currency would have a positive effect on net trade volumes, that is, export volumes minus import volumes.

The indirect effect via trade volume [third line of equation (21)] can be described as a function of the changes in the exchange rates as follows:

$$\tau_i^{ExJ}\hat{f}_i + \tau_i^{ExUS}\hat{g}_i + \tau_i^{Exj}\hat{h}_i - \tau_i^{ImJUS}\hat{Q}_i - \tau_i^{Imj}\hat{h}_j$$

$$= A^{i/Y}\hat{E}^{i/Y} + A^{i/\$}\hat{E}^{i/\$} + A^{j/Y}\hat{E}^{j/Y} + A^{j/\$}\hat{E}^{j/\$} \tag{22}$$

where $A^{i/Y} = \tau_i^{TJ}\varepsilon_j^i\varphi_j^i(1-\alpha_{i1}) - \tau_i^{TUS}\varepsilon_{US}^i\varphi_{US}^i\alpha_{i1} + \left(\tau_i^{TB}\varepsilon_j\varphi_j + \tau_i^{Imj}\varepsilon_i\varphi_i\right)\alpha_{i1},$

$A^{i/\$} = \tau_i^{TUS}\varepsilon_{US}^i\varphi_{US}^i(1-\alpha_{i2}) - \tau_i^{TJ}\varepsilon_j^i\varphi_j^i\alpha_{i2} + \left(\tau_i^{TB}\varepsilon_j\varphi_j + \tau_i^{Imj}\varepsilon_i\varphi_i\right)(1+\alpha_{i2}),$

$A^{j/Y} = -\left\{\tau_i^{TB}\varepsilon_j\varphi_j + \tau_i^{Imj}\varepsilon_i\varphi_i\right\}\alpha_{j1},$

$A^{j/\$} = -\left\{\tau_i^{TB}\varepsilon_j\varphi_j + \tau_i^{Imj}\varepsilon_i\varphi_i\right\}(1+\alpha_{j2}),$

$\tau_i^{TJ} \equiv \tau_i^{ExJ} - \tau_i^{ImJUS}w_J^i$, $\tau_i^{TUS} \equiv \tau_i^{ExUS} - \tau_i^{ImJUS}w_{US}^i$, $\tau_i^{TB} \equiv \tau_i^{Exj} - \tau_i^{ImJUS}w_j^i$ for $i =$ A, B and $j = B, A$ and $0 \leq \alpha_{i1} \equiv \frac{\omega_m^J E^{i/Y}P_m^Y}{C_i} \leq 1$, $0 \leq \alpha_{i2} \equiv \frac{\omega_m^{US}E^{i/\$}P_m^\$}{C_i} \leq 1$ for $i = A, B$. The signs of the parameters $\tau_i^{TJ}, \tau_i^{TUS}, \tau_i^{TB}$, and τ_i^{Exj} are positive if export industries are adding value to the parts imports by converting parts into products for export. Hence, we assume that these τ parameters are positive.

Exchange rates have effects on product prices, which change the relative prices of the products in the Japanese, the US, and Country A and B markets. The changes in the relative prices have effects on the demand for products in these markets. In our model, demand for products made in Country A or B is equivalent to that country's export volume. Since parts are imported from Japan and the United States, and some products are imported from the neighbor country, the exchange rates have effects on imports as well as exports.

In Equation (22), it is clear that the exchange rates of the neighbor country's currency vis-à-vis the yen and the dollar have unambiguous effects on trade volumes. The appreciation of the neighbor currency has positive effects on trade volume, as the competitiveness of home products increases. However, the exchange rates of the home currency vis-à-vis the yen and the dollar a priori have ambiguous effects on trade volumes.

If the exchange rate of the home currency vis-à-vis the yen, that is $A^{i/Y}$, is positive, depreciation will cause export volume to increase if the following inequality is satisfied:

$$\tau_i^{TJ} \varepsilon_J^i \varphi_J^i (1-\alpha_{i1}) + \left(\tau_i^{TB} \varepsilon_i \varphi_j + \tau_i^{Imj} \varepsilon_i \varphi_i \right) \alpha_{i1} > \tau_i^{TUS} \varepsilon_{US}^i \varphi_{US}^i \alpha_{i1} \qquad (23)$$

Similarly, the exchange rate of the home currency vis-à-vis the dollar, that is $A^{i/\$}$, is positive, if the following inequality is satisfied:

$$\tau_i^{TUS} \varepsilon_{US}^i \varphi_{US}^i (1-\alpha_{i2}) + \left(\tau_i^{TB} \varepsilon_j \varphi_j + \tau_i^{Imj} \varepsilon_i \varphi_i \right) (1+\alpha_{i2}) > \tau_i^{TJ} \varepsilon_J^i \varphi_J^i \alpha_{i2} \qquad (24)$$

The right-hand side of inequalities (23) and (24) means that the exchange rates have negative effects on export volumes into the US or Japanese market through increases in cost of imported parts in terms of the home currency. The left-hand side means positive effects, as the depreciation of the home currency increases export volumes through relative prices and decreases import volume of parts.

Thus, the effects of exchange rates on trade balances are ambiguous in our model, because parts are imported. Depreciation of the home currency against a foreign currency increases prices of imported parts in terms of the home currency. An increase in the domestic price of imported parts decreases optimal outputs, which in turn decreases export volumes as well as decreasing import volume of parts. The depreciation of the home currency has an adverse effect on the trade balance if the negative effect on exports via imported part costs is larger than the positive effects that depreciation of the home currency increase export volume through relative prices and decrease import volume of parts. In this case, the Marshall–Lerner condition is not satisfied even if the volume effect [third line of Equation (21)] dominates the *sum* of the direct price effect [first line of Equation (21)] and the PTM effects [second line of Equation (21)].

Thus, the dominance of the volume effect is necessary but not sufficient for the Marshall–Lerner condition to hold in our oligopoly model, where domestic firms import parts from Japan and the United States. In addition, for the Marshall–Lerner condition to hold, it must be supposed that the direct effect of exchange rates on export volume is larger than the effect via imported part costs on export volume. Hence, the Marshall–Lerner condition is satisfied in the model when the latter condition and the dominance of the volume effect are satisfied.

Next, let us examine the effects on home trade when the yen and dollar appreciate vis-à-vis both the home currency and the currency of the neighboring country, which is related to the stability of exchange rate policy of the two countries analyzed in the next section. These effects are the sum of $A^{i/Y}$ and $A^{j/Y}$ and that of $A^{i/\$}$ and $A^{j/\$}$, respectively. The following equation shows the condition that the yen appreciation (vis-à-vis both emerging market currencies) positive trade volume effects:

$$\tau_i^{TJ}\varepsilon_J^i\varphi_J^i(1-\alpha_{i1})-\tau_i^{TUS}\varepsilon_{US}^i\varphi_{US}^i\alpha_{i1}+\left(\tau_i^{TB}\varepsilon_j\varphi_j+\tau_i^{Imj}\varepsilon_i\varphi_i\right)\alpha_{i1}$$

$$>\left(\tau_i^{TB}\varepsilon_j\varphi_j+\tau_i^{Imj}\varepsilon_i\varphi_i\right)\alpha_{j1} \tag{25}$$

Similarly, the following equation shows the condition that the dollar appreciation (vis-à-vis both emerging market currencies) produces positive trade volume effects:

$$\tau_i^{TUS}\varepsilon_{US}^i\varphi_{US}^i(1-\alpha_{i2})-\tau_i^{TJ}\varepsilon_J^i\varphi_J^i\alpha_{i2}+\left(\tau_i^{TB}\varepsilon_j\varphi_j+\tau_i^{Imj}\varepsilon_i\varphi_i\right)(1+\alpha_{i2})$$

$$>\left(\tau_i^{TB}\varepsilon_j\varphi_j+\tau_i^{Imj}\varepsilon_i\varphi_i\right)(1+\alpha_{j2}) \tag{26}$$

Now, we examine several cases about import status:

(1) Country i imports parts from both Japan and the United States.
     Inequalities (23) and (24) may or may not be satisfied. Also, inequalities (25) and (26) may or may not be satisfied.
(2) Country i imports parts from Japan only $\left(\omega_m^{US}=0\right)$, $\alpha_{i2}=0$.
     Inequality (24) is satisfied, but inequality (23) may or may not be satisfied. Moreover, if the production function is symmetric among the neighbor countries—that is, the third term in the left-hand side and the right-hand side of inequality (25) cancel out—then inequality (25) is also satisfied.
(3) Country i imports parts from the United states only $\left(\omega_m^J=0\right)$, $\alpha_{i1}=0$.
     Inequality (23) is satisfied, but inequality (24) may or may not be satisfied. Moreover, if the production function is symmetric among the neighbor countries—that is, the third term in the left-hand side and the right-hand side of inequality (26) cancel out—then inequality (26) is satisfied.

4.　Exchange rate policies in a two-country model

In this section, we develop a two-country model to analyze how the exchange rate policy of one country can be affected by that of the other country. Interactions of exchange rate policies conducted emerge in the two-country model, because the competitiveness of home goods depends on the relative exchange rate vis-à-vis the neighbor's. First, we suppose the two countries have the same objective: to stabilize trade balances. The policy reaction function of Country i is derived in terms of the currency basket in order to stabilize fluctuations in trade balances, given the exchange rate policy of the neighbor country. As a result, it is theoretically possible that a coordination failure may occur.[7]

Coordination failure is the same as the prisoners' dilemma: if both countries adopt the dollar peg at the same time, neither country has any incentive to adopt a currency basket peg as long as the other country remains at the dollar peg. Both countries, however, would be better off if they simultaneously adopted the currency basket peg. Coordination failure means that one Nash equilibrium is inferior to another without a simultaneous movement by the other player.

For the sake of simplicity, in deriving a Nash equilibrium in the model, we assume that the dollar weight of the other country is instantly observable. This is a plausible assumption, because a simple regression [a la Frankel and Wei (1994)] using the dollar/yen exchange rate movements and the exchange rate movements of the other countries would reveal the dollar weight quickly. Of course, an inter-action of Country A guessing Country B's dollar weight and Country B's guessing Country A's dollar weight would make the convergence a little more complicated. The iteration of such mutual guessing can be simulated by the convergence pro-cess using the reaction function. On day two, Country A decides its dollar weight based on its observation of Country B's revealed dollar weight of day one, and then, on day three, Country B decides its dollar weight based on its observation of Country A's revealed dollar weight of day two, and so on. This process is illustrated in Figure 4.1 (see arrows).

We focus on the exchange rates of home currency vis-à-vis both the US dollar and the Japanese yen by assuming that the two countries trade not only with the neighboring country but also with the United States and Japan. Asian countries export their goods and services mainly to Japan, the United States, and neighboring Asian countries.

Where domestic firms import parts from the United States and Japan and compete with neighboring country firms in US and Japanese product markets as shown in the preceding sections, we can obtain the following equations from the micro-foundation framework. We express the effects of exchange rates on the

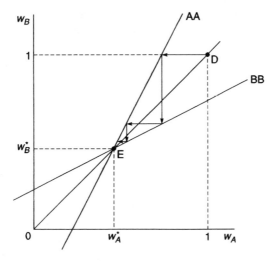

Figure 4.1 Convergence process in a stable equilibrium case of policy reaction functions

trade balances of Countries A and B in terms of rates of changes as follows:

$$\hat{T}_A = A^{A/Y}\hat{E}^{A/Y} + A^{A/\$}\hat{E}^{A/\$} + A^{B/Y}\hat{E}^{B/Y} + A^{B/\$}\hat{E}^{B/\$} \tag{27}$$

$$\hat{T}_B = B^{B/Y}\hat{E}^{B/Y} + B^{B/\$}\hat{E}^{B/\$} + B^{A/Y}\hat{E}^{A/Y} + B^{A/\$}\hat{E}^{A/\$} \tag{28}$$

where T_i is the trade balances of Country i; $E^{i/Y}$, exchange rate of currency i vis-à-vis the Japanese yen; $E^{i/\$}$, exchange rate of currency i vis-à-vis the US dollar; $A^{i/j}$, elasticity of trade balances of Country A in terms of the exchange rate of currency i vis-à-vis j; and $B^{i/j}$, elasticity of trade balances of Country B in terms of the exchange rate of currency i vis-à-vis j. Variables with a hut represent the rate of change in the relevant variable ($\hat{x} = \Delta x/x$).

As explained in the preceding section, Equations (27) and (28) include the three effects of exchange rates on trade balances: the direct price effect of exchange rates on trade balances, the indirect effect of exchange rates via PTM (pricing to market) behaviors of Country A and *B* firms, and the indirect effects of exchange rates on trade balances via export and import volumes. Under the Marshall–Lerner condition, the volume effect should dominate the *sum* of the direct price effect and the PTM effect. Accordingly, the volume effects of exchange rates should dominate in Equations (27) and (28) by the assumption of the Marshall–Lerner condition. For the qualitative analysis, we regard the signs of the *A* and *B* coefficients in Equations (27) and (28) as the signs of coefficients in the volume effects of exchange rates.

The coefficients ($A^{A/Y}$, $A^{A/\$}$, $B^{B/Y}$, and $B^{B/\$}$) on the exchange rates of the home currency vis-à-vis the yen and the dollar should be positive under the Marshall–Lerner condition. Exchange rates have negative effects on export volumes into the US or Japanese market through increases in the costs of imported parts in terms of the home currency; they also have direct positive effects on export volumes through relative prices and decreased import volume of parts. Thus, the effects of exchange rates on trade volumes are ambiguous because parts are imported in our model. The dominance of the volume effect is necessary but is not sufficient for the Marshall–Lerner condition to hold in our model. In addition, for the Marshall–Lerner condition to hold, it must be supposed that the direct effect of exchange rates on export volume is larger than the effect via imported part costs on export volume. Hence, the Marshall–Lerner condition is satisfied in the model when both the latter condition and the dominance of the volume effect are satisfied.

The coefficients ($A^{B/Y}$, $A^{B/\$}$, $B^{A/Y}$, and $B^{A/\$}$) on the exchange rates of the neighboring country's currency vis-à-vis the yen and the dollar are unambiguously negative in our model. The appreciation of the neighboring country's currency has positive effects on trade volume, as the competitiveness of home products would increase compared with the neighboring country's products.

However, the Marshall–Lerner condition cannot make clear whether coefficients on the exchange rates of the home currency vis-à-vis the yen and the dollar are larger or smaller than the absolute values of the neighboring country's currency vis-à-vis the yen and the dollar. Especially, in a general case where firms import parts from both Japan and the United States, it is not always true that coefficients on the exchange rates of the home currency are larger than those on the exchange rate of the neighboring country's currency ($A^{A/Y} > -A^{B/Y}$, $A^{A/\$} > -A^{B/\$}$, $B^{B/Y} > -B^{A/Y}$, and $B^{B/\$} > -B^{A/\$}$). As explained above, coefficients ($A^{A/Y}$, $A^{A/\$}$, $B^{B/Y}$, and $B^{B/\$}$ on the exchange rates of the home currency include an offsetting factor through imported parts costs in terms of the home currency. Accordingly, if the offsetting factor is relatively large, the coefficients may be smaller than the coefficients on the exchange rates of the neighboring country's currency, even though they are positive under the Marshall–Lerner condition.

We can have more definite relationships among the coefficients if we assume limited situations where firms imports parts from either Japan or the United States. In cases where firms import parts only from Japan, $A^{A/\$} > -A^{B/\$}$ for Country A and $B^{B/\$} > -B^{A/\$}$ for Country B. In contrast, in cases where firms import parts only from the United States, $A^{A/Y} > -A^{B/Y}$ for Country A and $B^{B/Y} > -B^{A/Y}$ for Country B.

We will analyze the interactions of exchange rate policies conducted by Countries A and B in the following two cases: one is a case where coefficients on the exchange rates of the home currency are larger than those on the exchange rates of the neighboring country's currency ($A^{A/Y} > -A^{B/Y}$, $A^{A/\$} > -A^{B/\$}$, $B^{B/Y} > -B^{A/Y}$, and $B^{B/\$} > -B^{A/\$}$), and the other is a case where coefficients on the exchange rates of the home currency are smaller than those on the exchange rate of the neighboring country's currency ($A^{A/Y} < -A^{B/Y}$, $A^{A/\$} < -A^{B/\$}$, $B^{B/Y} < -B^{A/Y}$, and $B^{B/\$} < -B^{A/\$}$).

A currency basket is defined as a weighted average of exchange rates of a home currency vis-à-vis the dollar and the yen. Thus, a currency basket peg means that a currency basket of nominal exchange rates is fixed at a certain level.[8] In other words, the rate of change in a currency basket, which is a weighted average of rates-of-change in the exchange rates, is equal to zero:

$$w_A \hat{E}^{A/\$} + (1 - w_A)\hat{E}^{A/Y} = 0 \tag{29}$$

$$w_B \hat{E}^{B/\$} + (1 - w_B)\hat{E}^{B/Y} = 0 \tag{30}$$

where w_i (for $i = A, B$) is a weight on the dollar in a currency basket for country i. We suppose a realistic case where $0 \leq w_i \leq 1$.[9]

When a country pegs its home currency to a currency basket, the relationships between the home currency vis-à-vis the dollar or the yen, and the yen vis-à-vis the dollar are shown as follows:

$$\begin{cases} \hat{E}^{A/\$} = (1 - w_A)\hat{E}^{Y/\$} \\ \hat{E}^{A/Y} = -w_A \hat{E}^{Y/\$} \end{cases} \tag{31}$$

$$\begin{cases} \hat{E}^{B/\$} = (1 - w_B)\hat{E}^{Y/\$} \\ \hat{E}^{B/Y} = -w_B \hat{E}^{Y/\$} \end{cases} \tag{32}$$

If the monetary authorities adopt a dollar peg system, and if the weight of the dollar in the currency basket is equal to unity, the exchange rate of the home currency vis-à-vis the dollar is fixed at a certain level, and the exchange rate of the home currency vis-à-vis the yen moves in parallel with that of the yen against the dollar. The home currency appreciates against the yen when the dollar appreciates against the yen.

In choosing weights for the dollar and the yen in the currency basket, both countries are assumed to be aiming to stabilize fluctuation in their own trade balances caused by changes in exchange rates.[10] We define optimality of exchange rate policy as the stabilization of fluctuations in trade balances in terms of the dollar under a currency basket peg system. We assume that each country minimizes the squared rate of change in its trade balances in terms of the dollar. That is, the countries have the following policy objective functions to minimize:

$$\hat{T}_A^2 = \left(A^{A/Y}\hat{E}^{A/Y} + A^{A/\$}\hat{E}^{A/\$} + A^{B/Y}\hat{E}^{B/Y} + A^{B/\$}\hat{E}^{B/\$} \right)^2 \tag{33}$$

$$\hat{T}_B^2 = \left(B^{B/Y}\hat{E}^{B/Y} + B^{B/\$}\hat{E}^{B/\$} + B^{A/Y}\hat{E}^{A/Y} + B^{A/\$}\hat{E}^{A/\$} \right)^2 \tag{34}$$

By substituting Equations (31) and (32) into Equations (33) and (34), respectively, the objective functions are shown in terms of weights for the exchange rates w_A and w_B.

$$\hat{T}_A^2 = \left\{ A^{A/\$} + A^{B/\$} - (A^{A/Y} + A^{A/\$})w_A - (A^{B/Y} + A^{B/\$})w_B \right\}^2 \hat{E}^{Y/\$^2} \tag{35}$$

$$\hat{T}_B^2 = \left\{ B^{B/\$} + B^{A/\$} - (B^{A/Y} + B^{A/\$})w_A - (B^{B/Y} + B^{B/\$})w_B \right\}^2 \hat{E}^{Y/\$^2} \tag{36}$$

From Equations (35) and (36), we can derive first-order conditions for minimizing the objective functions to obtain the following linear reaction functions:[11]

$$(A^{A/Y} + A^{A/\$})w_A + (A^{B/Y} + A^{B/\$})w_B = A^{A/\$} + A^{B/\$} \tag{37}$$

$$(B^{B/Y} + B^{B/\$})w_B + (B^{A/Y} + B^{A/\$})w_A = B^{B/\$} + B^{A/\$} \tag{38}$$

Equation (37) is a policy reaction function for Country A, which means that the monetary authority of Country A chooses an optimal weight for minimizing its objective function given a weight chosen by Country B. Also, Equation (38) is a policy reaction function for Country B. The monetary authority of Country B chooses an optimal weight for minimizing its policy objective function given a weight chosen by Country A. Thus, each country has to determine its own optimal weight in a currency basket while each is affected by the behavior of the other country.

Because both of the policy reaction functions are linear functions, there is a unique equilibrium pair of optimal weights for countries A and B. From Equations (37) and (38), we derive a pair of optimal weights for the dollar in a currency basket to stabilize the trade balances of both countries A and B at the same time:

$$w_A^* = \frac{(A^{A/\$}+A^{B/\$})(B^{B/Y}+B^{B/\$})-(A^{B/Y}+A^{B/\$})(B^{B/\$}+B^{A/\$})}{(A^{A/Y}+A^{A/\$})(B^{B/Y}+B^{B/\$})-(A^{B/Y}+A^{B/\$})(B^{A/Y}+B^{A/\$})} \qquad (39)$$

$$w_B^* = \frac{(A^{A/Y}+A^{A/\$})(B^{B/\$}+B^{A/\$})-(A^{A/\$}+A^{B/\$})(B^{A/Y}+B^{A/\$})}{(A^{A/Y}+A^{A/\$})(B^{B/Y}+B^{B/\$})-(A^{B/Y}+A^{B/\$})(B^{A/Y}+B^{A/\$})} \qquad (40)$$

If both countries adopt the optimal weights at the same time, trade balance fluctuation will be zero for both countries.

$$\hat{T}_{A(w_A=w_A^*,w_B=w_B^*)}^2 = \hat{T}_{B(w_A=w_A^*,w_B=w_B^*)}^2 = 0 \qquad (41)$$

From Equations (39) and (40), we obtain the result that the optimal weights w_A^* and w_B^* are always between 0 and 1 ($0 \le w_A^* \le 1$, $0 \le w_B^* \le 1$), both in the case where coefficients for the exchange rates of the home currency are larger than those for the exchange rate of the neighboring country's currency ($A^{A/Y} > -A^{B/Y}$, $A^{A/\$} > -A^{B/\$}$, $B^{B/Y} > -B^{A/Y}$, and $B^{B/\$} > -B^{A/\$}$) and in the case where coefficients for the exchange rates of the home currency are smaller than those for the exchange rates of the neighboring country's currency ($A^{A/Y} < -A^{B/Y}$, $A^{A/\$} < -A^{B/\$}$, $B^{B/Y} < -B^{A/Y}$, and $B^{B/\$} < -B^{A/\$}$).

5. Unstable equilibrium of optimal currency baskets

If Countries A and B could set w_A^* and w_B^*, respectively, at the same time, the trade balances of both countries would be stabilized. It is not always guaranteed, however, that the optimal weights for both countries are a stable equilibrium.

The condition for a stable equilibrium is

$$-\frac{A^{A/Y}+A^{A/\$}}{A^{B/Y}+A^{B/\$}} > -\frac{B^{A/Y}+B^{A/\$}}{B^{B/Y}+B^{B/\$}} \qquad (42)$$

This condition is satisfied if the coefficients of the exchange rates of the home currency are larger than those of the exchange rates of the neighboring country's currency ($A^{A/Y} > -A^{B/Y}$, $A^{A/\$} > -A^{B/\$}$, $B^{B/Y} > -B^{A/Y}$, and $B^{B/\$} > -B^{A/\$}$).

In this case, the pair of weights shall converge toward an equilibrium point implied by the optimal weights (w_A^*, w_B^*). The weights for both countries should converge toward their optimal equilibrium values.

Figure 4.1 shows a case where inequality (42) is satisfied. An equilibrium point with the optimal weights (w_A^*, w_B^*) is a stable one on a plane where policy reaction functions of Countries A and B are depicted as lines AA and BB, respectively. In this case, each country, A and B, gradually changes the weight of the dollar in its currency basket in order to stabilize its own trade balance, in response to the weight chosen by the other country. As a result, the weights for both countries can eventually reach an equilibrium point at the optimal weights (w_A^*, w_B^*).

On the other hand, if

$$-\frac{A^{A/Y}+A^{A/\$}}{A^{B/Y}+A^{B/\$}} < -\frac{B^{A/Y}+B^{A/\$}}{B^{B/Y}+B^{B/\$}}, \tag{43}$$

the pair of the optimal weights (w_A^*, w_B^*) is an unstable equilibrium. This condition is satisfied in the case where the coefficients of the exchange rates of the home currency are smaller than those of the exchange rates of the neighboring country's currency $(A^{A/Y} < -A^{B/Y}, A^{A/\$} < -A^{B/\$}, B^{B/Y} < -B^{A/Y},$ and $B^{B/\$} < -B^{A/\$})$. In this case, weights diverge from the optimal values once they are off the equilibrium point (w_A^*, w_B^*).

Figure 4.2 illustrates the policy reaction functions of both countries in a case where inequality (43) is satisfied. In this case, the equilibrium point with the optimal weights (w_A^*, w_B^*) is unstable. Suppose that each country, A and B, chooses its own weight to stabilize its own trade balance, in response to the weight chosen by the other country. The weights chosen by the two countries will tend to diverge from the optimal weights (w_A^*, w_B^*). Thus, the weight of the dollar increases and reaches a unity for both countries, assuming that the weight is realistically constrained between 0 and 1. Both countries would eventually adopt a full dollar peg system rather than the optimal currency basket peg system, even though they have been choosing their weights to stabilize their own trade balances.

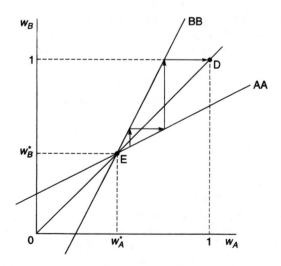

Figure 4.2 Unstable equilibrium case of policy reaction functions

Thus, if inequality (43) is satisfied, the optimal weight point is unstable. This makes it difficult for each country to sequentially change its exchange rate policy to an optimal exchange rate policy. Accordingly, it is natural that monetary authorities choose the dollar peg system rather than an optimal exchange rate regime in this case.

6. Multiple equilibria and coordination failure

Next, we consider a situation where monetary authorities try to shift their exchange rate regime from the current exchange rate regime to an optimal exchange rate regime. We analyze whether Countries A and B can make a direct shift from the current *de facto* dollar peg system to an optimal currency basket peg system in the state of stable equilibrium, which was analyzed in the previous section. The chances of a direct shift to an optimal currency basket peg system depend on whether each country can decrease fluctuations in trade balances under an optimal currency basket peg system in comparison with those under the current dollar peg system. In particular, the monetary authority of each country should care about fluctuations in trade balances in cases where it shifts to the optimal currency basket peg system while the other country keeps the dollar peg system.

We should compare trade balance fluctuations in the case where only one country adopts an optimal currency basket system with those in the case where both countries keep the dollar peg system. If both countries adopt the dollar peg $(w_A = w_B = 1)$ at the same time, fluctuations in trade balances are calculated as follows:

$$\hat{T}^2_{A(w_A=w_B=1)} = \left(A^{A/Y} + A^{B/Y}\right)^2 \hat{E}^{Y/\$^2} \tag{44}$$

$$\hat{T}^2_{B(w_A=w_B=1)} = \left(B^{B/Y} + B^{A/Y}\right)^2 \hat{E}^{Y/\$^2} \tag{45}$$

It is clear that in the case where both countries adopt the dollar peg system, the fluctuations in trade balances are larger than in the case where they adopt the optimal currency basket system, because in the latter case the fluctuations are zero. If $A^{A/Y} = -A^{B/Y}$ and $B^{B/Y} = -B^{A/Y}$, Equations (44) and (45) are zero, and the optimal exchange rate regime corresponds to the dollar peg system.

Next, we consider the possibility that both countries adopt the dollar peg system. One possible reason is that one country cannot adopt an optimal exchange rate policy because its losses increase if it alone adopts the basket while the other country keeps pegging its home currency to the dollar.

We consider how one country should behave if the other country adopts the dollar peg. For example, suppose that Country A adopts the above optimal currency basket peg $(w_A = w^*_A)$ while Country B adopts the dollar peg $(w_B = 1)$. In this case, the fluctuations in Country A's trade balance are as follows:

$$\hat{T}^2_{A(w_A=w_A^*,w_B=1)} =$$

$$\left\{ \frac{(A^{A/Y}+A^{A/\$})(B^{B/Y}-B^{A/\$})+(A^{A/\$}-A^{B/Y})(B^{A/Y}+B^{A/\$})}{(A^{A/Y}+A^{A/\$})(B^{B/Y}+B^{B/\$})-(A^{B/Y}+A^{B/\$})(B^{A/Y}+B^{A/\$})}(A^{B/Y}+A^{B/\$}) \right\}^2 \hat{E}^{Y/\$^2}$$

(46)

Here, we suppose that both countries have adopted the dollar peg system but contemplate two options: one is to keep the dollar peg system and the other is to jump to the optimal currency basket peg system. If Country B adopts the dollar peg ($w_B=1$), and Country A has the option to adopt the dollar peg ($w_A=1$) or the optimal currency basket peg ($w_A=w_A^*$), Country A compares the two options in terms of the projected fluctuations in its trade balance. Country A compares Equation (46) with Equation (44). It prefers the dollar peg to the optimal currency basket peg because the projected fluctuations in its trade balance are less with the dollar peg (Equation 6.1) than with the optimal currency basket peg (Equation 6.3) ($\hat{T}^2_{A(w_A=w_A^*,w_B=1)} > \hat{T}^2_{A(w_A=1,w_B=1)}$).

If Country B chooses the optimal currency basket peg ($w_B=w_B^*$) while Country A adopts the dollar peg ($w_A=1$), Country B would experience fluctuations in its trade balance:

$$\hat{T}^2_{A(w_A=1,w_B=w_B^*)} =$$

$$\left\{ \frac{(B^{B/Y}+B^{B/\$})(A^{A/Y}-A^{B/\$})+(B^{B/\$}-B^{A/Y})(A^{B/Y}+A^{B/\$})}{(A^{A/Y}+A^{A/\$})(B^{B/Y}+B^{B/\$})-(A^{B/Y}+A^{B/\$})(B^{A/Y}+B^{A/\$})}(B^{A/Y}+B^{A/\$}) \right\}^2 \hat{E}^{Y/\$^2}$$

(47)

The trade balance fluctuations in this case are larger than in the case where both countries adopt the dollar peg system ($\hat{T}^2_{B(w_A=1,w_B=w_B^*)} > \hat{T}^2_{B(w_A=1,w_B=1)}$).[13]

We can use Table 4.2 to explain how each Country selects its exchange rate policy. Table 4.2 shows a typical coordination game framework where there are two Nash equilibria. In this coordination game framework, once the participants fall into an inferior Nash equilibrium without coordination, they are forced to stay in it.

A situation where both countries adopt the dollar peg system is represented by the northwest cell in Table 4.2. We consider a case where both countries shift directly from the dollar peg system to their own optimal currency basket systems, which is represented by the southeast cell in Table 4.2. Given that the other country keeps the dollar peg system, each country compares the projected fluctuations in its trade balances in two cases: one where it keeps the dollar peg system and the other where it shifts to its optimal currency basket system. The latter case corresponds to the Northeast cell for Country A and the Southwest cell for Country B.

Table 4.2 Payoffs of exchange rate systems for two countries

Country B	Country A	
	Dollar peg	Optimal currency basket
Dollar peg	$\hat{T}^2_A(w_A=1, w_B=1)$	$\hat{T}^2_A(w_A=1w^*_A, w_B=1)$
	$\hat{T}^2_B(w_A=1, w_B=1)$	$\hat{T}^2_B(w_A=1w^*_A, w_B=1)$
Optimal currency basket	$\hat{T}^2_A(w_A=1, w_B=w^*_B)$	$\hat{T}^2_A(w_A=w^*_A, w_B=w^*_B)$
	$\hat{T}^2_B(w_A=1, w_B=w^*_B)$	$\hat{T}^2_B(w_A=w^*_A, w_B=w^*_B)$

$\hat{T}^2_A(w_A=1, w_B=1) < \hat{T}^2_A(w_A=w^*_A, w_B=1), \hat{T}^2_A(w_A=w^*_A, w_B=w^*_B) < \hat{T}^2_A(w_A=1, w_B=w^*_B)$

$\hat{T}^2_B(w_A=1, w_B=1) < \hat{T}^2_B(w_A=1, w_B=w^*_B), \hat{T}^2_B(w_A=w^*_A, w_B=w^*_B) < \hat{T}^2_B(w_A=w^*_A, w_B=1)$

Comparing the northwest and northeast cells, Country A should choose to keep the dollar peg system. Comparing the southwest and southeast cells, Country B should choose the same option. Therefore, both countries conclude that they should keep the dollar peg system, which is represented by the northwest cell.

Without a doubt, if both countries adopt their own optimal exchange rate regime, fluctuations in trade balances would be smaller than in cases where one country adopts a non-optimal exchange rate regime while the other adopts an optimal exchange rate regime. Our model has two equilibria, an optimal currency basket equilibrium and a dollar peg equilibrium. If both countries choose the dollar peg system, they are forced to maintain it at the dollar peg equilibrium, even though their optimal currency basket system would be preferable for minimizing fluctuations of trade balances. In this sense, history has decided the current exchange rate regime.

Accordingly, without coordination it is difficult for the monetary authorities of the two countries to shift directly from the current exchange rate regime to their optimal exchange rate regime. Faced with the prospect of coordination failure, the monetary authorities cannot escape from the current dollar peg system. To adopt the optimal exchange rate regime, they must coordinate with one another.

7.   Conclusion

We examined the question of how emerging market economies that export goods to the United States, Japan, and neighboring countries should choose their exchange rate regime. The optimal exchange rate regime is defined as one that minimizes fluctuation of the trade balance caused by fluctuation of the yen–dollar exchange rate. One might object to this framework on the grounds that the Asian currency crises were caused largely by capital movements, and not by the trade account problem. There are two reasons why trade account stabilization is important. First, one of the important triggers that caused the sudden reversal of capital flows (or attacks by speculators) in Thailand was the large current account deficit (about 8 percent of GDP in 1996), caused partly by the overvalued baht. The trade balance is important because it affects confidence in the exchange rate regime. Second, when capital movements are large, this alone may cause an overvaluation of the currency and/or a current account deficit. To judge whether the exchange rate is misaligned, one needs a benchmark. An exchange rate that is calculated to stabilize the real exchange rate gives such a benchmark. The calculation of such a basket value gives a good reference to answer the question whether capital flows are excessively large or small, causing misalignment.

We can draw some policy implications from these conclusions. First, real effective exchange rate must be managed if the Asian region—which relies on exports to Japan, the United States, and other regions—wants to avoid a boom-and-bust cycle due to under- or overvalued exchange rates. A basket currency regime would be particularly helpful. Second, the choice of exchange rate regime (or weights in the basket) may depend on a neighboring country's choice of regime. There may be coordination failure. If a neighboring country chooses the dollar peg, the choice is the dollar peg, and the neighboring country decides the choice in the same manner. However, if two countries make their decisions simultaneously, both would be better off to move to a basket currency regime with a greater weighting of the yen. Third, to help each country calculate a basket tailored to its own needs, it may be helpful to calculate and publish the typical currency basket unit for the region. Such a currency unit (say, the Asian Currency Unit, or ACU) would have [specific] weights for the US dollar, the yen, and the euro. Coordination failure might be avoided if each Asian country managed its own currency within a reasonable band around the ACU. We leave the calculation of such a currency unit, and simulations of the trade balances under the basket system, for future work.

Although this chapter simplifies many aspects of the real world, we believe that the essential points are very relevant to the real world. Asian countries would benefit from coordination with each other in choosing an exchange rate regime.

Appendix (Proof of $\hat{T}^2_{A(w_A=w_B=1)} < \hat{T}^2_{A(w_A=w^*_A, w_B=1)}$)

We prove that in a case of stable equilibrium $\hat{T}^2_{A(w_A=w_B=1)} < \hat{T}^2_{A(w_A=w^*_A, w_B=1)}$. To satisfy the following condition of stable equilibrium case, we assume that $A^{A/Y} > -A^{B/Y}$, $A^{A/\$} > -A^{B/\$}$, $B^{B/Y} > -B^{A/Y}$, and $B^{B/\$} > -B^{A/\$}$:

$$-\frac{A^{A/Y}+A^{A/\$}}{A^{B/Y}+A^{B/\$}} > -\frac{B^{A/Y}+B^{A/\$}}{B^{B/Y}+B^{B/\$}} \tag{A.1}$$

From Equations (44) and (46),

$$\hat{T}^2_{A(w_A=w^*_A, w_B=1)} - \hat{T}^2_{A(w_A=w_B=1)}$$

$$= \left[\left\{ \frac{(A^{A/Y}+A^{A/\$})(B^{B/Y}-B^{A/\$})+(A^{A/\$}-A^{B/Y})(B^{A/Y}+B^{A/\$})}{(A^{A/Y}+A^{A/\$})(B^{B/Y}+B^{B/\$})+(A^{B/Y}-A^{B/\$})(B^{A/Y}+B^{A/\$})}(A^{B/Y}+A^{B/\$}) \right\}^2 \right.$$

$$\left. -(A^{A/Y}+A^{B/Y})^2 \right] \hat{E}^{Y/\$^2}$$

Our assumption of $A^{A/Y} > -A^{B/Y}$ makes $(A^{A/Y}+A^{B/Y})$ in the above equation positive. Therefore, $\hat{T}^2_{A(w_A=w_B=1)} < \hat{T}^2_{A(w_A=w^*_A, w_B=1)}$ if the following inequality holds:

$$\frac{(A^{A/Y}+A^{A/\$})(B^{B/Y}-B^{A/\$})+(A^{A/\$}-A^{B/Y})(B^{A/Y}+B^{A/\$})}{(A^{A/Y}+A^{A/\$})(B^{B/Y}+B^{B/\$})-(A^{B/Y}+A^{B/\$})(B^{A/Y}+B^{A/\$})}(A^{B/Y}+A^{B/\$}) > A^{A/Y}+A^{B/Y}$$

We can arrange the difference between the right-hand side and the left-hand side of the above inequality in the following way:

$$\frac{(A^{A/Y}+A^{A/\$})(B^{B/Y}-B^{A/\$})+(A^{A/\$}-A^{B/Y})(B^{A/Y}+B^{A/\$})}{(A^{A/Y}+A^{A/\$})(B^{B/Y}+B^{B/\$})-(A^{B/Y}+A^{B/\$})(B^{A/Y}+B^{A/\$})}(A^{B/Y}+A^{B/\$})-(A^{A/Y}+A^{B/Y})$$

$$=\frac{1}{\Delta}\Big[\big\{(A^{A/Y}+A^{A/\$})(B^{B/Y}-B^{A/\$})+(A^{A/\$}-A^{B/Y})(B^{A/Y}+B^{A/\$})\big\}(A^{B/Y}+A^{B/\$})$$

$$-\big\{(A^{A/Y}+A^{A/\$})(B^{B/Y}+B^{B/\$})-(A^{B/Y}+A^{B/\$})(B^{A/Y}+B^{A/\$})\big\}(A^{A/Y}+A^{A/\$})\Big]$$

$$=\frac{1}{\Delta}\Big[(A^{A/Y}+A^{A/\$})\big\{(B^{B/Y}-B^{A/\$})(A^{B/Y}+A^{B/\$})-(B^{B/Y}+B^{B/\$})(A^{A/Y}+A^{B/Y})\big\}$$

$$+(A^{B/Y}+A^{B/\$})(B^{A/Y}+B^{A/\$})(A^{A/Y}+A^{A/\$})\Big]$$

$$=\frac{1}{\Delta}(A^{A/Y}+A^{A/\$})\big\{(B^{B/Y}-B^{A/\$})(A^{B/Y}+A^{B/\$})-(B^{B/Y}+B^{B/\$})(A^{A/Y}+A^{B/Y})$$

$$+(A^{B/Y}+A^{B/\$})(B^{A/Y}+B^{A/\$})\big\}$$

$$=\frac{1}{\Delta}(A^{A/Y}+A^{A/\$})\big\{(A^{B/Y}+A^{B/\$})(B^{B/Y}+B^{A/Y})-(B^{B/Y}+B^{B/\$})(A^{A/Y}+A^{B/Y})\big\}$$

where $\Delta \equiv (A^{A/Y}+A^{A/\$})(B^{B/Y}+B^{B/\$})-(A^{B/Y}+A^{B/\$})(B^{A/Y}+B^{A/\$})<0$ from inequality (42).

Under the Marshall–Lerner condition, in equations (27) and (28), the coefficients ($A^{A/Y}$, $A^{A/\$}$, $B^{B/Y}$, and $B^{B/\$}$) on the exchange rates of the home currency vis-à-vis the yen and the dollar should be positive. Moreover, coefficients ($A^{B/Y}$, $A^{B/\$}$, $B^{A/Y}$, and $B^{A/\$}$) on the exchange rates of the neighboring country's currency vis-à-vis the yen and the dollar are unambiguously negative. Accordingly, in the stable equilibrium case the difference is positive.

Therefore, in the stable equilibrium case, $\hat{T}^2_{A(w_A=w_B=1)} < \hat{T}^2_{A(w_A=w^*_A,w_B=1)}$. If both countries adopt the dollar peg system at the same time, fluctuations of trade balances are smaller than in the case where only the home country adopts the optimal currency basket peg system while the other country maintains the dollar peg system.

Notes

1 An earlier version of this study was presented at the CEPII-KIEP-ADBI conference, December 17–18, 1999. The authors are grateful to Gang Yi, Kenichi Ohno, Koichi Hamada, Takashi Misumi, and other participants of the conference, and to the anonymous referees, for their useful and constructive comments. The views expressed here are the authors' own, and not necessarily those of the institutions with which the authors were affiliated at present or in the past.

2 Before the currency crisis, several Asian countries including Thailand and Korea claimed that they were adopting a basket system, or a managed float system. However, the actual movements of exchange rates suggest that the weight of the dollar was quite high. See Frankel and Wei (1994). In that sense, we call the pre-crisis regime the *de facto* dollar peg.

3 The so-called 'two-corner solution' has become a popular view among some researchers and policy makers in the post-crisis discussions. (See Eichengreen (1999), for example.) According to this view, the only regimes that are stable in the long run are the free floating (ultimate flexibility), and a currency board (ultimate inflexibility). Any intermediate regime—managed float or fixed exchange rate regime without a currency board—is unstable. Advocates of the two-corner solution cite the fact that Hong Kong and Argentina, both currency board economies, survived the currency crisis of the neighboring economies.

It is not advisable for countries that export substantial volumes to Japan as well as the United States to adopt an exchange rate regime pegged to the US dollar. Hong Kong seems to be an exception, as it is a small open country with lots of reexports and with high labor and price flexibility of domestic markets. The currency board of the Hong Kong type is not suitable for other Asian economies.

Would a free-floating exchange rate be appropriate for other Asian economies? If one believes that the market will (most of the time) determine the exchange rate at the level (most) consistent with fundamentals, then the free floating rate is advisable. However, if one believes that the market will (too often) drive the exchange rate to a level (clearly) misaligned with the fundamentals, then policy actions in the domestic market and some direct interventions to the exchange rate market may be called for. The latter view is more convincing in the view of the following evidence. First, even advanced countries find it necessary to intervene occasionally. Foreign exchange rates sometimes become misaligned with fundamentals. The US dollar in 1984–85 and the yen in 1995 are obvious example of overvaluation. Misalignment needs to be corrected by intervention and some policy adjustment. Second, the worst of the Asian crises, say November 1997 to January 1998, came long after the Asian economies moved to flexible exchange rate regimes. When contagious crises feed each other among the regional economies, free floating regimes could cause a downward spiral of the region's currencies. Thus, a devaluation of a currency could bring down the currencies of trade- and investment-related countries. Those who praise China as a barrier stopping a contagious spiral of devaluation in the region by maintaining a fixed exchange rate should also be advocating some sort of managed float in times of crisis.

4 Flanders and Helpman (1979), Lipschitz and Sundararajan (1980), and Flanders and Tishler (1981) emphasized only the real side of the economy in modeling the currency basket peg issue. On the other hand, Turnovsky (1982) and Bhandari (1985) used a general equilibrium macroeconomic model that included capital mobility.

5 Ohno (1989) examined the pass-through effects of exchange rates on export pricing behavior in manufacturing after taking into account prices of raw materials. Marston (1990) modeled a similar pricing to market model.

6 In our model, Japanese and US suppliers of parts are not assumed to price to market, because many suppliers exist and they behave competitively. Parts are more difficult to differentiate compared to brand-name products.

7 Bénassy-Quéré (1999) and Ohno (1999) analyzed pegging the US dollar as a coordination failure.

8 A currency basket of nominal exchange rates is fixed at a specific level because we suppose that economies experience no inflation. The monetary authorities should adopt a crawling currency basket system if the economies experience positive rates of inflation that are different from those in the United States and Japan.

9 We limit our discussion to realistic cases, though it is theoretically possible to suppose $1 < w_i$.

10 This assumption was made in Ito et al. (1998). Alternatively, we may assume that the monetary authorities minimize the absolute variation of the trade account to GDP ratio. Bénassy-Quéré (1999) assumed that the monetary authorities seek to stabilize both their external competitiveness and the real price of their external debt.

11 We can obtain linear reaction functions because we assume quadratic functions of the rate of change in trade balances. It is usual to consider fluctuations of trade balances as a second order of moment though it is, in general, unnecessary to limit the second order of moment. We obtain nonlinear functions if we assume a more general form of objective functions.

12 See Appendix for our proof of the inequality $\hat{T}^2_{A(w_A=w^*_A,w_B=1)} > \hat{T}^2_{A(w_A=1,w_B=1)}$.

13 Equations (44) and (45) show that $\hat{T}^2_{A(w_A=w_B=1)}$ and $\hat{T}^2_{B(w_A=w_B=1)}$ are symmetric. Equations (46) and (47) shows that $\hat{T}^2_{A(w_A=w^*_A,w_B=1)}$ and $\hat{T}^2_{B(w_A=1,w_B=w^*_B)}$ are symmetric. Accordingly, we can apply the proof of inequality $\hat{T}^2_{A(w_A=w^*_A,w_B=1)} > \hat{T}^2_{A(w_A=1,w_B=1)}$ for Country A to a proof of inequality $\hat{T}^2_{B(w_A=1,w_B=w^*_B)} > \hat{T}^2_{B(w_A=1,w_B=1)}$ for Country B.

References

Bénassy-Quéré, A. (1999). Optimal pegs for East Asian currencies. *Journal of the Japanese and International Economies*, 13(1), 44–60.

Bhandari, J. S. (1985). Experiments with the optimal currency composite. *Southern Economic Journal*, 51(3): 711–730.

Eichengreen, B. (1999). *Toward a New International Financial Architecture: A Practical Post-Asia Agenda*. Washington, DC: Institute for International Economics.

Flanders, M. J. and Helpman, E. (1979). An optimal exchange rate peg in a world of general floating. *The Review of Economic Studies*, 46(3), 533–542.

Flanders, M. J. and Tishler, A. (1981). The role of elasticity optimism in choosing an optimal currency basket with applications to Israel. *Journal of International Economics*, 11(3), 395–406.

Frankel, J. and Wei, S. J. (1994). Yen bloc or dollar bloc? Exchange rate policies of the east Asian economies. In T. Ito and A. O. Krueger, eds., *Macroeconomic Linkage: Savings, Exchange Rates, and Capital Flows*, Chicago: University of Chicago Press, pp. 295–355.

Ito, T. Ogawa, E. and Sasaki, Y. N. (1998). How did the dollar peg fail in asia? *Journal of the Japanese and International Economies*, 12(4), 256–304.

Lipschitz, L. and Sundararajan, V. (1980). The optimal basket in a world of generalized floating. *IMF Staff papers*, 27(1), 80–100.

Marston, R. C. (1990). Pricing to market in Japanese manufacturing. *Journal of International Economics*, 29(3/4), 217–236.

Ogawa, E. and Ito, T. (2000). On the desirability of a regional basket currency arrangement. NBER Working papers, no. 8002.

Ohno, K. (1989). Export pricing behavior in manufacturing: A U.S.-Japan comparison. *IMF Staff Chapters*, 36(3), 550–579.

Ohno, K. (1999). Exchange rate management in developing Asia: reassessment of the pre-crisis soft dollar zone. ADB Institute, Working Paper Series, No.1.

Turnovsky, S. J. (1982). A determination of the optimal currency basket. *Journal of International Economics*, 12(3–4), 333–354.

5 Economic interdependence and international coordination in East Asia[1]

Eiji Ogawa

1. Introduction

The Asian currency crisis of 1997 taught several lessons. Before the currency crisis, monetary authorities in many East Asian countries adopted a de facto dollar peg system. As the US dollar appreciated from 1995 to 1997, this de facto dollar peg system dragged these currencies higher as well, hurting export competitiveness by causing an appreciation in the effective exchange rates of these countries, which trade with Japan, the European Union, and other countries as well as the United States. Accordingly, one of the lessons is that the de facto dollar peg system was dangerous for East Asian countries (Williamson 2000).

In recent years, however, as McKinnon (2000) has pointed out, links with the US dollar have returned to the pre-crisis situation for some East Asian countries. Ogawa (2002b) estimated weights for the US dollar in a possible currency basket for some East Asian countries, using a method devised by Frankel and Wei (1994). Analytical results show that some countries have increased the linkages of their home currencies with the US dollar in recent years.

It is important to consider what factors restored the linkages between East Asian currencies and the US dollar. These factors include the inertia of the US dollar as a key currency in the world economy, the US dollar as a nominal anchor, the appreciation of the Japanese yen against the US dollar, and trade competition within the region, which led to coordination failure in choosing an exchange rate system. In this chapter, we focus on coordination failure in choosing an exchange rate system.

In Ogawa and Ito (2002), we used a two-country model to analyze theoretically why monetary authorities maintained the dollar peg system instead of adopting other exchange rate regimes that might have been more favorable. We showed that coordination failure among the monetary authorities contributed to their decisions to retain the dollar peg system. Moreover, we made an empirical analysis to investigate whether the monetary authorities, in fact, met with coordination failure in choosing an optimal exchange rate system among the ASEAN5 countries, China, and Korea.

2.   Recent return to de facto dollar pegs

This section shows that East Asian currencies have increased their linkages with the US dollar in recent years. When we compare the recent movements of these currencies against the US dollar and against the Japanese yen, we see that the exchange rates fluctuated more widely against both the US dollar and the Japanese yen during the crisis from July 1997 to the end of 1998 than before the crisis. During the currency crisis, Thailand, Indonesia, Malaysia, and Korea experienced overshooting of their exchange rates (Table 5.1).

Exchange rates stabilized in 1999 and 2000. However, we see differences in the patterns of fluctuation against the US dollar and against the Japanese yen. Rates vis-à-vis the Japanese yen fluctuated more widely than those against the US dollar. It seems that some East Asian countries returned to the same kind of de facto dollar peg system they had before the currency crisis, even though the de facto dollar peg system was at least a contributory factor to the currency crisis.

Ogawa (2002b) analyzed empirically how much weight the monetary authorities gave the US dollar in their conduct of exchange rate policy. McKinnon (2000) and Kawai and Akiyama (2000) used the Frankel and Wei (1994) method to conduct a similar analysis. Each came to the conclusion that East Asian countries have returned to a de facto dollar peg system.

In estimating the weight of the US dollar, the sample period was divided into half-year sub-periods. Weights for major currencies (US dollar, Japanese yen, the Deutsche mark, and British pound) in possible currency baskets for the period from January 1997 to September 2000 were estimated. East Asian currencies were regressed against the Swiss franc for various sub-periods in 1997–2000, using daily data and other high-frequency data from *Datastream* and other sources.

The log differences of the exchange rates of the local currencies were regressed against the Swiss franc *vs.* the log differences of the exchange rates of the major currencies against the Swiss franc.

$$\Delta \log e^{home/SF} = a_0 + a_1 \Delta \log e^{USD/SF} + a_2 \Delta \log e^{JPY/SF} + a_3 \Delta \log e^{DM/SF}$$

$$+ a_4 \Delta \log e^{BP/SF} + \varepsilon_t \tag{1}$$

In regressing the exchange rates of local currencies against those of major currencies, the variables that were significantly negative were omitted.

Table 5.1 shows the results of the estimation of weights in a possible currency basket with log differences using daily data. In Thailand's case, the weight of the US dollar was 0.990 in January–June 1997, before the currency crisis. This weight decreased during the currency crisis, from July 1997 to June 1998, but since July 1998 it has increased again. We observe similar movements for the currencies of Indonesia, Malaysia, the Philippines, Singapore, and Korea. Thus, from

Table 5.1 Estimation of weights in a currency basket (daily data; log differences)

Currency	Period	US dollar	Yen	DM	B pound
Thailand	Jan–Jun 1997	0.990***	0.049***	–	−0.001
	Jul–Dec 1997	0.932**	0.020	0.550	−0.268
	Jan–Jun 1998	0.471	0.148	0.727	0.311
	Jul–Dec 1998	1.004***	0.082	0.146	−0.039
	Jan–Jun 1999	0.998***	0.043	−0.079	−0.088
	Jul–Dec 1999	1.145***	−0.040	0.032	−0.147
	Jan–Jun 2000	0.908***	0.027	−0.116	0.090
	Jan–Sep 2000	0.896***	0.035	−0.121	0.119**
Indonesia	Jan–Jun 1997	0.999***	0.014	0.024	0.025
	Jul–Dec 1997	0.843	−0.152	−0.390	0.458
	Jan–Jun 1998	−0.203	1.974**	2.071	0.890
	Jul–Dec 1998	0.841*	0.277	0.244	0.063
	Jan–Jun 1999	1.159***	0.298*	0.144	–
	Jul–Dec 1999	0.477	0.411**	0.660	–
	Jan–Jun 2000	0.942***	0.129	0.266	−0.009
	Jan–Sep 2000	1.012***	0.118	0.890***	0.165
Philippines	Jan–Jun 1997	0.999***	−0.001	−0.002	0.000
	Jul–Dec 1997	1.232***	−0.137	0.094	−0.08
	Jan–Jun 1998	0.656**	0.082	−0.346	0.403
	Jul–Dec 1998	1.127***	−0.026	0.001	−0.040
	Jan–Jun 1999	0.996***	−0.027	0.030	0.060
	Jul–Dec 1999	1.046***	−0.073	0.244	0.166
	Jan–Jun 2000	0.938***	−0.043	0.096	0.064
	Jan–Sep 2000	0.872***	−0.005	−0.100	0.055
Malaysia	Jan–Jun 1997	1.030***	0.023	−0.070	−0.071
	Jul–Dec 1997	0.650**	0.303*	0.602*	−0.026
	Jan–Jun 1998	0.867*	0.341	−0.654	0.976
	Jul–Dec 1998	1.027***	0.050	0.136	−0.078
	Jan–Jun 1999	1.000***	0.000	0.000	0.000
	Jul–Dec 1999	1.000***	0.000	0.000	0.000
	Jan–Jun 2000	1.000***	0.000	0.000	0.000
	Jan–Sep 2000	1.000***	0.000	0.000	0.000
Singapore	Jan–Jun 1997	0.902***	0.095***	0.030	0.015
	Jul–Dec 1997	0.833***	0.050	−0.040	0.145*
	Jan–Jun 1998	0.747***	0.209**	0.318	0.115
	Jul–Dec 1998	0.903***	0.232***	0.088	0.012
	Jan–Jun 1999	0.915***	0.072***	0.303***	−0.091
	Jul–Dec 1999	0.997***	0.021	−0.049	−0.052
	Jan–Jun 2000	0.929***	0.005	0.108	0.052
	Jan–Sep 2000	0.948***	0.001	0.038	0.051
Korea	Jan–Jun 1997	1.009***	0.049*	0.042	0.012
	Jul–Dec 1997	0.590	1.104**	0.256	0.391
	Jan–Jun 1998	0.536	0.045	1.228	0.122
	Jul–Dec 1998	1.015***	0.063	0.083	–
	Jan–Jun 1999	1.008***	−0.012	−0.250	0.043
	Jul–Dec 1999	0.951***	0.043	−0.146	−0.002
	Jan–Jun 2000	1.027***	−0.061	−0.061	0.016
	Jan–Sep 2000	0.975***	–	0.009	0.015

continued

Table 5.1—Continued

Currency	Period	US dollar	Yen	DM	B pound
Taiwan	Jan–Jun 1997	0.990***	−0.013	−0.037	−0.000
	Jul–Dec 1997	1.020***	−0.026	0.178	−0.084
	Jan–Jun 1998	0.895***	0.082	0.087	−0.001
	Jul–Dec 1998	0.957***	0.099***	−0.060	−0.008
	Jan–Jun 1999	0.974***	0.021	0.095	–
	Jul–Dec 1999	1.000***	0.008	0.041	−0.015
	Jan–Jun 2000	0.971***	–	0.038	−0.006
	Jan–Sep 2000	0.981***	–	0.022	−0.013

Source: Ogawa (2002b).
***Significance level of 1%; **significance level of 5%; *significance level of 10%.
Period [Jan–Jun 1997]: 01:02:1997 to 06:30:1997.
Period [Jul–Dec 1997]: 07:02:1997 to 12:31:1997.
Period [Jan–Jun 1998]: 01:02:1998 to 06:30:1998.
Period [Jul–Dec 1998]: 07:02:1998 to 12:31:1998.
Period [Jan–Jun 1999]: 01:04:1999 to 06:30:1999.
Period [Jul–Dec 1999]: 07:02:1999 to 12:31:1999.
Period [Jan–Jun 2000]: 01:04:2000 to 06:30:2000.
Period [Jan–Sep 2000]: 01:04:2000 to 09:15:2000.

an empirical analysis, we arrive at the conclusion that linkages of East Asian currencies with the US dollar have returned to 1. In other words, we found that the weight of the US dollar has increased or has been increasing toward 1 in most East Asian countries.

Next, we should consider why monetary authorities have returned to the de facto dollar peg system if they intended to intervene in foreign exchange markets to target (or peg) their home currency to the US dollar. As noted above, some factors include the inertia of the US dollar as a key currency (Ogawa 2002a), the US dollar's role as a nominal anchor, the appreciation of the Japanese yen against the US dollar, and trade competition within the region, leading to coordination failure in choosing an exchange rate system. Throughout this chapter, the focus is on coordination failure in exchange rate policy.

3.   Currencies of neighboring countries and their effects on trade balances

East Asian countries are economically interdependent in the field of international trade. They have close trade relationships with one another, and they also compete with one another in trade with the US and Japan. In these circumstances, the exports of each of these countries can be affected by the exchange rates of neighboring countries' currencies as well as the US dollar. In this sense, they have economic interdependences in a field of international trade, not only in exchange rate of the home currency (Tables 5.2 a–d).

We estimate the elasticity of exports with respect to the exchange rates of home currencies and the currencies of neighboring countries. We regress the exports with

Table 5.2a Estimation of export equations (1980:Q1 to 1997:Q2)

ASEAN5

Exports	Indonesia	t-value	Thailand	t-value	Singapore	t-value	Malaysia	t-value	Philippines	t-value
$E^{A/\$}(a+b)$	0.277	1.924*	−0.111	−0.113	0.309	0.917	−0.498	−1.923*	−0.023	−0.579
$E^{B/\$}(c+d)$	−2.356	−5.432***	0.056	0.081	0.344	1.391	0.361	2.008*	−0.038	−0.186
$E^{¥/\$}(-(b+d))$	−0.400	−2.953***	0.965	3.516***	0.251	2.029***	0.088	1.158	−0.009	−0.146

***Significant level of 1%; *Significant level of 10%

Table 5.2b Estimation of export equations (1980:Q1 to 2000:Q1)

ASEAN5

Exports	Indonesia	t-value	Thailand	t-value	Singapore	t-value	Malaysia	t-value	Philippines	t-value
$E^{A/\$}(a+b)$	0.281	2.931***	0.028	0.063	0.282	0.928	−0.551	−3.843***	−0.021	−0.335
$E^{B/\$}(c+d)$	−2.303	−5.487***	0.316	0.712	−0.101	−1.137	0.293	2.800***	0.005	0.059
$E^{¥/\$}(-(b+d))$	−0.375	−2.922***	0.935	3.715***	0.227	2.119**	0.102	1.507	−0.053	−0.624

***Significant level of 1%; **Significant level of 5%;

Table 5.2c Estimation of export equations (1981:Q1 to 1997:Q2)

| | ASEAN5+China+Korea | | | | | | | | | | | | | |
| | Indonesia | | Thailand | | Singapore | | Malaysia | | Philippines | | Korea | | China | |
Exports		t-value		t-value		t-value		t-value		t-value		t-value		t-value
$E^{A/\$}(a+b)$	0.562	1.992*	0.308	1.077	0.944	1.929*	−1.446	−3.040***	0.010	0.070	0.022	1.037	−0.026	−1.078
$E^{B/\$}(c+d)$	−0.028	−0.046	−0.245	−0.820	0.528	1.394	0.716	1.994*	0.546	0.911	0.002	0.089	−0.113	−0.848
$E^{¥/\$}(-(b+d))$	−0.237	−0.868	−0.061	−0.641	0.361	2.013**	0.308	2.350**	0.154	0.688	−0.003	−0.227	−0.024	−0.702

***Significant level of 1%; **Significant level of 5%; *Significant level of 10%

Table 5.2d Estimation of export equations (1981:Q1 to 2000:Q1)

| | ASEAN5+China+Korea | | | | | | | | | | | | | |
| | Indonesia | | Thailand | | Singapore | | Malaysia | | Philippines | | Korea | | China | |
Exports		t-value		t-value		t-value		t-value		t-value		t-value		t-value
$E^{A/\$}(a+b)$	0.008	0.073	−0.047	−0.640	0.596	1.207	−0.850	−2.206**	−0.038	−0.222	−0.013	−0.768	−0.051	−0.890
$E^{B/\$}(c+d)$	−0.798	−1.409	0.130	1.069	−0.268	−1.216	0.617	1.704*	0.186	0.527	0.002	0.082	0.093	1.086
$E^{¥/\$}(-(b+d))$	−0.034	−0.135	0.109	2.719***	0.380	1.999**	0.331	2.249**	0.001	0.004	0.018	1.333	−0.061	−0.774

***Significant level of 1%; **Significant level of 5%; *Significant level of 10%

respect to both sets of exchange rates according to the following Equation:

$$\hat{X}_t^A = a\hat{E}_t^{A/\$} + b\hat{E}_t^{A/Y} + c\hat{E}_t^{B/\$} + d\hat{E}_t^{B/Y} \tag{2}$$

where X^A represents exports of country A; $E^{A/\$}$, exchange rate of home currency vis-à-vis the US dollar; $E^{A/Y}$, exchange rate of home currency vis-à-vis the Japanese yen; $E^{B/\$}$, exchange rate of neighboring country currencies vis-à-vis the US dollar; and $E^{A/Y}$, exchange rate of neighboring country currencies vis-à-vis the Japanese yen. Variables with a hat represent the rate of change in the relevant variable ($\hat{x} = \Delta x/x$). Coefficients (a and b) on home currency exchange rates are expected to be positive, while coefficients (c and d) on exchange rates of neighboring country currencies are expected to be negative.

Exchange rates vis-à-vis the Japanese yen were determined by arbitrage between the yen/dollar exchange rates and the exchange rates for each regional currency against the US dollar. Accordingly, we can rewrite Equation (2) as follows:

$$\hat{X}_t = a\hat{E}_t^{A/\$} + b(\hat{E}_t^{A/\$} - \hat{E}_t^{Y/\$}) + c\hat{E}_t^{B/\$} + d(\hat{E}_t^{B/\$} - \hat{E}_t^{Y/\$})$$

$$= (a+b)\hat{E}_t^{A/\$} + (c+d)\hat{E}_t^{B/\$} - (b+d)\hat{E}_t^{Y/\$} \tag{3}$$

We estimate a polynomial distributed lag model for Equation (3):

$$\hat{X}_t = \sum_{k=0}^{8} (a_k + b_k)\hat{E}_{t-k}^{A/\$} + \sum_{k=0}^{8} (c_k + d_k)\hat{E}_{t-k}^{B/\$} - \sum_{k=0}^{8} (b_k + d_k)\hat{E}_{t-k}^{Y/\$} \tag{4}$$

We use third-degree polynomial distributed lags that are extended back for eight periods with far constraint for our regression. We use the Maximum Likelihood Method to correct for serially correlated errors.

We used quarterly data for the ASEAN5 countries (Indonesia, Malaysia, the Philippines, Singapore, Thailand), China, and Korea. We made two groups for the estimation: one group consisting of the ASEAN5 countries, and another group consisting of the ASEAN5 countries plus China and Korea. First, we regard the ASEAN5 countries as neighboring countries. Next, we regard the group of ASEAN5+China+Korea as neighboring countries. For the exchange rates of neighboring country currencies, we use the trade-weighted average of these exchange rates. The data set was taken from the *International Financial Statistics* CD-ROM (IMF). The data are seasonally adjusted with ESMOOTH instructions in RATS version 4.30. We used real exchange rates as the exchange rates in Equation (4). We used WPI data to calculate real exchange rates.

For the ASEAN5 group, we set two sample periods: one from Q1 1980 to Q2 1997, and the other from Q1 1980 to Q1 2000, to take into account the effects of the Asian currency crisis starting in July 1997. We estimate export equations for the sample period from Q1 1980 to Q2 1997. For the sample period from Q1 1980 to Q1 2000, we eliminate the effects of the currency crisis on export equations by placing a crisis dummy in export equations for the crisis period, and a post-crisis dummy in export equations for the period after the crisis. The crisis dummy is set at 1 for the period from Q2 1997 to Q4 1998, and the post-crisis dummy is set at 1 for the period from Q1 1999 to Q1 2000.

For the group ASEAN5+China+Korea, because of the constraints of Chinese trade data, we set two sample periods: Q1 1981 to Q2 1997, and Q1 1981 to Q1 2000. For the period Q1 1981 to Q1 2000 we again placed a crisis dummy and a post-crisis dummy in the export Equations to eliminate the effects of the currency crisis on export Equations.

Tables 5.2a–d show the results of these estimations. The coefficients of $E^{B/\$}(c+d)$ correspond to the effects of the neighboring country currencies (the other ASEAN5 country currencies or the other countries of ASEAN5+ China+Korea) on exports. Tables 5.2a and b show the results when the neighboring countries are the other ASEAN5 countries. Tables 5.2c and d show the results when the neighboring countries are the other countries of the group ASEAN5+China+Korea as neighboring countries.

When the group of neighboring countries is defined as the other AESAN5 countries, their currencies had significant negative effects on Indonesia's exports during both of the periods under review. For Singapore and the Philippines, the currencies of the other ASEAN5 countries had negative effects on exports, but they were statistically insignificant during these two periods. For Malaysia, by contrast, currencies of the other ASEAN5 countries had significantly positive effects on exports during both of the periods under study.

When the group of neighboring countries is defined as the other countries of ASEAN5+China+Korea are regarded as neighboring countries, their currencies had negative effects on the exports of Indonesia, Thailand, and China in the period from 1981 to 1997, and on the exports of Indonesia and Singapore in the period from 1981 to 2000, but they were statistically insignificant. For Malaysia, by contrast, currencies of the neighboring countries in this group had significantly positive effects on exports of during both of the periods under study. The neighboring country currencies had positive but insignificant effects on exports of the other countries (Figure 5.1).

4.   Coordination failure in choosing an optimal exchange rate system

Monetary authorities may meet with situations where circumstances force them to keep the prevailing exchange rate system instead of adopting an optimal exchange rate system. Such a situation is related to a kind of coordination failure. We might suppose, for example, that all East Asian countries are currently employing the de facto dollar peg system, and that each knows it should adopt a currency basket system order to stabilize fluctuations of its trade balances. Companies in these countries compete with one another in both Japan and the US (Figure 5.2).

In such a situation, if one country switches to a currency basket system while the others keep the dollar peg system, the country with a currency basket system might

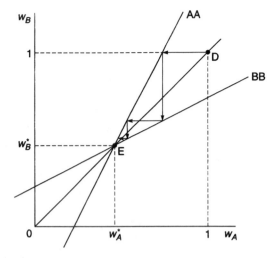

Figure 5.1 Stable equilibrium of policy reaction functions

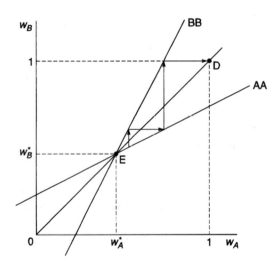

Figure 5.2 Unstable equilibrium of policy reaction functions

face increased fluctuations in its trade balance. If the US dollar depreciates against the Japanese yen, the related appreciation of the home currency of the country in question erodes the price competitiveness of firms in that country. On the other hand, if the US dollar depreciates against the Japanese yen, the related depreciation of the home currency of the country in question improves the price competitiveness of firms in that country. This is why the country that acted alone in adopting a currency basket system faces increased volatility in its trade balance. This might lead monetary authorities of that country to conclude that they must keep the dollar peg. This line of thinking may persuade monetary authorities in many countries to keep the dollar peg.

Ogawa and Ito (2002) used a two-country model and a game-theory framework to analyze coordination failure in choosing an optimal exchange rate system. We analyzed the theoretical possibilities of coordination failures by comparing losses in two situations:[2] one where both monetary authorities adopted the dollar peg at the same time, and another where one country adopted an optimal currency basket peg while the other country adopted the dollar peg.

We express the above effects of exchange rates on the trade balances of Countries A and B in terms of rates of change as follows:

$$\hat{T}_A = A^{A/Y}\hat{E}^{A/Y} + A^{A/\$}\hat{E}^{A/\$} + A^{B/Y}\hat{E}^{B/Y} + A^{B/\$}\hat{E}^{B/\$} \tag{5}$$

$$\hat{T}_B = B^{B/Y}\hat{E}^{B/Y} + B^{B/\$}\hat{E}^{B/\$} + B^{A/Y}\hat{E}^{A/Y} + B^{A/\$}\hat{E}^{A/\$} \tag{6}$$

where T_i is the trade balance of Country i; $A^{i/j}$, elasticity of the trade balance of Country A in terms of the exchange rate of currency i against currency j; $B^{i/j}$, elasticity of trade balance of Country B in terms of the exchange rate of currency i vis-à-vis currency j.

The volume effects of the exchange rates should dominate in Equations (5) and (6), under the assumption of the Marshall–Lerner condition. For the qualitative analysis, we regard the signs of coefficients A and B in Equations (5) and (6) as the signs of the coefficients in the volume effects of exchange rates.

Coefficients ($A^{A/Y}$, $A^{A/\$}$, $B^{B/Y}$, and $B^{B/\$}$) on the exchange rates of the home currency vis-à-vis the Japanese yen and the US dollar should be positive under the Marshall–Lerner condition. Coefficients ($A^{B/Y}$, $A^{B/\$}$, $B^{A/Y}$, and $B^{A/\$}$) on the exchange rates of the neighboring country's currency vis-à-vis the Japanese yen and the US dollar are unambiguously negative in our model. The appreciation of the neighboring country's currency has a positive effect on the home country's trade volume, as the competitiveness of home products increases compared with the neighboring country's products.

In constructing a currency basket, both countries are assumed to choose weights for the US dollar and the Japanese yen in a currency basket in order to stabilize exchange-rate-related fluctuations in their own trade balances. In our view, the optimal exchange rate policy would be a currency basket peg system aimed at stabilizing trade balances, as denominated in US dollars. We suppose that monetary authorities in each country control the weights of currencies in the basket with the aim of minimizing the squared rate of change in the US dollar-denominated trade balance, subject to the following equations:

$$w_A\hat{E}^{A/\$} + (1 - w_A)\hat{E}^{A/Y} = 0 \tag{7}$$

$$w_B\hat{E}^{B/\$} + (1 - w_B)\hat{E}^{B/Y} = 0 \tag{8}$$

where w_i (for $i = A, B$) is the weight of the US dollar in a currency basket for Country i. We suppose a realistic case where $0 \leq w_i \leq 1$.

We can derive the first-order conditions for minimizing the objective functions to obtain the following linear reaction functions:

$$(A^{A/Y} + A^{A/\$})w_A + (A^{B/Y} + A^{B/\$})w_B = A^{A/\$} + A^{B/\$} \tag{9}$$

$$(B^{B/Y} + B^{B/\$})w_B + (B^{A/Y} + B^{A/\$})w_A = B^{B/\$} + B^{A/\$} \tag{10}$$

There is a unique equilibrium pair of optimal weights for Countries A and B because both of the policy reaction functions are linear functions. From Equations (9) and (10), we can derive a pair of optimal weights (w_A^*, w_B^*) for the US dollar in a currency basket to stabilize the trade balances of both Countries A and B. If the monetary authorities of both Countries A and B could, at the same time, set w_A^* and w_B^*, respectively, trade balances would be stabilized in both countries. However, it is not always guaranteed that the optimal weights for the both countries are a stable equilibrium.

The condition for a stable equilibrium is

$$-\frac{A^{A/Y} + A^{A/\$}}{A^{B/Y} + A^{B/\$}} > -\frac{B^{A/Y} + B^{A/\$}}{B^{B/Y} + B^{B/\$}} \tag{11}$$

In this case, the pair of weights converges toward an equilibrium point implied by the optimal weights (w_A^*, w_B^*) as shown in Figure 5.1. The weights for both countries should converge to their optimal equilibrium values.

On the other hand, if

$$-\frac{A^{A/Y} + A^{A/\$}}{A^{B/Y} + A^{B/\$}} < -\frac{B^{A/Y} + B^{A/\$}}{B^{B/Y} + B^{B/\$}} \tag{12}$$

the pair of optimal weights (w_A^*, w_B^*) is an unstable equilibrium. In this case, weights diverge from the optimal weights once they are off the equilibrium point (w_A^*, w_B^*) as shown in Figure 5.2.

Suppose each Country A and B, chooses its own weighting to stabilize its own trade balance, given the weighting chosen by the other country. The weights chosen by each country should diverge from the optimal weights (w_A^*, w_B^*). In this way, the weight of the US dollar increases and approaches unity for both countries, provided the weight is realistically constrained between 0 and 1. Eventually, both countries effectively adopt a full dollar peg system rather than the optimal currency basket peg, even though their aim has been to choose weights to stabilize their own trade balances. Thus, if inequality (12) is satisfied, an optimal weight point is unstable. In this situation, it is difficult for monetary authorities to change to an optimal exchange rate policy.

Next, we analyze whether Countries A and B can shift directly from the dollar peg system to an optimal currency basket peg system. The shift to an optimal currency basket peg depends on whether the monetary authorities in each country can produce more stable trade balances using the optimal currency basket peg system, compared with the dollar peg system. Each country should be especially careful about fluctuations in trade balances if it alone shifts to the optimal currency basket peg system while the other country keeps the dollar peg system.

If both countries adopt the dollar peg ($w_A = w_B = 1$) at the same time, fluctuations in Country A's trade balance are calculated as follows:

$$\hat{T}^2_{A(w_A=w_B=1)} = (A_1 - A_3)^2 \hat{E}^{Y/\$^2} \tag{13}$$

If Country A adopts the optimal currency basket peg ($w_A = w_A^*$) while Country B adopts the dollar peg ($w_B = 1$), fluctuations in Country A's trade balance are calculated as follows:

$$\hat{T}^2_{A(w_A=w_A^*, w_B=1)} = \left\{ \frac{(A_1+A_2)(B_1+B_4) - (A_1+A_4)(B_3+B_4)}{(A_1+A_2)(B_1+B_2) - (A_3+A_4)(B_3+B_4)} (A_3+A_4) \right\}^2 \hat{E}^{Y/\$^2} \tag{14}$$

If Country A is free to choose whether to adopt the dollar peg ($w_A = 1$) or the optimal currency basket peg ($w_A = w_A^*$), given that Country B adopts the dollar peg ($w_B = 1$), the monetary authority of Country A is likely to compare the two options in terms of the potential fluctuation in trade balances. The monetary authority of Country A compares Equation (14) with Equation (13). If the adoption of the dollar peg [Equation (13)] is likely to result in a more stable trade balance, compared with the adoption of the optimal currency basket peg [Equation (14)], Country A is likely to prefer the dollar peg (Tables 5.5a and b).

Country B is likely to behave in the same way, because we assumed symmetry for the economies of both countries. Thus, both countries are likely to keep pegging their currencies to the dollar if their trade balances fluctuate widely with the optimal currency basket peg. This is called coordination failure. Only if the two countries coordinate policy to adopt the optimal currency basket peg at the same time can they peg their currencies to the optimal currency basket (Tables 5.6a and b).

5.   Empirical analysis of coordination failure

5.1.   Methodology

We empirically analyze whether the ASEAN5 countries have stable or unstable equilibrium in choosing an optimal exchange rate system, and whether they are likely to meet with coordination failure.

We use the results of the export estimating Equation (4) for each of the ASEAN5 countries. We also need an import estimating equation for each country, and export and import estimating equations for neighboring countries.

We regress imports against the exchange rates of both the home currency and neighboring currencies according to the following regression equations:

$$\hat{M}_t = e\hat{E}_t^{A/\$} + f\hat{E}_t^{A/Y} \tag{15}$$

where M represents imports. Parameters e and f are expected to be negative.

The exchange rates for each currency vis-à-vis the Japanese yen are determined by arbitrage between the yen–dollar exchange rates and the exchange rates of each currency vis-à-vis the US dollar. Accordingly, we can rewrite Equation (15) as follows:

$$\hat{M}_t = e\hat{E}_t^{A/\$} + f(\hat{E}_t^{A/\$} - \hat{E}_t^{Y/\$}) = (e+f)\hat{E}_t^{A/\$} - f\hat{E}_t^{Y/\$} \tag{16}$$

We estimate a polynomial distributed lag model for Equation (16) similar to the export estimation Equation (4):

$$\hat{M}_t = \sum_{k=0}^{8}(e_k + f_k)\hat{E}_{t-k}^{A/\$} - \sum_{k=0}^{8} f_k \hat{E}_{t-k}^{Y/\$} \tag{17}$$

We derive export and import estimating Equations for neighboring countries. We use an arithmetic average of the other ASEAN5 countries for the neighboring countries.

The elasticity of the trade balance in terms of the exchange rates of the home currency vis-à-vis the US dollar or the Japanese yen is calculated as the weighted sum of the elasticities of exports and imports. We can regard the elasticity in Equation (5) as the weighted average of coefficients in Equations (2) and (15):

$$A^{A/\$} = \frac{\overline{X}}{\overline{X}+\overline{M}}a - \frac{\overline{M}}{\overline{X}+\overline{M}}e \tag{18a}$$

$$A^{A/Y} = \frac{\overline{X}}{\overline{X}+\overline{M}}b - \frac{\overline{M}}{\overline{X}+\overline{M}}f \tag{18b}$$

where $\overline{X}$ is the average of exports during a sample period, and $\overline{M}$, the average of imports during a sample period.

However, we cannot identify the coefficients (a, b, e, f) in the estimation Equations (4) and (17). For this reason, we calculate the slopes of the reaction functions of the home country and the neighboring country, AA and BB, according to the following equations:

$$\frac{A^{A/Y} + A^{A/\$}}{A^{B/Y} + A^{B/\$}} = \frac{\frac{\overline{X}}{X+M}(a+b) - \frac{\overline{M}}{X+M}(e+f)}{(c+d)} \tag{19a}$$

$$\frac{B^{A/Y} + B^{A/\$}}{B^{B/Y} + B^{B/\$}} = \frac{(c+d)}{\frac{\overline{X}}{X+M}(a+b) - \frac{\overline{M}}{X+M}(e+f)} \tag{19b}$$

In this way, we use estimated coefficients in both the export Equation (4) and the import Equation (17), to calculate the slopes of the reaction functions of the home country and the neighboring country, respectively.

5.2.   ASEAN5

We estimate the case of the ASEAN5, using quarterly data for the ASEAN5 countries (Indonesia, Malaysia, the Philippines, Singapore, and Thailand). We define the group of neighboring countries for any ASEAN country as the other members of the ASEAN5. We use the trade-weighted average of exchange rates for the neighboring countries' currencies. We set two analytical periods, to take into account the effects of the Asian currency crisis. One period is from Q1 1980 to Q2 1997, and the other is from Q1 1980 to Q1 2000. For the latter analytical period, we use both a crisis dummy and a post-crisis dummy, as explained in Section 3.

Tables 5.3a and b show the sums of coefficients for the listed variables, with lags in export and import equations for a home country and neighboring countries.

Table 5.3a(1) Estimation of export and import equations (1980:Q1 to 1997:Q2)

	ASEAN5					
	Indonesia		*Thailand*		*Singapore*	
Home country (Country A)						
Exports		*t-value*		*t-value*		*t-value*
$E^{A/\$}(a+b)$	0.277	1.924*	−0.111	−0.113	0.309	0.917
$E^{B/\$}(c+d)$	−2.356	−5.432***	0.056	0.081	0.344	1.391
$E^{\yen/\$}(-(b+d))$	−0.400	−2.953***	0.965	3.516***	0.251	2.029***
Imports						
$E^{A/\$}(e+f)$	−0.303	−1.630	−1.511	−1.801*	−0.385	−1.864*
$E^{\yen/\$}(-f)$	0.525	2.210**	0.215	0.632	−0.162	−2.058**
Neighboring countries (Country B)						
Exports						
$E^{B/\$}(a+b)$	−0.233	−0.469	0.701	1.528	0.445	1.640
$E^{A/\$}(c+d)$	0.335	3.004***	−0.437	−0.728	0.062	0.167
$E^{\yen/\$}(-(b+d))$	0.187	1.436	0.160	1.054	0.122	0.867
Imports						
$E^{B/\$}(e+f)$	−0.949	−4.332***	−0.703	−2.772***	−0.467	−1.610
$E^{\yen/\$}(-f)$	−0.067	−0.844	0.265	2.233**	0.428	2.318**

***Significant level of 1%; **Significant level of 5%; *Significant level of 10%

Table 5.3a(2) Estimation of export and import equations (1980:Q1 to 1997:Q2)

	ASEAN5			
	Malasiya		Philippines	
Home country (Country A)				
Exports		*t-value*		*t-value*
$E^{A/\$}(a+b)$	−0.498	−1.923*	−0.023	−0.579
$E^{B/\$}(c+d)$	0.361	2.008*	−0.038	−0.186
$E^{¥/\$}(-(b+d))$	0.088	1.158	−0.009	−0.146
Imports				
$E^{A/\$}(e+f)$	0.437	0.542	−0.147	−2.177**
$E^{¥/\$}(-f)$	0.122	0.519	−0.102	−0.931
Neighboring countries (Country B)				
Exports				
$E^{B/\$}(a+b)$	0.348	1.276	−0.128	−1.127
$E^{A/\$}(c+d)$	−0.556	−1.410	−0.014	−0.159
$E^{¥/\$}(-(b+d))$	0.205	1.766*	0.152	1.303
Imports				
$E^{B/\$}(e+f)$	−0.669	−2.515**	−0.377	−2.883***
$E^{¥/\$}(-f)$	0.321	2.343**	0.268	1.864*

***Significant level of 1%; **Significant level of 5%; *Significant level of 10%

Table 5.3b(1) Estimation of export and import equations (1980:Q1 to 2000:Q1)

	ASEAN5					
	Indonesia		Thailand		Singapore	
Home country (Country A)						
Exports		*t-value*		*t-value*		*t-value*
$E^{A/\$}(a+b)$	0.281	2.931***	0.028	0.063	0.282	0.928
$E^{B/\$}(c+d)$	−2.303	−5.487***	0.316	0.712	−0.101	−1.137
$E^{¥/\$}(-(b+d))$	−0.375	−2.922***	0.935	3.715***	0.227	2.119**
Imports						
$E^{A/\$}(e+f)$	−0.195	−2.271**	−0.686	−2.402**	−0.661	−3.922***
$E^{¥/\$}(-f)$	0.445	2.338**	0.250	0.792	−0.230	−3.443***

continued

Table 5.3b(1)—Continued

	ASEAN5					
	Indonesia		Thailand		Singapore	
Neighboring countries (Country B)						
Exports		*t-value*		*t-value*		*t-value*
$E^{B/\$}(a+b)$	−0.853	−2.337**	0.520	2.327**	0.035	0.340
$E^{A/\$}(c+d)$	0.151	2.194**	−0.696	−3.169***	−0.027	−0.086
$E^{\yen/\$}(-(b+d))$	0.116	0.899	0.086	0.642	0.146	1.176
Imports						
$E^{B/\$}(e+f)$	−0.865	−4.400***	−0.606	−3.870***	−0.377	−2.619***
$E^{\yen/\$}(-f)$	−0.033	−0.348	0.278	2.507**	0.365	2.237**

***Significant level of 1%; **Significant level of 5%;

Table 5.3b(2) Estimation of export and import equations (1980:Q1 to 2000:Q1)

	ASEAN5			
	Malaysia		Philippines	
Home country (Country A)				
Exports		*t-value*		*t-value*
$E^{A/\$}(a+b)$	−0.551	−3.843***	−0.021	−0.335
$E^{B/\$}(c+d)$	0.293	2.800***	0.005	0.059
$E^{\yen/\$}(-(b+d))$	0.102	1.507	−0.053	−0.624
Imports				
$E^{A/\$}(e+f)$	−0.384	−1.248	−0.150	−2.271**
$E^{\yen/\$}(-f)$	0.350	1.628	−0.088	−0.861
Neighboring countries (Country B)				
Exports				
$E^{B/\$}(a+b)$	0.343	2.076**	−0.061	−0.460
$E^{A/\$}(c+d)$	−0.678	−2.986***	−0.055	−0.619
$E^{\yen/\$}(-(b+d))$	0.159	1.496	0.190	1.533
Imports				
$E^{B/\$}(e+f)$	−0.609	−3.399***	−0.355	−2.176**
$E^{\yen/\$}(-f)$	0.354	2.477**	0.266	1.782*

***Significant level of 1%; **Significant level of 5%; *Significant level of 10%

Some of the coefficients have their expected sign, and we find this significant. Thailand and Malaysia showed the expected signs for coefficients for neighboring countries. A few coefficients for neighboring countries, however, have the wrong sign.

Tables 5.4a and b show the slopes of policy reaction functions for a home country and neighboring countries. We can judge whether an equilibrium of policy reaction functions is stable or unstable using inequalities (11) and (12). In the period from Q1 1980 to Q2 1997, only Indonesia shows an unstable equilibrium in policy reaction functions of the home country and neighboring countries. In the period from Q1 1980 to Q1 2000, Indonesia, Thailand, and Malaysia show unstable equilibrium. All other cases show stable equilibrium in policy reaction functions.

Next, we investigate whether the ASEAN5 countries could shift directly from the dollar peg system to an optimal exchange rate system, which is related to the idea of coordination failure in choosing an exchange rate system. For this purpose, we calculate the fluctuations of trade balances in two cases: one where both the home country and neighboring countries adopt the dollar peg system, and another where the home country adopts the optimal exchange rate system while the neighboring countries adopt the dollar peg system. It is possible to compare the fluctuations of the trade balances in the two cases. Tables 5.4a and b show the results of the calculations.

Among the four countries with a stable equilibrium during the analytical period from Q1 1980 to Q2 1997, only Malaysia showed smaller fluctuations of trade balances when the dollar peg system is adopted by all countries than when the optimal exchange rate system is adopted, given the neighboring countries' dollar

Table 5.4a Stability of equilibrium and coordination failure (1980:Q1 to 1997:Q2)

| | *ASEAN5* | | | | |
	Indonesia	Thailand	Singapore	Malaysia	Philippines
Stability condition					
Slope of AA	0.122	−13.474	−1.012	1.301	1.948
Slope of BB	−0.887	0.622	−0.136	1.087	0.111
Stable or unstable	Unstable	Stable	Stable	Stable	Stable
Optimal weight					
w_A^*	0.823	0.507	−0.623	6.241	0.809
w_B^*	0.367	1.075	1.530	7.372	1.493
Fluctuation in trade balance					
$\hat{T}^2_{A(w_A=w_A^*,w_b=1)}$	2.220	0.00002	0.033	5.276	0.0003
$\hat{T}^2_{A(w_A=w_b=1)}$	2.071	0.134	0.147	0.026	0.001
Coordination failure	Yes	None	None	Yes	None

Table 5.4b Stability of equilibrium and coordination failure (1980:Q1 to 2000:Q1)

	ASEAN5				
	Indonesia	Thailand	Singapore	Malaysia	Philippines
Stability condition					
Slope of AA	0.106	−1.197	4.754	0.351	−15.520
Slope of BB	−4.356	1.237	0.125	1.416	0.378
Stable or unstable	Unstable	Unstable	Stable	Unstable	Stable
Optimal weight					
w_A^*	0.156	0.065	0.763	0.041	0.595
w_B^*	0.316	0.624	1.629	0.577	1.283
Fluctuation in trade balance					
$\hat{T}^2_{A(w_A=w_A^*,w_b=1)}$	2.483	0.014	0.004	0.015	0.000002
$\hat{T}^2_{A(w_A=w_b=1)}$	1.874	0.223	0.031	0.001	0.001
Coordination failure	Yes	None	None	Yes	None

peg system. For both of the two countries (Singapore and the Philippines) with a stable equilibrium during the analytical period from Q1 1980 to Q1 2000, fluctuations of trade balances are larger in the case where the dollar peg system is adopted by all countries. If we limit the group of neighboring countries to the ASEAN5, there is no possibility of facing coordination failure in choosing an exchange rate system.

The results of this analysis imply that Indonesia, Thailand, and Malaysia cannot shift from the dollar peg system to an optimal exchange rate system, because they may meet with coordination failure in choosing an optimal exchange rate system.

5.3.   *ASEAN5+China+Korea*

Next, we add China and Korea to the ASEAN5 countries and conduct the same empirical analysis of both equilibrium stability and coordination failure in exchange rate policy. We define each country's neighboring countries as the remaining members of the group ASEAN5+China+Korea. We use the trade-weighted average exchange rates for the currencies of the neighboring countries. We could derive export and import estimating equations only for the period from Q1 1981 to Q1 2000, because of the limitations of the Chinese trade data. In both our export and import estimating equations, we use a crisis dummy and a post-crisis dummy to take into account the effects of the Asian currency crisis.

Table 5.5a shows the sums of the coefficients for the listed variables with lags in export and import equations for each home country and its neighboring countries during the analytical period from Q1 1981 to Q2 1997. Table 5.5b shows the sums

Table 5.5a(1) Estimation of export and import equations (1981:Q1 to 1997:Q2)

	ASEAN5+China+Korea					
	Indonesia		Thailand		Singapore	
Home country (Country A)						
Exports		*t-value*		*t-value*		*t-value*
$E^{A/\$}(a+b)$	0.562	1.992*	0.308	1.077	0.944	1.929*
$E^{B/\$}(c+d)$	−0.028	−0.046	−0.245	−0.820	0.528	1.394
$E^{\yen/\$}(-(b+d))$	−0.237	−0.868	−0.061	−0.641	0.361	2.013**
Imports						
$E^{A/\$}(e+f)$	0.115	1.545	−0.894	−1.090	−0.221	−1.355
$E^{\yen/\$}(-f)$	−0.100	−1.379	0.050	0.154	−0.102	−1.565
Neighboring countries (Country B)						
Exports						
$E^{B/\$}(a+b)$	0.542	1.970*	1.410	3.284***	0.761	2.190**
$E^{A/\$}(c+d)$	0.353	2.838***	−0.862	−1.463	0.758	1.544
$E^{\yen/\$}(-(b+d))$	0.183	1.582	0.204	1.162	0.363	2.009*
Imports						
$E^{B/\$}(e+f)$	−0.098	−0.937	0.001	0.010	0.060	0.731
$E^{\yen/\$}(-f)$	−0.064	−1.259	−0.036	−0.762	−0.050	−1.059

***Significant level of 1%; **Significant level of 5%; *Significant level of 10%

Table 5.5a(2) Estimation of export and import equations (1981:Q1 to 1997:Q2)

	ASEAN5+China+Korea			
	Malaysia		Philippines	
Home country (Country A)				
Exports		*t-value*		*t-value*
$E^{A/\$}(a+b)$	−1.446	−3.040***	0.010	0.070
$E^{B/\$}(c+d)$	0.716	1.994*	0.546	0.911
$E^{\yen/\$}(-(b+d))$	0.308	2.350**	0.154	0.688
Imports				
$E^{A/\$}(e+f)$	0.557	1.015	−0.193	−2.654**
$E^{\yen/\$}(-f)$	−0.048	−0.308	−0.187	−1.707*

continued

Table 5.5a(2)—Continued

	ASEAN5+China+Korea			
	Malaysia		*Philippines*	
Neighboring countries (Country B)				
Exports				
$E^{B/\$}(a+b)$	0.996	2.975***	1.190	3.075***
$E^{A/\$}(c+d)$	−0.744	−1.217	−0.068	−0.670
$E^{¥/\$}(-(b+d))$	0.367	2.385**	0.266	1.658
Imports				
$E^{B/\$}(e+f)$	−0.015	−0.166	−0.019	−0.190
$E^{¥/\$}(-f)$	−0.042	−0.973	−0.051	−1.189

***Significant level of 1%; **Significant level of 5%; *Significant level of 10%

Table 5.5a(3) Estimation of export and import equations (1981:Q1 to 1997:Q2)

	ASEAN5+China+Korea			
	Korea		*China*	
Home country (Country A)				
Exports		*t-value*		*t-value*
$E^{A/\$}(a+b)$	0.022	1.037	−0.026	−1.078
$E^{B/\$}(c+d)$	0.002	0.089	−0.113	−0.848
$E^{¥/\$}(-(b+d))$	−0.003	−0.227	−0.024	−0.702
Imports				
$E^{A/\$}(e+f)$	−0.263	−2.310**	−0.045	−0.419
$E^{¥/\$}(-f)$	−2.310	−2.310**	−0.109	−0.687
Neighboring countries (Country B)				
Exports				
$E^{B/\$}(a+b)$	0.863	2.568**	0.790	1.397
$E^{A/\$}(c+d)$	−0.213	−0.555	0.206	1.984*
$E^{¥/\$}(-(b+d))$	0.179	0.752	0.500	2.764***
Imports				
$E^{B/\$}(e+f)$	−0.289	−1.570	−0.957	−6.739***
$E^{¥/\$}(-f)$	−0.024	−0.628	0.008	0.105

***Significant level of 1%; **Significant level of 5%; *Significant level of 10%

Table 5.5b(1) Estimation of export and import equations (1981:Q1 to 2000:Q1)

	ASEAN5+China+Korea					
	Indonesia		Thailand		Singapore	
Home country (Country A)						
Exports		*t-value*		*t-value*		*t-value*
$E^{A/\$}(a+b)$	0.008	0.073	−0.047	−0.640	0.596	1.207
$E^{B/\$}(c+d)$	−0.798	−1.409	0.130	1.069	−0.268	−1.216
$E^{¥/\$}(-(b+d))$	−0.034	−0.135	0.109	2.719***	0.380	1.999**
Imports						
$E^{A/\$}(e+f)$	−0.082	−1.986*	−0.624	−2.094**	−0.483	−2.452**
$E^{¥/\$}(-f)$	0.043	0.376	0.347	0.904	−0.143	−1.736**
Neighboring countries (Country B)						
Exports						
$E^{B/\$}(a+b)$	0.252	0.957	−0.016	−3.509***	0.157	0.994
$E^{A/\$}(c+d)$	−0.082	−1.261	−0.970	−3.250***	−0.668	−1.834*
$E^{¥/\$}(-(b+d))$	0.396	3.112***	0.313	1.932**	0.418	2.594**
Imports						
$E^{B/\$}(e+f)$	−0.608	−3.450***	−0.303	−4.198***	−0.281	−3.949***
$E^{¥/\$}(-f)$	−0.053	−0.436	−0.016	−0.288	−0.029	−0.413

***Significant level of 1%; **Significant level of 5%; *Significant level of 10%

Table 5.5b(2) Estimation of export and import equations (1981:Q1 to 2000:Q1)

	ASEAN5+China+Korea			
	Malaysia		Philippines	
Home country (Country A)				
Exports		*t-value*		*t-value*
$E^{A/\$}(a+b)$	−0.850	−2.206**	−0.038	−0.222
$E^{B/\$}(c+d)$	0.617	1.704*	0.186	0.527
$E^{¥/\$}(-(b+d))$	0.331	2.249**	0.001	0.004
Imports				
$E^{A/\$}(e+f)$	−0.356	−1.300	−0.008	−1.382
$E^{¥/\$}(-f)$	0.120	0.615	−0.025	−2.722***

continued

Table 5.5b(2)—Continued

	ASEAN5+China+Korea		
	Malaysia		Philippines
Neighboring countries (Country B)			
Exports			
$E^{B/\$}(a+b)$	1.069	4.130***	0.099	0.376
$E^{A/\$}(c+d)$	−1.308	−3.843***	−0.222	−1.922*
$E^{\yen/\$}(-(b+d))$	0.514	3.823***	0.416	2.545**
Imports			
$E^{B/\$}(e+f)$	−0.432	−4.391***	−0.514	−4.840***
$E^{\yen/\$}(-f)$	−0.007	−0.087	−0.018	−0.232

***Significant level of 1%; **Significant level of 5%; *Significant level of 10%

Table 5.5b(3) Estimation of export and import equations (1981:Q1 to 2000:Q1)

	ASEAN5+China+Korea		
	Korea		China
Home country (Country A)			
Exports		*t-value*		*t-value*
$E^{A/\$}(a+b)$	−0.013	−0.768	−0.051	−0.890
$E^{B/\$}(c+d)$	0.002	0.082	0.093	1.086
$E^{\yen/\$}(-(b+d))$	0.018	1.333	−0.061	−0.774
Imports			
$E^{A/\$}(e+f)$	−0.307	−6.661***	−0.111	−1.330
$E^{\yen/\$}(-f)$	−0.176	−3.215***	−0.124	−1.093
Neighboring countries (Country B)			
Exports			
$E^{B/\$}(a+b)$	0.705	2.634**	−0.104	−0.527
$E^{A/\$}(c+d)$	−0.616	−2.733***	0.229	2.572**
$E^{\yen/\$}(-(b+d))$	0.337	1.963*	0.564	3.364***
Imports			
$E^{B/\$}(e+f)$	−0.300	−4.451***	−0.852	−5.946***
$E^{\yen/\$}(-f)$	−0.005	−0.154	0.066	0.610

***Significant level of 1%; **Significant level of 5%; *Significant level of 10%

of the coefficients for the listed variables with lags in export and import Equations for each home country and its neighboring countries during the analytical period from Q1 1981 to Q1 2000. Significantly, some of the coefficients have the expected sign. Equally significantly, however, some coefficients have the wrong sign for the neighboring countries.

Tables 5.6a and b show the slopes of policy reaction functions for each home country and its neighboring countries during the two analytical periods. We can judge whether an equilibrium of policy reaction functions is stable or unstable according to inequalities (11) and (12). Singapore, Malaysia, and China exhibit an unstable equilibrium in policy reaction functions of the home and neighboring countries during the period from Q1 1981 to Q2 1997. Indonesia, Singapore, Malaysia, the Philippines, and China exhibit an unstable equilibrium in the period from Q1 1981 to Q1 2000. Thailand and Korea exhibit a stable equilibrium in their policy reaction functions. The equilibrium changed from stable to unstable for Singapore and the Philippines through the addition of China and Korea to the ASEAN5 group.

We investigate coordination failure in choosing an exchange rate system, that is, whether the group comprising the ASEAN5, China, and Korea can shift directly from the dollar peg system to an optimal exchange rate system when the other countries in the group are regarded as neighbors. Table 5.6 compares the fluctuations of trade balances in two cases: one where all of the countries adopt the dollar peg system and another where one country adopts an optimal exchange rate system while its neighbors adhere to the dollar peg system.

Table 5.6a Stability of equilibrium and coordination failure (1981:Q1 to 1997:Q2)

	ASEAN5+China+Korea						
	Indonesia	Thailand	Singapore	Malaysia	Philippines	Korea	China
Stability condition							
Slope of AA	9.792	2.526	−1.078	1.423	−0.208	−71.233	0.069
Slope of BB	−1.096	1.105	−2.117	1.466	0.111	0.368	−0.236
Stable or unstable	Stable	Stable	Unstable	Unstable	Stable	Stable	Unstable
Optimal weight							
w_A^*	1.263	1.764	0.350	−23.920	−1.112	−7.057	0.119
w_B^*	−0.216	2.172	0.752	−35.198	0.558	−1.959	0.808
Fluctuation in trade balance							
$\hat{T}^2_{A(w_A=w_A^*, w_b=1)}$	0.0012	0.083	0.0171	672.3859	0.0582	0.00003	0.0005
$\hat{T}^2_{A(w_A=w_b=1)}$	0.0116	0.034	0.2507	0.2774	0.2315	1.323	0.0002
Coordination failure	None	Yes	None	Yes	None	None	Yes

Table 5.6b Stability of equilibrium and coordination failure (1981:Q1 to 2000:Q1)

	ASEAN5+China+Korea						
	Indonesia	Thailand	Singapore	Malaysia	Philippines	Korea	China
Stability condition							
Slope of AA	0.049	−2.382	2.004	0.440	0.064	−72.635	−0.285
Slope of BB	0.192	1.140	3.070	1.739	0.732	1.220	−0.612
Stable or unstable	Unstable	Stable	Unstable	Unstable	Unstable	Stable	Unstable
Optimal weight							
w_A^*	0.762	1.056	0.981	0.089	0.584	0.342	0.395
w_B^*	0.522	1.361	1.403	−0.065	0.331	0.458	0.400
Fluctuation in trade balance							
$\hat{T}^2_{A(w_A=w_A^*,w_b=1)}$	0.1454	0.002	0.0117	0.4319	0.0155	0.000001	0.003
$\hat{T}^2_{A(w_A=w_b=1)}$	0.1384	0.004	0.0140	0.1683	0.0143	0.010	0.005
Coordination failure	Yes	None	None	Yes	Yes	None	None

Thailand, which exhibits a stable equilibrium in policy reaction functions, coordination failure in choosing an exchange rate system emerges during the period from Q1 1981 to Q2 1997. In contrast, we can find no coordination failure in the case of Korea, which also has a stable equilibrium.

This analytical result implies that the ASEAN countries and China are forced to adopt the dollar peg system because they have an unstable equilibrium or coordination failure in choosing an exchange rate system. Within the group ASEAN5, South Korea, and China, only South Korea can shift directly from the dollar peg system to its optimal exchange rate system.

6. Conclusion

It is often said that the de facto dollar peg system is dangerous for East Asian countries, because they trade with Japan, the EU, and each other as well as with the United States. Under the de facto dollar peg system, movement in the yen–dollar exchange rate caused trade imbalances. In addition, before the currency crisis, the de facto dollar peg system stimulated capital inflows to the countries that would later be affected by the crisis. When we look at exchange rate movements for East Asian currencies during the post-crisis period from 1999 to the present, we see that exchange rates against the US dollar have stabilized, while exchange rates against the yen have fluctuated. It seems some countries have been returning to the de facto dollar peg system they adopted before the currency crisis.

Coordination failure in exchange rate policies among these countries may be one factor fueling this trend. Even if we suppose that a currency basket is the optimal system for East Asian countries, to prevent another currency crisis in the future, monetary authorities may face coordination failure. If coordination failure prevents them from adopting the optimal currency basket system, they must make arrangements for international coordination in their exchange rate policies, if they are to achieve crisis-proof currency basket systems.

Notes

1 This chapter is part of the Kobe Research Project. I wish to express my sincere thanks to Masahiro Kawai, Helmut Reisen, Helmut Wagner, and participants at seminars at the ADB, the Central Bank of the Philippines, the ECB, the CEPII, and University of Hagen, for their useful comments. I also wish to thank Yu Yongding for providing data on China, and to Hayato Nakata for his research assistance.
2 Bénassy-Quéré (1999) and Ohno (1999) analyzed pegging the US dollar as a coordination failure.

References

Bénassy-Quéré, A. (1999). Optimal pegs for East Asian currencies. *Journal of the Japanese and International Economies*, **13**(1), 44–60.

Frankel, J. A. and Wei, S. (1994). Yen bloc or dollar bloc? exchange rate policies of the East Asian economies. In T. Ito and A. O. Krueger, eds., *Macroeconomic Linkage: Savings, Exchange Rates, and Capital Flows*, Chicago: University of Chicago Press, pp. 295–355.

Kawai, M. and Akiyama, S. (2000). Implications of the currency crisis for exchange rate arrangements in emerging East Asia. World Bank, May.

McKinnon, R. I. (2000). After the crisis, the East Asian dollar standard resurrected: an interpretation of high-frequency exchange rate pegging. August.

Ogawa, E. (2002a). "The US dollar in the international monetary system after the Asian crisis," Japan Bank for International Cooperation Institute, JBICI Discussion Paper, No. 1.

Ogawa, E. (2002b). Should East Asian countries return to dollar peg again? In P. Drysdale and K. Ishigaki, eds., *East Asian Trade and Financial Integration: New Issues*. Canberra: Asia Pacific Press, pp. 159–184.

Ogawa, E and Ito, T. (2002). On the desirability of a regional basket currency arrangement. *Journal of the Japanese and International Economies,* **16**(3), 317–334.

Ohno, K. (1999). Exchange rate management in developing Asia: reassessment of the pre-crisis soft dollar zone. ADB Institute, Working Paper Series, No. 1.

Williamson, J. (2000). *Exchange Rate Regimes for East Asia: Reviving the Intermediate Option.* Washington, DC: Institute for International Economics.

6   A case for a coordinated basket for Asian countries

Takatoshi Ito

1.   Introduction

Exchange rate policy is an important pillar of macroeconomic policy for any country, but this is especially true for small, open economies. The value and volatility of any currency affects flows of both trade and investment. A stable exchange rate promotes trade and investment, but it sometimes invites excessive capital inflows. A flexible exchange rate is important so that authorities and markets can make adjustments in response to domestic and external shocks. However, excessive flexibility can itself become a shock to the economy. Indeed, the market sometimes overshoots, and exchange rates may sustain misalignment. A fixed exchange rate regime with capital mobility may limit the degree of freedom in monetary policy, while a free-floating regime with capital mobility may expose exporters and importers to the whims of large investment funds abroad.

The de facto dollar peg in place before the Asian currency crisis of 1997 was one of the reasons why East Asian countries fell into financial crisis. Asian countries pegged their currencies to the US dollar, but their exports and imports were diversified, so third-currency fluctuations—for example a change in the value of their currency against the yen or the euro—had a profound effect on their export competitiveness, which is easily is affected by fluctuations in real effective exchange rates. Another problem associated with fixed exchange rates in emerging market economies with liberalized capital flows is that short-term borrowers (local corporations and banks) and lenders (foreign banks) may fail to realize the importance of risk premiums for the remote but possible event of devaluation. The failure to fully grasp this risk makes both lenders and borrowers behave irrationally. Borrowers think that dollar-denominated loans with lower interest rates are cheaper than local currency loans, while lenders think that borrowers, often with high growth performance, are safe and free from default risk. Borrowers realize only too late that devaluation has made their debt unsustainable, and then lenders realize that even very creditworthy borrowers may default in the midst of a currency crisis. This is basically what happened in Asia from the mid-1990s to the crisis in 1997–98 [See Ito (1999a, 1999b, 2000) for details].

After the currency crisis that erupted in Thailand in July 1997, all East Asian countries except China and Hong Kong floated their currencies. In the first six months of the crisis, all of these currencies depreciated significantly, although there were differences in the timing and speed of their falls. Most currencies hit the bottom in mid-January 1998, and then started to appreciate. The Indonesian rupiah was an exception, staying quite weak for the rest of 1998; the magnitude of its eventual recovery was much less than the other currencies. From July 1997 to the summer of 1998, the movement of these Asian currencies was much less closely tied to the US dollar than before, and the correlation with the yen increased. By the summer of 1998, however, many Asian countries began to attempt to regain some stability in the exchange rate of their currencies vis-à-vis the US dollar. As an extreme case, Malaysia returned to a fixed exchange rate against the US dollar in September 1998. The correlation between Asian currencies and the US dollar increased in 1999 and 2000. Similar trends were observed for other emerging market economies. Calvo and Reinhart (2000) coined the phrase 'fear of floating' for the emerging economies, even after the crises in Asia, Russia, Brazil, and Turkey. Had emerging market economies missed the lesson that these currency crises had originated from fixed exchange rates? Or is there any inherent reason why emerging market economies prefer exchange rate stability vis-à-vis the US dollar?

Many observers (Bénassy-Quéré, 1999; Ito *et al.* 1998; Williamson, 2000, to name a few) think that a basket currency regime may be the most desirable exchange rate regime for emerging market economies with diverse trading partners. They propose that Asian countries should make their exchange rates reflect the weighted average of trading partners' exchange rates, thus fluctuating against the US dollar.

Ogawa and Ito (2002) have argued that groups of emerging market economies often encounter a coordination problem when they try to stabilize real effective exchange rates. For example, when Thailand calculates its real effective exchange rate, the formula should include the neighbor's exchange rate, say Malaysia's. When Malaysia calculates its real effective exchange rate, the Thai exchange rate should be in the calculation. If Malaysia decides to adopt a dollar peg (for political reasons), then the de facto weight of the dollar in the real effective exchange rate of the Thai baht suddenly increases, and Thailand becomes more likely to adopt a dollar peg as well (or at least increase the weighting of the dollar in its exchange rate). Under these circumstances, Malaysia and Thailand should solve the problem jointly, choosing weights for major currencies, and excluding each other's exchange rate from the formula. A joint decision would produce better results than the uncoordinated Nash solution, in that Thailand would regard Malaysia's exchange rate as a given, and Malaysia would regard the Thai exchange rate as a given. Ogawa and Ito (2002) showed how to calculate such a coordinated basket. They also showed that there may be multiple equilibria, and that letting the market grope for the right values for the common basket could result in a bad equilibrium.

This chapter will extend Ogawa and Ito's (2002) results to a multi-country model. The following types of exchange rate movements will be examined: (1) actual exchange rate movements, (2) uncoordinated, individual basket exchange rate movements, and (3) coordinated, individual basket exchange rate movements.

2. Exchange rate movements in Asia before and after the Asian currency crisis

Figures 6.1 and 6.2 show the nominal exchange rates (vis-à-vis the US dollar) of the East Asian countries from January 1990 to December 2004. Since the movement in the Indonesian rupiah dwarfs the others, Figure 6.1 includes Indonesia and Figure 6.2 does not. One can observe that, except for the large devaluation of the Chinese yuan in 1994, exchange rates were relatively stable between January 1990 and June 1997, reflecting the adoption of the de facto dollar peg.

Ever since the currency crisis that started in July 1997, Asian currencies have fluctuated widely. Except for the Indonesian rupiah, the value of which dropped to one-sixth its pre-crisis value, Asian currencies have been fluctuating within 100 and 200 (where 100 equals the average value for 2000).

Table 6.1 shows the correlation between Asian currencies and the US dollar (by showing the exchange rates of these currencies against the Swiss franc). This shows that the correlation of Asian currencies with the US dollar was, in general, quite high before July 1997. China had a one-time devaluation in 1994, so its correlation coefficient is low; except for that event, however, its correlation would

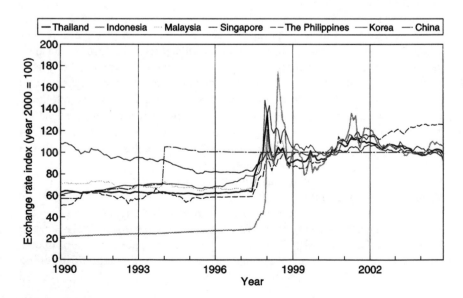

Figure 6.1 Nominal exchange rates against US dollar Index: Jan. 1990–Dec. 2004.

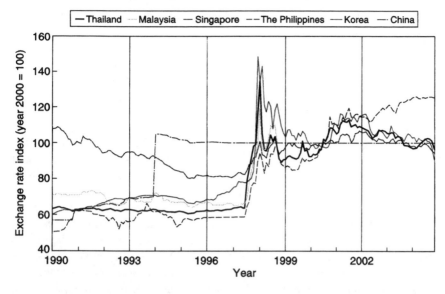

Figure 6.2 Nominal exchange rates against US dollar (excluding Indonesia) Index: Jan. 1990–Dec. 2004.

Table 6.1 Correlation coefficients of Asian currencies with the US dollar, monthly data

	THB	*INR*	*MLR*	*SND*	*PHP*	*KRW*	*CHY*
1990:1–1997:1	0.995	0.911	0.922	0.374	0.855	0.897	0.792
1997:7–1998:12	0.133	−0.095	0.343	0.639	0.469	0.146	1.000
1999:1–2001:12	0.165	−0.084	1.000	0.901	−0.288	0.702	1.000
2001:1–2003:12	0.964	0.541	1.000	0.990	0.985	0.956	1.000
2002:1–2004:12	0.956	0.879	1.000	0.992	0.990	0.913	1.000

Notes:
Each currency is defined vis-à-vis the Swiss Franc and similarly with US dollar.

have been much higher (close to 0.95). The correlation of the Singapore dollar with the US dollar is low, because the Monetary Authority of Singapore has tacitly been following the basket regime. For all East Asian currencies except the Singapore dollar, the correlation with the US dollar declined significantly in the immediate post-crisis period, July 1997 to December 1998. This is when the Asian currencies were floating rather freely. The correlation with the US dollar increased again, however, in January 1999 to December 2001. The correlation of the Thai currency to the US dollar in 1999–2000 was lower than before the crisis, but higher than in the immediate post-crisis period. For most currencies other than the Indonesian rupiah, after 2001 the correlation with the US dollar rose above 0.90. Especially in Singapore, the correlation with the US dollar became extremely high. This is surprising, given that Singapore's resilience to regional currency crises is often credited to its basket currency regime.

One obvious question is, why do East Asian countries seem to gravitate back toward exchange rate stability vis-à-vis the US dollar, even though the adoption of a basket currency regime appears to offer obvious advantages. The series of currency crises in the second half of the 1990s clearly demonstrated that fixed exchange rates were inappropriate. One reason for East Asian nations' persistence in the pursuit of exchange rate stability against the dollar may have been coordination failure. Malaysia's decision to adopt the US dollar peg in September 1998 changed the optimal basket weights for Thailand, Singapore, Indonesia, and other neighboring countries. Moreover, as these countries raised the weighting of the dollar in their currency calculations, this process became a kind of a feed-back loop. Thailand took into account the increased dollar weights that Singapore and Indonesia were using, as well as Malaysia, and Singapore and Indonesia did the same. (Chapter 3 of this book shows empirical evidence for this theoretical inference.) A joint decision-making process might have led them to choose lower weights for the US dollar, but instead their sequential decisions regarding the dollar peg appears to have led these countries away from coordinated equilibrium. This is the coordination failure shown in the Ogawa and Ito model.

3.   Theory: uncoordinated basket and coordinated basket

This section reviews the Ogawa and Ito model, and then presents its extension to a multi-country model. Ogawa and Ito (2002) showed in a two-country example how the dollar peg weight of Country A is related to the dollar peg weight of Country B, when each country is trying to minimize the volatility of trade balances.

Ogawa and Ito showed that the dollar weight of Country A, w_A, is a reaction function of the dollar weight of Country B, w_B, and the dollar weight of Country B is a reaction function of the dollar weight of Country A.

$$(A^{A/Y} + A^{A/\$})w_A + (A^{B/Y} + A^{B/\$})w_B = A^{A/\$} + A^{B/\$}$$

$$(B^{B/Y} + B^{B/\$})w_B + (B^{A/Y} + B^{A/\$})w_A = B^{B/\$} + B^{A/\$}$$

Thus, each country has to determine the optimal weights in its currency basket while being simultaneously affected by the behavior of the other country.

There is a unique equilibrium pair of optimal weights for Countries A and B because both of the policy reaction functions are linear functions. From the above equations, we can derive a pair of optimal weights for the dollar in a currency basket to stabilize the trade balances of both Countries A and B at the same time:

$$w_A^* = \frac{(A^{A/\$} + A^{B/\$})(B^{B/Y} + B^{B/\$}) - (A^{B/Y} + A^{B/\$})(B^{B/\$} + B^{A/\$})}{(A^{A/Y} + A^{A/\$})(B^{B/Y} + B^{B/\$}) - (A^{B/Y} + A^{B/\$})(B^{A/Y} + B^{A/\$})}$$

$$w_B^* = \frac{(A^{A/Y} + A^{A/\$})(B^{B/\$} + B^{A/\$}) - (A^{A/\$} + A^{B/\$})(B^{A/Y} + B^{A/\$})}{(A^{A/Y} + A^{A/\$})(B^{B/Y} + B^{B/\$}) - (A^{B/Y} + A^{B/\$})(B^{A/Y} + B^{A/\$})}$$

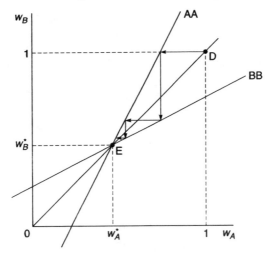

Figure 6.3 Interdependence of the dollar weights: a stable case.

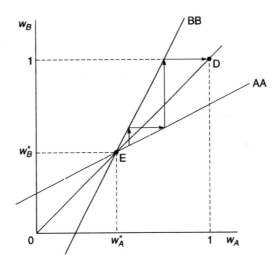

Figure 6.4 Interdependence of the dollar weights: an unstable case.

The reaction functions are shown in the Figures 6.3 and 6.4. The slopes of the reaction functions determine whether the optimal weights (w_A^*, w_B^*) can be a stable or an unstable equilibrium. When a crisis and floating (as in 1997–98) temporarily lower the dollar weight, if the real world is at unstable equilibrium, sooner or later the dollar weights will increase again (as they did in 1999–2001).

As shown in Figure 6.4, sequential decisions will bring the dollar weights to the joint dollar peg solution (1,1), which is inferior to the interior equilibrium. Therefore, in cases of unstable equilibria, simple floating does not eliminate the dollar peg. Exchange rate regimes in Asia demonstrate a pronounced tendency to gravitate back to a de facto dollar peg.

Now, let us extend the model to an *n*-country framework. First, we assume that the optimal weight of the other currencies corresponds to the trade weight. (More precisely, it should be the trade weight adjusted for the price elasticity of exports. See Ito *et al.* (1998).) Second, let us define Europe as the group of 11 countries that joined to create Euro in January 1999, and calculate past theoretical values for the euro by fixing the weights.[2] Let us limit our study to the US, Japan, the Euro 11, and the seven Asian countries mentioned below. We will define total exports as exports to these countries, and calculate the export share (adding up to 1): a_{ij} is the share of Country j in exports from Country i. The exchange rates of the US dollar, Japanese yen, and the euro are measured *vs.* the Swiss franc:

$$Y_{USD} = \text{US dollar/CHF}$$

$$Y_{JPY} = \text{Japanese yen/CHF}$$

$$Y_{EUR} = \text{euro/CHF}$$

Let us define the exchange rate of the East Asian countries vis-à-vis the Swiss franc (CHF = Swiss Franc) for seven countries.

$$X_{THB} = \text{Thai baht/CHF}$$

$$X_{INR} = \text{Indonesian rupiah/CHF}$$

$$X_{MLR} = \text{Malaysian ringgit/CHF}$$

$$X_{SND} = \text{Singapore dollar/CHF}$$

$$X_{PHP} = \text{Philippine peso/CHF}$$

$$X_{KRW} = \text{Korean won/CHF}$$

$$X_{CNY} = \text{Chinese yuan/CHF}$$

Each exchange rate is nominal, if the nominal rate is used; each exchange rate is real if it is adjusted for the changes in the CPI.

$x = (\log X_{THB}, \log X_{INR}, \log X_{MLR}, \log X_{SND}, \log X_{PHP}, \log X_{KRW}, \log X_{CNY})'$ is a column vector of the nominal exchange rates.

$A = \{a_{ij}\}$, a 7 × 7 trade share matrix with 0s in the diagonal.

$y = (\log Y_{USD}, \log Y_{JPY}, \log Y_{EUR})'$ is a column vector of the major currencies outside the regional grouping.

B = a 7 × 3 matrix of trade shares with the United States, Japan, and Europe;

the actual exchange rates are denoted as x^a and y^a, and the uncoordinated exchange rate as x^u. The uncoordinated exchange rate is defined by the following formula.

$$x^u = Ax^a + By^a$$

The uncoordinated basket is defined as the exchange rate that considers the changes in the (USD, JPY, EUR), and Asian currencies as given. When the dollar, yen, and euro fluctuate, the exchange rate of Country i moves through the direct impact of By^a. This effect ignores how the Asian currencies would be affected by the changes in the major currencies. The changes in Asian currencies other than currency i also affect the currency of Country i through Ax^a.

$I =$ a 7×7 identity matrix, that is, having 1 at the diagonal, and 0 off-diagonal.

Then the coordinated basket is defined by the following equation:

$$x^c = Ax^c + By^a$$

The coordinated basket rate, x^c, is calculated with knowledge of the outside currencies, y^a, only, and the actual rate of the regional currencies are irrelevant. Hence,

$$(I - A)x^c = By^a$$

and

$$x^c = (1 - A)^{-1} \cdot By^a$$

The calculation of x^c assumes that the inverse matrix exists. Otherwise, the coordinated rate cannot be calculated.

Let us call the currencies that join in forming the coordination as inside-basket currencies and those that do not as outside-basket currencies. The coordinated coefficients can be adopted when all the participating countries are willing to submit their trade weighted weights on all currencies (including inside- and outside-basket currencies), and then go through the calculation of deriving another set of coefficients on outside-basket currencies only, taking into account direct and indirect weights on outside-basket currencies. They all have to agree on the same procedure, since deviation from the procedure by any one country will have an indirect influence on all other currencies. This action needs policy coordination.

This illustrates the importance of policy coordination, because when one a country changes the weights in its basket, there are repercussions for the basket systems of other countries. The cooperating countries have to calculate the sum of direct and indirect weights of the outside currencies against which their currencies float.

Define

$$C = (I - A)^{-1} \cdot B$$

The C matrix (7×3) is the coordinated basket matrix. Each row of the C matrix is the coordinated basket solution for each of the major currencies. For example, (c_{11}, c_{12}, c_{13}) is the weight that the Thai baht should put on ($\log Y_{USD}$, $\log Y_{JPY}$, $\log Y_{EUR}$), (c_{12}, c_{22}, c_{23}) is the weight the Indonesian rupiah should put on ($\log Y_{USD}$, $\log Y_{JPY}$, $\log Y_{EUR}$), and so on. These weights include both the direct and indirect effects of changes in the major currencies.

4.　Estimates of the coordinated and uncoordinated basket

To calculate basket currencies, it is necessary to choose the relative weighting of the currencies against which the currency will float. Here, we use the trade weight (sum of exports to Country j and imports from Country j divided by the total trade volume of Country k). We calculate the trade weights based on the International Monetary Fund's Direction of Trade (DOT) data. We interpolate the annual DOT data as monthly data. We calculate the basket values by applying the monthly weights to monthly exchange rates taken from the International Monetary Fund's International Financial Statistics (IFS).

Figures 6.5–6.11 show the actual movements the national currency exchange rate vis-à-vis Swiss franc and uncoordinated basket currencies, in nominal terms, from January 1990 to November 2004, with the benchmark in year 2000 (that is, in year 2000, the actual and basket rates were assumed to be identical). We can observe the following general trends across the countries. For most countries in East Asia, after 1995 the uncoordinated basket value of the currency was more depreciated than the actual exchange rate. In other words, the actual nominal exchange rate was overvalued compared to the basket currency value that are

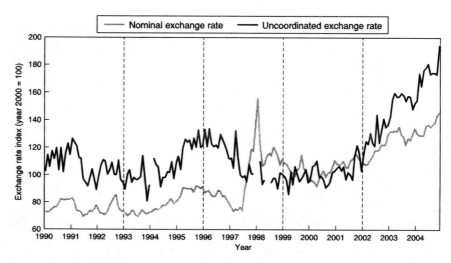

Figure 6.5 Thailand, Jan. 1990–Nov. 2004 Nominal exchange rate and uncoordinated exchange rate.

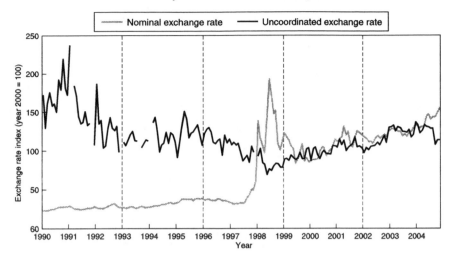

Figure 6.6 Indonesia, Jan. 1990–Nov. 2004 Nominal exchange rate and uncoordinated exchange rate.

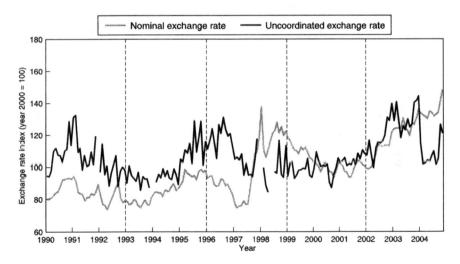

Figure 6.7 Malaysia, Jan. 1990–Nov. 2004 Nominal exchange rate and uncoordinated exchange rate.

calculated with year 2000 as a benchmark. This is partly due to the de facto dollar peg policy that these countries had adopted before the currency crisis. The nominal exchange rate vis-à-vis the US dollar appreciated slightly after 2000, while the uncoordinated value of the exchange rate depreciated. The difference between the uncoordinated basket and the actual rate was large for Thailand, the Philippines, and Malaysia before the crisis. For Korea, China, and Singapore, there

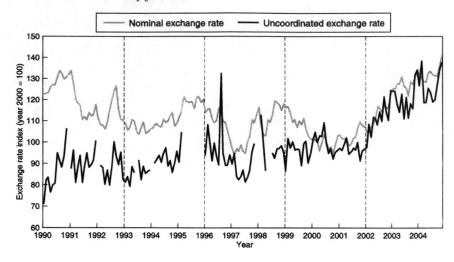

Figure 6.8 Singapore, Jan. 1990–Nov. 2004 Nominal exchange rate and uncoordinated exchange rate.

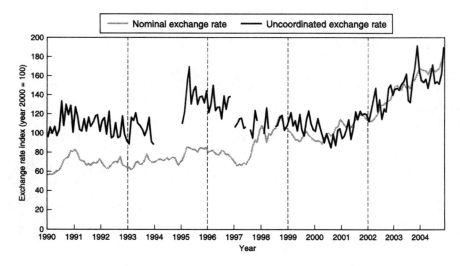

Figure 6.9 The Philippines, Jan. 1990–Nov. 2004 Nominal exchange rate and uncoordinated exchange rate.

was little serious currency misalignment before the currency crisis of 1997. This confirms that the currencies of some Asian nations were overvalued before the crisis, which hurt their exports. However, the result is slightly counter-intuitive in that one of the most seriously affected crisis countries, namely Korea, does not show serious misalignment, while Singapore, known to have a basket system, still had a misalignment, compared to the uncoordinated basket. The result of

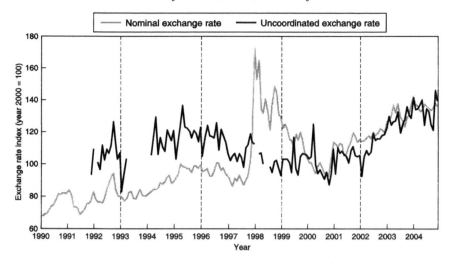

Figure 6.10 Korea, Jan. 1990–Nov. 2004 Nominal exchange rate and uncoordinated exchange rate.

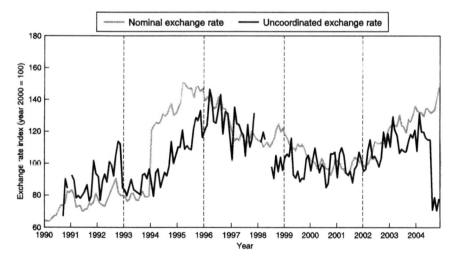

Figure 6.11 China, Jan. 1990–Nov. 2004 Nominal exchange rate and uncoordinated exchange rate.

Indonesia cannot be appropriately interpreted, as the country experienced large inflation during the crisis and comparison of the nominal exchange rate before and after the crisis is misleading.

Figures 6.12–6.18 show the movements of actual and coordinated basket currencies from January 1990 to November 2004. The actual exchange rates did not diverge much from the coordinated basket currencies in the post-crisis period

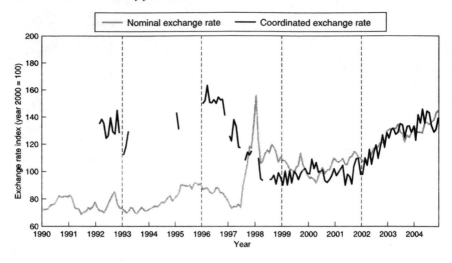

Figure 6.12 Thailand, Jan. 1990–Nov. 2004 Nominal exchange rate and coordinated exchange rate.

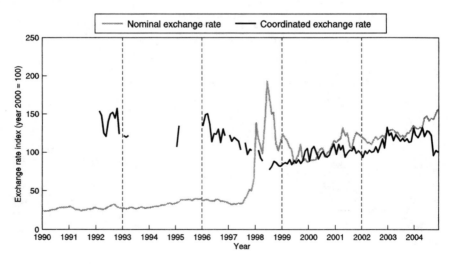

Figure 6.13 Indonesia, Jan. 1990–Nov. 2004 Nominal exchange rate and coordinated exchange rate.

of 1999–2003. The gaps in the line of coordinated exchange rate in the graph represents periods when the inverse matrix could not have been calculated.

The coordinated basket values show that when the dollar-yen and dollar-euro rates fluctuated, Asian currencies collectively moved more or less in the same direction and the actual exchange rate tracks the coordinated basket rather well for some countries.

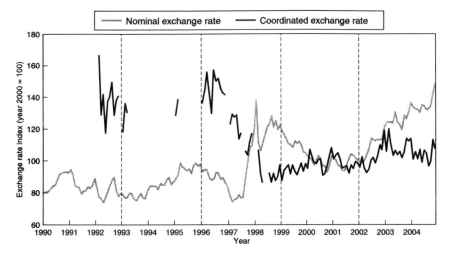

Figure 6.14 Malaysia, Jan. 1990–Nov. 2004 Nominal exchange rate and coordinated exchange rate.

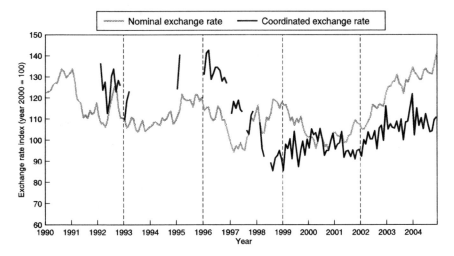

Figure 6.15 Singapore, Jan. 1990–Nov. 2004 Nominal exchange rate and coordinated exchange rate.

Similar to the previous result, the currencies of China, Malaysia and Singapore, and Thailand were found to have been undervalued compared to the coordinated baskets from 2003 to 2004.

According to new measures that take into account the indirect effects of neighbors' exchange rates, we judge the actual exchange rates just before the crisis to have been overvalued. The degree of misalignment was more for coordinated

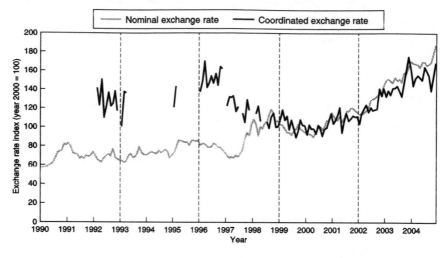

Figure 6.16 The Philippines, Jan. 1990–Nov. 2004 Nominal exchange rate and coordinated exchange rate.

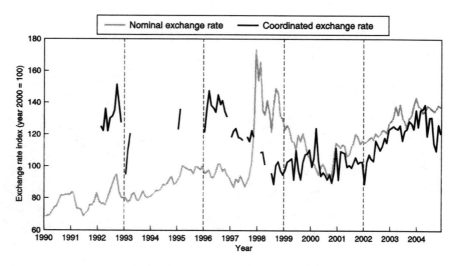

Figure 6.17 Korea, Jan. 1990–Nov. 2004 Nominal exchange rate and coordinated exchange rate.

basket values than for uncoordinated basket values. Only China and Singapore had the exchange rate relatively close to cooperative basket value before the crisis. It was not recognised before the crisis that the currencies in the region were vastly overvalued if proper (coordinated) basket concept was used.

There were interesting developments in the post-crisis period. The weight of the dollar increased for all currencies, and the deviations between coordinated and

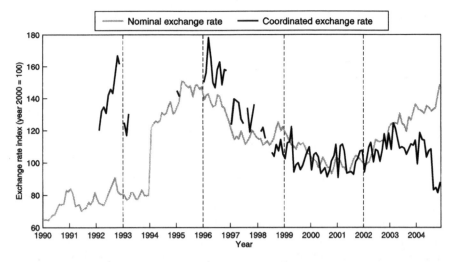

Figure 6.18 China, Jan. 1990–Nov. 2004 Nominal exchange rate and coordinated exchange rate.

uncoordinated baskets became smaller. This seems to imply that baskets weights were chosen with coordination. Immediately after the crisis, the deviations of the coordinated and uncoordinated exchange rates diverged because the Indonesian rupiah depreciated steeply. If Asian countries had coordinated the basket, their currencies would have depreciated more than they actually did, prolonging the crisis. Therefore, during the deep crisis, the currencies in crisis may have been supported by coordinated intervention, or cut off from the basket of regional currencies, to prevent the spillover of the crisis.

These results imply some aspects of basket currencies that may be relevant in both normal and crisis periods. Basket currencies are designed to prevent both over-valuation and under-valuation of a currency relative to the real effective exchange rate. During normal times, with no turbulent crisis, gradual fluctuations among the major currencies could affect the real effective exchange rates of currencies in the region. Basket currencies, which are designed to track real effective exchange rates, could help avoid this problem. If neighboring countries adopt non-basket currencies, however, basket currencies might not be the best solution for the region. Coordinated basket currencies would be more flexible, because they would avert the possibility that neighboring countries might fix exchange rates at inappropriate levels. This intuitive conclusion, however, was not clearly demonstrated by Asian currencies during the period 1995–97. In this exercise, the coordinated basket was calculated backwardly with a benchmark of year 2000, so that the deviation shown in this paper clearly benefitted from hindsight.

During periods of turbulence, uncoordinated baskets may precipitate competitive devaluations, where one currency clearly deviates from its long-run value due to political or market turmoil, leading others to do so as well. This was clearly shown in Asia cases in 1997–1998 due to the steep fall in the Indonesian rupiah. This kind of contagion could be prevented by adopting coordinated basket currencies that use only major currencies in a basket.

5.   Summary and policy recommendations

This chapter shows two ways of calculating basket currency values for Asian countries, one with coordination and one without. The results are mixed. Although the coordinated solution is the more defensible solution theoretically, it does not explain the actual result that exchange rates were overvalued before the Asian currency crisis. In the post-crisis period, however, the coordinated solution might have been better than the uncoordinated one, and actually it would have pointed to greater appreciation than actually occurred. That is because the uncoordinated basket would have produced steep depreciation for countries other than Indonesia, sparked by the sharp depreciation of the rupiah. The coordinated solution would have resulted in a more stable exchange rate. In other words, coordination might have produced more stable exchange rate dynamics in the post-crisis period.

Exchange rate policy coordination among Asian countries is desirable, to produce stability in real effective exchange rate systems. It would help avert competitive devaluations by calculating stable real effective exchange rates based solely on major currencies outside the region. In a sense, this is close to what was practiced in Europe before the introduction of the euro—group members fixed exchange rates relative to one another, and allowed the joint basket to float against the outside world.

If countries were to apply the method proposed in this chapter, coordination could become complex. One way to make this method more practical might be to introduce a common basket, or an Asian currency unit. Each country could peg its currency to this Asian currency unit, within a trading band. If deviations in the idiosyncratic weights (coordinated solution) on (yen, dollar, euro) from ones in the common basket are small enough, as shown in this chapter, it might be easier to adopt the common basket, both politically and practically. Coordination comes automatically with the common basket. More coordination can be achieved by the introduction of the Asian currency unit. This would be the next step in the search for the best exchange rate arrangement for the region.

Another important topic to be explored further is whether the yen could be within the region of policy coordination under consideration rather than outside the region. In this chapter, we have considered a region that consists of Asia excluding Japan. The analogy of Europe may suggest, however, that Japan should coordinate with other Asian countries to float their currencies jointly against the US dollar and the euro. Future research should aim at exploring the potential advantages and pitfalls of having Japan join the regional coordination.

Notes

1 The Euro 11 are: Austria, Belgium, France, Germany, Italy, Luxemburg, the Netherlands, Finland, Ireland, Portugal, and Spain.

References

Bénassy-Quéré, A. (1999). Optimal pegs for East Asian currencies. *Journal of the Japanese and International Economies*, **13**(1), 44–60.

Calvo, G. A. and Reinhart, C. M. (2000). Fear of Floating. NBER working paper, No. 7993, November.

Ito, T. (1999a). Asian currency crisis: its origin and backgrounds. *Journal Development Assistance*, **5**(1), 108–141.

Ito, T. (1999b). Capital flows in East and Southeast Asia. In M. Feldstein, ed., *International Capital Flows*, NBER-University of Chicago Press, Chicago: pp. 111–32.

Ito, T. (2000). Capital Flows in Asia. In S. Edwards, ed., *Capital Flows and the Emerging Economies*, NBER-University of Chicago Press, Chicago: pp. 255–296.

Ito, T., Ogawa, E., and Sasaki, Y. N. (1998). How did the dollar peg fail in Asia. *Journal of the Japanese and International Economies*, **12**, 256–304.

Ogawa, E. and Ito, T. (2002). On the desirability of a regional basket currency arrangement. *Journal of the Japanese and International Economies*, **16**(3), 317–334.

Williamson, J. (2000). *Exchange Rate Regimes for Emerging Markets: Reviving the Intermediate Option*. Washington, DC: Institute for International Economics, September.

7 A common currency basket in bond markets in East Asia[1]

Eiji Ogawa and Junko Shimizu

1. Introduction

There is said to be both an abundance of savings in East Asia and profitable investment opportunities in East Asian emerging market countries. However, there is a problem of how efficiently savings can be matched with investments within East Asia. One solution might be to establish and activate regional bond markets in East Asia. The establishment of regional bond markets, however, might give rise to another problem: foreign exchange risks. Both borrowers and lenders in East Asia could face foreign exchange risks if bonds are denominated in a foreign currency in the regional bond markets.

Bond issuers in international bond markets ordinarily select an international currency for their bonds. The US dollar is the dominant international currency in the world economy. Any time a bond issuer issues a bond in a currency other than its own local currency, it faces the risk of currency volatility. Similarly, investors face foreign exchange risk if they invest in bonds denominated in currencies other than their own.

Risk-averse bond issuers and investors prefer to minimize foreign exchange risk. In the interest of reducing foreign exchange risk, it might be desirable for them to select other currencies when issuing and investing in bonds. However, in terms of liquidity, network externalities might be at work in bond markets. As a result, both investors and issuers of regional bonds as well as international bonds face a trade-off between foreign exchange risks and liquidity.

Several authors have discussed whether monetary authorities in East Asia should engage in regional cooperation in exchange rate regimes and the possible creation of a regional currency, to prevent another currency crisis (Ito *et al.* 1999, Bénassy-Quéré 1999, Williamson 2000, Ogawa and Ito 2002, and Ogawa, Ito, and Sasaki 2004). It has been suggested that a common currency basket is needed for regional cooperation. In this chapter, we propose that a regional currency is equivalent to a currency basket.

This study aims to investigate the advantages and disadvantages of choosing a regional currency over an international currency, taking into account both foreign exchange risks and liquidity. This chapter is composed of the following sections. Section 1 reviews the current situation of East Asian financial markets and movement toward intra-regional cooperation. Section 2 investigates what kind of currency is desirable for bond issuers and investors in terms of foreign exchange risk. Section 3 considers liquidity in regional bond markets from the viewpoint of denomination currency. Section 4 summarizes our results and conclusions.

2.   Current situation

2.1.   *Overview of East Asian financial markets*

Since the Asian currency crisis, we have recognized that, to solve the so-called double mismatch problem, East Asian countries need to develop local bond markets. Before the crisis, the financial systems of Asian economies relied heavily on the banking sector, and banks concentrated their business on long-term loans to domestic firms by making short-run borrowings in terms of foreign currency from foreign banks. The fact that these transactions contained both a maturity mismatch and a currency mismatch was a central cause of the crisis. The maturity mismatch resulted from the practice of using short-term capital funding to meet long-term financial needs. The currency mismatch was caused by borrowing foreign currencies, particularly the US dollar, and converting them to local currencies. To avoid the recurrence of double mismatching and to mobilize an abundance of intraregional money effectively, Asian countries should develop their bond markets.

The recent economic recovery in East Asia also emphasizes the significance of bond market development. One conspicuous phenomenon in recent years has been the increase of official foreign reserves held by East Asian countries. Figure 7.1 shows that foreign reserves held by 10 East Asian countries swelled to more than 50 percent of world reserves by 2001 from only 11 percent in 1980. Asia's foreign reserves have not been deployed in domestic and regional markets, however, a large proportion of these reserves is currently invested in US and European bond markets.

Meanwhile, dependence on domestic savings is another feature of East Asian countries. Table 7.1 shows the savings–investment balance of East Asian countries. In all cases except Indonesia, the Philippines and Taiwan, the gross domestic savings ratio in East Asian countries exceeds 30 percent of GDP—the highest level in the world, including the industrialized countries. In Malaysia, China, and Singapore, the ratios exceeded 40 percent in 2003. In the nine Asian economies (four ASEAN countries, the NIEs, and China), the average savings ratio was above 30 percent, which was higher than the average for other developing countries. To use these high domestic savings effectively, it is necessary to develop local bond market to match savings and investments.

Since the currency crisis, the development of bond markets has become one of the most urgent tasks in regional financial cooperation. After Asian countries recovered from the currency crisis, their bond markets began to expand quickly. Table 7.2 shows the domestic market capitalization in East Asian markets, indicating that many Asian markets have expanded to some degree. Korea and Malaysia,

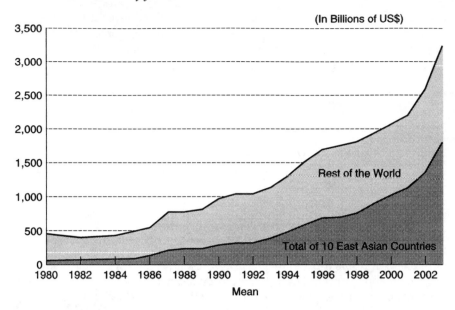

Figure 7.1 Foreign Reserves in 10 East Asian Countries.
Source: IFS and Taiwan Central Bank. Ten East Asian Countries include
ASEAN5 plus Japan, China, Hong Kong, Korea, and Taiwan.

Table 7.1 Savings-investment balance of East Asian countries

	Gross domestic savings			Gross domestic capital formation			Saving–investment balance		
	1995	2000	2003	1995	2000	2003	1995	2000	2003
China	42.5	39.0	42.7	40.8	36.3	44.4	1.7	2.6	−1.7
Hong Kong	29.1	31.7	31.6	34.7	28.1	22.8	−5.5	3.6	8.7
Indonesia	30.6	25.6	21.5	31.9	16.1	16.0	−1.3	9.5	5.5
Korea	36.5	33.9	32.8	37.7	31.0	29.4	−1.1	2.9	3.4
Malaysia	39.7	47.2	42.9	43.6	27.2	21.8	−3.9	20.0	21.1
Philippines	14.5	17.3	20.1	22.5	21.2	18.7	−7.9	−3.9	1.4
Singapore	50.2	47.9	46.7	34.2	32.0	13.4	16.1	15.9	33.3
Thailand	37.3	33.2	33.1	42.1	22.8	25.2	−4.8	10.4	7.9
Taiwan	25.9	24.4	23.5	25.3	22.9	17.2	0.6	1.5	6.3
East Asia average	34.0	33.3	32.8	34.8	26.4	23.2	−0.7	6.9	9.6
Developing countries total	26.9	26.6	NA	27.2	24.5	NA	−0.8	2.1	NA

Source: Key Indicators 2004, Asian Development Bank, UN World Economic and Social Survey 2004.
NA, not available.

Table 7.2 Domestic market capitalization in East Asian markets

Plase of Exchange	(in Millions of US$)			
	End 1990	*End 1995*	*End 2000*	*End 2003*
Hong Kong	83,386	303,705	623,398	714,597
Jakarta	8,081	66,454	26,813	54,659
Japan (Tokyo)	2,928,534	3,545,307	3,157,222	2,953,098
Korea	110,301	181,955	148,361	298,248
Bursa Malaysia	47,869	213,757	113,155	160,970
Philippines	6,632	58,780	25,261	23,190
Shanghai	NA	NA	NA	360,106
Shenzhen	NA	NA	NA	152,872
Singapore	34,269	150,959	155,126	148,503
Taiwan	98,927	187,206	247,597	379,060
Thailand	20,777	135,774	29,217	119,017

Source : World Federation of Exchanges.
NA, not available.

in particular, have completely recovered, and now exceed the pre-crisis level. Two Chinese markets, Shanghai and Shenzhen, hold enormous potential for the near future. However, their domestic market capitalization is still far lower than Tokyo's.

Table 7.3 shows that the value of bonds listed in East Asian markets is still very small compared with Japanese bond markets. One exception is Korea, where the value of bonds has increased substantially; their value in 2003 was over three times the 1995 value.

Table 7.4 shows the size of government bond markets in East Asian countries, indicating that, except for Japan, these markets are not so large. These government bond markets lack benchmarks and have a small scale of issuance. Before the Asian

Table 7.3 Value of bonds listed in East Asian markets

Exchange	(in Millions of US$)			
	End 1990	*End 1995*	*End 2000*	*End 2003*
Bursa Malaysia	541	3,497	1,563	2,205
Hong Kong	657	NA	89,401	56,536
Korea	NA	162,421	335,718	509,877
Osaka	953,624	1,917,468	2,535,507	4,462,898
Philippines	-	-	0	543
Shanghai	NA	NA	NA	70,761
Shenzhen	NA	NA	NA	2,358
Singapore	98,698	150,539	218,792	276,195
Taiwan	NA	31,813	48,455	77,467
Thailand	148	1,945	-	3,550
Tokyo	978,895	1,969,068	2,548,332	NA

Source: World Federation of Exchanges.
NA, not available.

Table 7.4 Government bond market outstanding of East Asian countries

	In local currency	In Millions of US dollar
Singapore[1]	63,050 (S$ million)	37,125
Thailand[2]	742,176 (Baht million)	18,731
Malaysia[3]	130,800 (RM million)	34,403
Indonesia[4]	386,522 (IDR billion)	45,892
Philippines[5]	512,646 (PHP million)	9,234
Korea[6]	105,332 (Won billion)	88,403
Hong Kong[7]	120,152 (HK$ million)	15,476
China[8]	870,866 (Yuan million)	105,210
Japan[9]	9437,564 (Yen billion)	4,082,890

Notes:
We use closing rate of foreign exchange rates against the US dollar in 2003 to couvert the outstanding in local currency into the US dollar. The details of each data are follows:
1. Dec, 2003. Total outstanding of Bills and Bonds of Singapore Government Securities by MAS.
2. Dec, 2003. ThaiBDC Trading and Outstanding of Government securities by BOT.
3. Dec, 2003. Balances of Conventional Malaysian Government Securities by Bank Negara Malaysia.
4. Nov, 2003. Market capitalization of government bond in Surabaya Stock Exchange by Bank Indonesia.
5. May, 2003. Claims on National Government Securities by Central Bank of Philippines.
6. Nov, 2003. Outstanding amounts of Monetary Stabilisation Bonds (public offerings) by Bank of Korea.
7. Dec, 2003. Outstanding amount of Exchange Fund Bills and Notes by Hong Kong Monetary Authority.
8. Total in 2002. Turnover of Spot Trading of T-Bond Transaction by People's Bank of China.
9. Sept, 2003 Outstanding amounts of Government Bonds by Ministry of Finance HP.

currency crisis, these countries had scant experience in issuing government bonds, and their bonds were mostly short-term. This made it difficult to foster benchmark bonds in these countries.

2.2. *Asian bond fund initiative*

As discussed previously, bond markets in East Asia are not adequately developed, and individual countries face some obstacles to developing their local bond market. We recognize that to establish bond markets in East Asian countries, a wide range of regional financial cooperation would be indispensable.

The first movement toward regional cooperation was within ASEAN plus three. The Asian bond market initiative was proposed at a meeting in December 2002, at which Japan played a central role. Second, the EMEAP (Executives' Meeting of East Asia and Pacific Central Banks) Group, comprising 11 central banks and monetary authorities in the East Asia and Pacific region, jointly launched the Asian Bond Fund (ABF). All EMEAP members agreed in principle to invest in the fund. The fund, which had an initial size of about US Ineqn 1 billion, invested in a basket of US dollar-denominated bonds issued by Asian sovereign and quasi-sovereign institutions in EMEAP economies other than Japan, Australia, and New Zealand. The launch of the US dollar ABF was an important step in regional cooperation aimed at promoting bond markets in the region. The EMEAP Group has been active in promoting efficient financial intermediation in the region, and the launch of the ABF will facilitate the channeling back into the region of a small portion of the very sizeable official reserves held by the Asian economies.

Although the Asian Bond Fund1 was started in US dollars, other types of Asian bonds, including currency-basket bonds, could be launched in the near future.[2] It is important to recognize the advantages and disadvantages for both issuer and investor of choosing a regional currency over an international currency.

3. Foreign exchange risk

3.1. *Methodology and data*

We investigate how much foreign exchange risk investors and bond issuers face when they invest in or issue bonds denominated in various currencies. Our analysis focuses on the volatility of investment returns and borrowing costs for bonds denominated in various foreign currencies. We compare those volatilities for each of the East Asian countries in terms of the three major currencies (the US dollar, the euro, and the Japanese yen) and a currency basket. The currency basket is composed of the three major currencies. Regarding the basket shares, we have assigned weights corresponding to the East Asian countries' trade-weights for the United States, Japan, and the euro area countries.

There are three types of basket shares related to the trade-weight, as follows. The basket shares based on trade-weight I and trade-weight II depend on the calculation methods of Ogawa and Kawasaki (2003). These trade-weights are the share of total amount of trade between ASEAN+2 (Korea and Taiwan) and the US, Japan, and the euro area countries. The difference between trade-weight I and trade-weight II is whether the trade-weight includes the trade amount of the seven sampled East Asian countries against the rest of the world. Trade-weight I is the share of the total trade for the seven East Asian countries with only the three major countries. Trade-weight II includes the amount of trade with the rest of the world and adds it to the share of the United States. We use the average share of monthly results from January 1988 to December 2001. The currency basket shares of trade-weight I (US dollar : Japanese yen : euro) are 42.4 percent, 34.7 percent, 22.9 percent, and the currency basket shares of trade-weight II are 63.4 percent, 23.3 percent, 13.3 percent, respectively.

We apply another type of currency basket share based on trade volume, called trade-intensity, which is calculated by the method of Petri (1993).[3] The index of trade-intensity, which measures the bilateral trade linkages among countries (or regions), is defined as follows:

$$I_{j,k} = (T_{j,k}/T_j)/(T_k/T_w)$$

where $I_{j,k}$ is the index of trade-intensity between country j and country k, $T_{j,k}$ is the volume of country j's trade with country k, T_j is the total volume of Country j's trade, T_k is the total volume of Country k's trade, and T_w is the volume of total world trade. In other words, the index of trade-intensity measures the closeness of bilateral trade linkage, adjusted for the relative volume in world trade.[4] A situation where the index of trade-intensity is a unity can be interpreted as a neutral bilateral trade relationship. Values over a unity mean that the trade relationship between Countries j and k is biased toward stronger interdependence than their trade with the rest of the world. Values under a unity mean their trade relationship is biased toward weaker interdependence than their trade with the rest of the world. In this chapter, we use the result of 2000.[5] All trade data are from Directions of Trade (IMF), except the data for Taiwan, which are from the National Statistics of Taiwan.

As discussed earlier, we have made three kinds of currency basket for each of the East Asian currencies separately by year, and for the entire sample period. Applying these different currency baskets, we can investigate whether issuing bonds denominated in any particular currency basket might contribute to lessening the volatility of borrowing costs and investment returns, and which type of currency basket might be most effective in decreasing the volatility for each of the East Asian countries.

We used three-month money market rates and daily closing exchange rates to calculate foreign borrowing costs and foreign investment returns.[6] The time series data are used to calculate the means and standard deviations of the borrowing costs and the investment returns, because volatility is defined as standard deviation. The daily rates of borrowing costs and investment returns in terms of home currency are regarded as the sum of daily interest rates and daily rates of change in exchange rates.

The daily interest rate is converted from the annualized three-month money market rate according to the following formula:

$$\text{Daily interest rate} = \exp^{1/360 \log(1+\text{annual rate})}$$

where represents an exponential function.

The daily rates of change in exchange rates are computed as the rate of change in exchange rates from one business day to the next consecutive business day.

$$\text{Daily rates of change in exchange rates} = \frac{e_{t+1} - e_t}{e_t} \times 100$$

where e_t is the exchange rate for a period t.

Our analytical period covers January 1, 1999 to September 30, 2004. The data set includes 1496 observations for the analytical period. The exchange rate data represent bilateral rates for East Asian currencies in terms of the US dollar. We calculated cross rates for East Asian currencies vis-à-vis the Japanese yen and the euro using the exchange rates for the Japanese yen, the euro, and East Asian currencies vis-à-vis the US dollar.

We first investigated the daily rates of foreign borrowing costs for the seven East Asian countries: Singapore, Thailand, Malaysia, the Philippines, Indonesia, Taiwan, and Korea. For each country, we calculated seven different types of foreign borrowing costs for the entire sample period, based on the issuance of bonds denominated in terms of four single currencies, including the home currency, the US dollar, the euro, the Japanese yen, and in terms of three currency-basket types.

Similarly, we investigated the daily rates of foreign investment return for investors in the United States, the euro area, and Japan. For investors, we calculated the daily rates of return based on investment in bonds denominated in terms of the US dollar, the euro, the Japanese yen, and eight different types of currency basket for each of the seven East Asian countries.[7]

3.2. Results—Borrowing costs for bond issuers in seven East Asian countries

Tables 7.5–7.11 show the means and standard deviations for the daily rates of foreign borrowing costs when borrowers in each of the seven East Asian countries issued bonds denominated in terms of the home currency, US dollar, euro, Japanese yen, and three different types of currency basket. The results show that, in all East Asian countries, the standard deviation is lowest for home-currency-denominated bonds. Issuing bonds in local currency, however, has not been common practice in East Asia. For pragmatic reasons, the US dollar has been the common currency for foreign borrowings. Accordingly, we compare the means and standard deviations for issuing bonds denominated in terms of the US dollars with those in terms of the currency basket.

Our results indicate that the currency-basket-denominated bonds could decrease the volatility of borrowing costs for all East Asian countries. Especially with the currency basket, volatilities of borrowing costs are far lower than those in terms of the euro and the Japanese yen. This means that daily movements of borrowing costs in the three major currencies offset each other. Accordingly, borrowing by issuing currency-basket-denominated bonds can help reduce volatility of borrowing costs, compared with issuing single-currency-denominated bonds.

Figures 7.2–7.8 plot the relationships between means and standard deviations of borrowing costs for the seven East Asian countries, which are arranged in the above tables. We discuss each country's results separately.

For Singapore, the standard deviation of borrowing costs is 0.710 percent for issuing bonds denominated in the euro, which is the most volatile of the three major currencies. The standard deviation of borrowing costs is 0.565 percent for issuing bonds denominated in the Japanese yen, which is the cheapest but second-riskiest among the three major currencies. The standard deviation of borrowing costs is 0.011 percent for issuing bonds denominated in the US dollar, which is the lowest among three major currencies. Of the three types of basket share used for bonds in the currency basket, bonds using trade-weight II exhibit the lowest standard deviation of borrowing costs, 0.241 percent, which is lower than the standard deviation of borrowing costs for bonds denominated in US dollars, and much

Table 7.5 Borrowing cost in Singapore (daily, %)

Singapore		Single currency type				Currency basket type		
Borrowing in terms of		Home currency	USD	Euro	Yen	Trade-weight T	Trade-weight U	Trade-intensity
Max	1999–2004	0.008	1.560	3.508	3.128	1.278	1.372	1.822
Min	1999–2004	0.001	−1.585	−2.111	−3.364	−1.282	−1.382	−1.759
Mean	1999–2004	0.004	0.011	0.016	0.005	0.010	0.010	0.008
Std. Dev.	1999–2004	0.002	0.278	0.619	0.565	0.281	0.241	0.345
	1999	0.001	0.326	0.600	0.799	0.377	0.322	0.493
	2000	0.001	0.224	0.734	0.576	0.279	0.226	0.344
	2001	0.002	0.280	0.703	0.541	0.304	0.258	0.345
	2002	0.000	0.275	0.523	0.475	0.237	0.206	0.281
	2003	0.000	0.260	0.530	0.426	0.231	0.208	0.270
	2004	0.001	0.294	0.578	0.465	0.210	0.192	0.262

1. Daily rates are calculated by authors. Sample period is 1/1/1999-9/30/2004. All data of exchange rate and interest rate are from Data stream.
2. The basket share of Trade-weight T is the share of total trade amount of ASEAN+2 (Korea and Taiwan) against US, Japan and 12 Euro countries. We use the average share of monthly results in the period of Jan. 1998 to Dec. 2000 . Data are from Directions of Trade (IMF). As a result, the basket ratio is US: Japan: Euro = 42.4%: 34.7%: 22.9%.
3. The basket share of Trade-weight II is the share of total trade amount of ASEAN+2 (Korea and Taiwan) against US+rest of the world, Japan and 12 Euro countries. We use the average ratio of monthly results in the period of Jan. 1988 to Dec. 2001. All trade data except Taiwan are from Directions of Trade (IMF). The data of Taiwan are from National Statistics of Taiwan. As a result, the basket ratio is US Japan: Euro = 63.4%: 23.3%: 13.3%.
4. The basket ratio of Trade-intensity is calculated by the method of Petri (1993). We use the result of 2000 and the ratios are US Japan : Euro = 1.03 : 1.88 : 0.36 = 31.5% : 57.5% : 11.0%.

150

Table 7.6 Borrowing cost in Thailand (daily, %)

Thailand		Single currency type				Currency basket type		
Borrowing in terms of		Home currency	USD	Euro	Yen	Trade-weight T	Trade-weight U	Trade-intensity
Max	1999–2004	0.016	3.284	4.695	5.137	3.953	3.677	4.422
Min	1999–2004	0.003	−3.261	−3.432	−4.265	−3.372	−3.332	−3.404
Mean	1999–2004	0.007	0.018	0.023	0.013	0.017	0.018	0.015
Std. Dev.	1999–2004	0.003	0.427	0.717	0.674	0.448	0.417	0.508
	1999	0.001	0.616	0.767	0.955	0.637	0.609	0.735
	2000	0.001	0.476	0.885	0.696	0.511	0.480	0.548
	2001	0.000	0.301	0.756	0.583	0.363	0.309	0.410
	2002	0.000	0.454	0.591	0.647	0.442	0.425	0.501
	2003	0.001	0.307	0.594	0.482	0.314	0.285	0.353
	2004	0.000	0.248	0.641	0.550	0.285	0.227	0.360

1. Daily rates are calculated by authors. Sample period is 1/1/1999-9/30/2004. All data of exchange rate and interest rate are from Data stream.
2. The basket share of Trade-weight T is the share of total trade amount of ASEAN+2 (Korea and Taiwan) against US, Japan and 12 Euro countries. We use the average share of monthly results in the period of Jan. 1998 to Dec. 2000 . Data are from Directions of Trade (IMF). As a result, the basket ratio is US : Japan : Euro = 42.4% : 34.7% : 22.9%.
3. The basket share of Trade-weight U is the share of total trade amount of ASEAN+2 (Korea and Taiwan) against US+rest of the world, Japan and 12 Euro countries. We use the average ratio of monthly results in the period of Jan. 1988 to Dec. 2001. All trade data except Taiwan are from Directions of Trade (IMF). The data of Taiwan are from National Statistics of Taiwan. As a result, the basket ratio is US : Japan : Euro = 63.4% : 23.3% : 13.3%.
4. The basket ratio of Trade-intensity is calculated by the method of Petri (1993). We use the result of 2000 and the ratios are US : Japan : Euro = 1.43 : 2.97 : 0.39 = 29.9% : 0.39 = 29.9% : 8.1%.

Table 7.7 Borrowing cost in Malaysia (daily, %)

Malaysia		Single currency type				Currency basket type		
Borrowing in terms of		Home currency	USD	Euro	Yen	Trade-weight T	Trade-weight U	Trade-intensity
Max	1999–2004	0.017	0.214	3.390	2.891	1.143	0.806	1.932
Min	1999–2004	0.008	−0.320	−2.231	−3.876	−1.454	−0.961	−2.375
Mean	1999–2004	0.009	0.009	0.014	0.004	0.008	0.009	0.106
Std. Dev.	1999–2004	0.002	0.024	0.634	0.651	0.296	0.191	0.425
	1999	0.004	0.033	0.564	0.852	0.344	0.228	0.547
	2000	0.000	0.003	0.723	0.620	0.267	0.171	0.392
	2001	0.000	0.014	0.687	0.619	0.292	0.187	0.405
	2002	0.000	0.018	0.549	0.619	0.292	0.188	0.411
	2003	0.000	0.034	0.587	0.511	0.260	0.167	0.342
	2004	0.000	0.024	0.683	0.626	0.314	0.202	0.420

1. Daily rates are calculated by authors. Sample period is 1/1/1999-9/30/2004. All data of exchange rate and interest rate are from Data stream.
2. The basket share of Trade-weight T is the share of total trade amount of ASEAN+2 (Korea and Taiwan) against US, Japan and 12 Euro countries. We use the average share of monthly results in the period of Jan. 1998 to Dec. 2000 . Data are from Directions of Trade (IMF). As a result, the basket ratio is US Japan : Euro = 42.4% : 34.7% : 22.9%.
3. The basket share of Trade-weight U s the share of total trade amount of ASEAN+2 (Korea and Taiwan) against US+rest of the world, Japan and 12 Euro countries. W e use the average ratio of monthly results in the period of Jan. 1988 to Dec. 2001. All trade data except Taiwan are from Directions of Trade (IMF). The data of Taiwan are from National Statistics of Taiwan. As a result, the basket ratio is US : Japan : Euro = 63.4% : 23.3% : 13.3%.
4. The basket ratio of Trade-intensity is calculated by the method of Petri (1993). We use the result of 2000 and the ratios are US : Japan : Euro = 1.17 : 2.54 : 0.33 = 29.0% : 62.9% : 8.1%.

Table 7.8 Borrowing cost in Philippines (daily, %)

Philippines		Single currency type				Currency basket type		
Borrowing in terms of		Home currency	USD	Euro	Yen	Trade-weight T	Trade-weight U	Trade-intensity
Max	1999–2004	0.040	3.703	4.012	4.435	3.907	3.839	4.027
Min	1999–2004	0.016	−10.487	−11.380	−9.721	−10.426	−10.427	−10.124
Mean	1999–2004	0.023	0.035	0.040	0.030	0.034	0.034	0.032
Std. Dev.	1999–2004	0.005	0.543	0.827	0.809	0.597	0.560	0.636
1999		0.004	0.444	0.685	0.880	0.502	0.455	0.594
2000		0.006	0.612	0.965	0.904	0.688	0.649	0.732
2001		0.003	0.872	1.150	1.024	0.913	0.886	0.921
2002		0.001	0.411	0.613	0.679	0.448	0.412	0.498
2003		0.000	0.391	0.698	0.619	0.455	0.415	0.481
2004		0.000	0.214	0.677	0.607	0.329	0.251	0.383

1. Daily rates are calculated by authors. Sample period is 1/1/1999-9/30/2004. All data of exchange rate and interest rate are from Data stream.
2. The basket share of Trade-weight T is the share of total trade amount of ASEAN+2(Korea and Taiwan) against US, Japan and 12 Euro countries. We use the average share of monthly results in the period of Jan. 1998 to Dec. 2000 . Data are from Directions of Trade (IMF). As a result, the basket ratio is US Japan Euro = 42.4% : 34.7% : 22.9%.
3. The basket share of Trade-weight U s the share of total trade amount of ASEAN+2 (Korea and Taiwan) against US+rest of the world, Japan and 12 Euro countries. We use the average ratio of monthly results in the period of Jan. 1988 to Dec. 2001. All trade data except Taiwan are from Directions of Trade (MF). The data of Taiwan are from National Statistics of Taiwan. As a result, the basket ratio is US : Japan : Euro = 63.4% : 23.3% : 13.3%.
4. The basket ratio of Trade-intensity is calculated by the method of Petri (1993). We use the result of 2000 and the ratios are US : Japan : Euro = 1.58 : 2.54 : 0.36 = 35.3% : 56.7% : 8.0%.

Table 7.9 Borrowing cost in Indonesia (daily, %)

Indonesia		Single currency type				Currency basket type		
Borrowing in terms of		Home currency	USD	Euro	Yen	Trade-weight T	Trade-weight U	Trade-intensity
Max	1999–2004	0.110	7.467	8.961	6.856	7.584	7.515	7.111
Min	1999–2004	0.000	−8.581	−9.092	−9.612	−9.056	−8.890	−9.385
Mean	1999–2004	0.035	0.026	0.031	0.020	0.025	0.025	0.022
Std. Dev.	1999–2004	0.017	1.111	1.290	1.239	1.133	1.116	1.179
	1999	0.027	1.837	1.917	1.925	1.831	1.825	1.868
	2000	0.002	1.000	1.309	1.131	1.038	1.014	1.072
	2001	0.004	1.343	1.591	1.499	1.403	1.373	1.446
	2002	0.005	0.712	0.820	0.898	0.729	0.710	0.815
	2003	0.004	0.437	0.698	0.624	0.474	0.444	0.547
	2004	0.003	0.513	0.793	0.716	0.538	0.507	0.622

1. Daily rates are calculated by authors. Sample period is 1/1/1999- 9/30/2004. All data of exchange rate and interest rate are from Data stream.
2. The basket share of Trade-weight T is the share of total trade amount of ASEAN+2 (Korea and Taiwan) against US, Japan and 12 Euro countries. We use the average share of monthly results in the period of Jan. 1998 to Dec. 2000 . Data are from Directions of Trade (IMF). As a result, the basket ratio is US : Japan : Euro=42.4% : 34.7% : 22.9%.
3. The basket share of Trade-weight II s the share of total trade amount of ASEAN+2 (Korea and Taiwan) against US+rest of the world, Japan and 12 Euro countries. We use the average ratio of monthly results in the period of Jan. 1988 to Dec. 2001. All trade data except Taiwan are from Directions of Trade (MF). The data of Taiwan are from National Statistics of Taiwan. As a result, the basket ratio is US : Japan : Euro = 63.4% : 23.3% : 13.3%.
4. The basket ratio of Trade-intensity is calculated by the method of Petri (1993). We use the result of 2000 and the ratios are US : Japan : Euro = 0.87 : 3.6 : 0.4 = 17.9% : 73.9% : 8.2%.

Table 7.10 Borrowing cost in Taiwan (daily, %)

Taiwan		Single currency type				Currency basket type		
Borrowing in terms of		Home currency	USD	Euro	Yen	Trade-weight T	Trade-weight U	Trade-intensity
Max	1999–2004	0.016	3.341	3.390	5.387	3.695	3.492	4.580
Min	1999–2004	0.002	−3.186	−3.362	−4.269	−3.274	−3.142	−3.638
Mean	1999–2004	0.009	0.014	0.018	0.008	0.013	0.013	0.010
Std. Dev.	1999–2004	0.005	0.311	0.672	0.700	0.403	0.346	0.531
1999		0.000	0.160	0.564	0.842	0.351	0.253	0.586
2000		0.001	0.570	0.885	0.854	0.624	0.592	0.717
2001		0.002	0.294	0.729	0.699	0.414	0.349	0.536
2002		0.001	0.197	0.514	0.583	0.279	0.211	0.415
2003		0.001	0.153	0.586	0.506	0.274	0.202	0.372
2004		0.000	0.281	0.690	0.631	0.369	0.305	0.477

1. Daily rates are calculated by authors. Sample period is 1/1/1999–9/30/2004. All data of exchange rate and interest rate are from Data stream.

2. The basket share of Trade-weight I is the share of total trade amount of ASEAN+2(Korea and Taiw an) against US, Japan and 12 Euro countries. We use the average share of monthly results in the period of Jan. 1998 to Dec. 2000 .Data are from Directions of Trade (IMF). As a result, the basket ratio is US : Japan : Euro=42.4% : 34.7% : 22.9%.

3. The basket share of Trade-weight II s the share of total trade amount of ASEAN+2(Korea and Taiw an) against US+rest of the world, Japan and 12 Euro countries. We use the average ratio of monthly results in the period of Jan. 1988 to Dec. 2001. All trade data except Taiwan are from Directions of Trade (IMF). The data of Taiwan are from National Statistics of Taiwan. As a result, the basket ratio is US : Japan : Euro = 63.4% : 23.3% : 13.3%.

4. The basket ratio of Trade-in tensity is calculated by the method of Petri (1993). We use the result of 2000 and the ratios are US : Japan : Euro = 1.03 : 2.97 : 0.36 = 23.6% : 68.1% : 8.3%.

Table 7.11 Borrowing cost in Korea (daily, %)

Korea		Single currency type				Currency basket type		
Borrowing in terms of		Home currency	USD	Euro	Yen	Trade-weight T	Trade-weight U	Trade-intensity
Max	1999–2004	0.022	4.447	4.359	4.374	4.402	4.419	4.397
Min	1999–2004	0.010	−3.975	−4.068	−3.876	−3.693	−3.784	−3.470
Mean	1999–2004	0.015	0.007	0.012	0.002	0.007	0.007	0.004
Std. Dev.	1999–2004	0.003	0.512	0.809	0.733	0.544	0.512	0.576
	1999	0.002	0.422	0.683	0.895	0.503	0.449	0.613
	2000	0.000	0.552	0.988	0.762	0.610	0.573	0.622
	2001	0.002	0.523	0.918	0.682	0.561	0.526	0.559
	2002	0.000	0.586	0.722	0.716	0.571	0.559	0.596
	2003	0.001	0.556	0.756	0.675	0.563	0.546	0.581
	2004	0.001	0.352	0.713	0.609	0.391	0.346	0.432

1. Daily rates are calculated by authors. Sample period is 1/1/1999–9/30/2004. All data of exchange rate and interest rate are from Data stream.
2. The basket share of Trade-weight I is the share of total trade amount of ASEAN+2 (Korea and Taiwan) against US, Japan and 12 Euro countries. We use the average share of monthly results in the period of Jan. 1998 to Dec. 2000 . Data are from Directions of Trade(IMF). As a result, the basket ratio is US : Japan : Euro=42.4% : 34.7% : 22.9%.
3. The basket share of Trade-w eight II s the share of total trade amount of ASEAN+2 (Korea and Taiwan) against US+rest of the world, Japan and 12 Euro countries. We use the average ratio of monthly results in the period of Jan. 1988 to Dec. 2001. All trade data except Taiwan are from Directions of Trade (IMF). The data of Taiwan are from National Statistics of Taiwan. As a result, the basket ratio is US : Japan : Euro = 63.4% : 23.3% : 13.3%.
4. The basket ratio of Trade-intensity is calculated by the method of Petri (1993). We use the result of 2000 and the ratios are US : Japan : Euro = 1.36 : 2.4 : 0.33 = 33.3% : 58.7% : 8.1%.

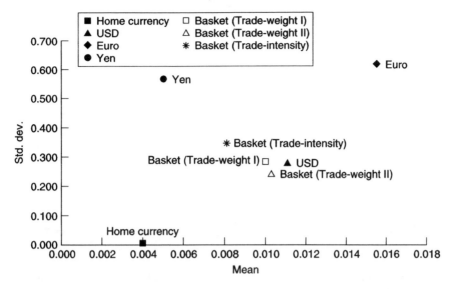

Figure 7.2 Mean and standard deviation of borrowing cost in Singapore.

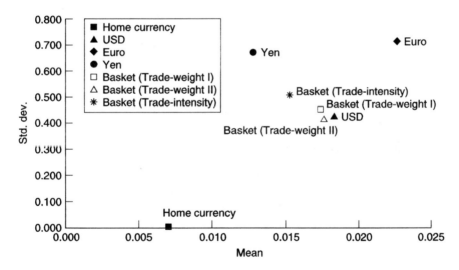

Figure 7.3 Mean and standard deviation of borrowing cost in Thailand.

lower than bonds denominated in terms of the euro or the yen. The second-lowest standard deviation of borrowing costs for currency-basket-denominated bonds is for bonds using trade-weight I, 0.281 percent, which is lower than bonds denominated in terms of the euro or the yen, but a bit higher than US dollar bonds. The standard deviation of borrowing costs for currency-basket-denominated bonds with shares based on trade-intensity is 0.345 percent, higher than that of US dollar

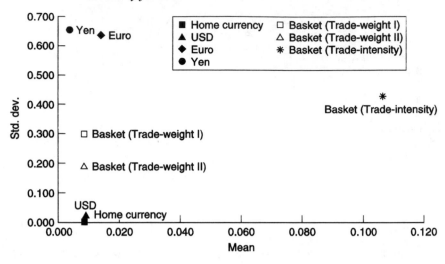

Figure 7.4 Mean and standard deviation of borrowing cost in Malaysia.

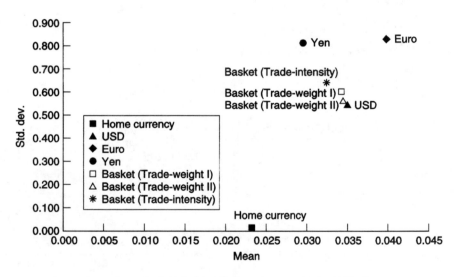

Figure 7.5 Mean and standard deviation of borrowing cost in the Philippines.

bonds. This suggests that basket shares based on trade-intensity do not contribute to reduced volatility of foreign borrowing costs in Singapore. Still, the mean borrowing costs for issuing currency-basket-denominated bonds are all lower than those of US-dollar-denominated bonds, suggesting that currency-basket bonds could lower borrowing costs. Comparing the differences in annual volatility between US-dollar-denominated bonds and currency-basket-denominated bonds, we see that currency-basket-denominated bonds made a larger contribution to decreasing

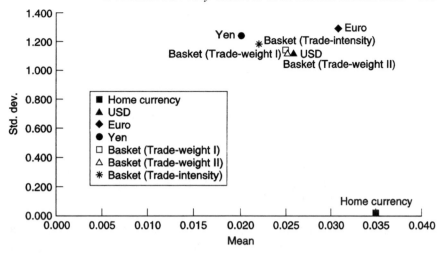

Figure 7.6 Mean and standard deviation of borrowing cost in Indonesia.

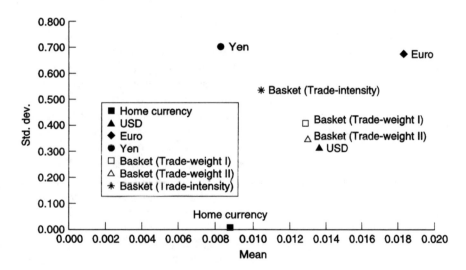

Figure 7.7 Mean and standard deviation of borrowing cost in Taiwan.

volatility by 2004. This suggests that issuing currency-basket-denominated bonds became more useful in decreasing the volatility of daily foreign borrowing costs in Singapore.

Results for Thailand were almost the same as for Singapore. For issuing euro-denominated bonds, the most volatile of the three major currencies, the standard deviation of borrowing costs is 0.717 percent. For issuing Japanese yen-denominated bonds, the standard deviation of borrowing costs is a less-volatile

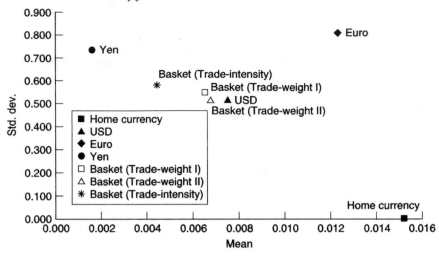

Figure 7.8 Mean and standard deviation of borrowing cost in Korea.

0.674 percent. For US-dollar-denominated bonds, the standard deviation of borrowing costs is 0.427 percent, the lowest among the three major currencies.

Of the three types of basket share in the currency-basket-denominated bonds, the lowest standard deviation of borrowing costs was for bonds based on trade-weight II, 0.417 percent, which is lower than the standard deviation of borrowing cost for US-dollar-denominated bonds, and much lower than euro- and Japanese yen-denominated bonds. The standard deviation for currency-basket- denominated bonds with shares based on trade-intensity is 0.508 percent, higher than bonds denominated in US dollars or other currency baskets. This suggests that basket shares based on trade-intensity do not contribute to decreasing volatility of foreign borrowing costs in Thailand. On the other hand, mean borrowing costs are lower for all currency-basket-denominated bonds than for US-dollar-denominated bonds. Comparing the differences in annual volatility for US-dollar-denominated bonds and currency-basket-denominated bonds, we see that currency-basket-denominated bonds' contribution to volatility reduction grew in 2004. This suggests that issuing currency-basket-denominated bonds became more useful in decreasing the volatility of foreign borrowing costs in Thailand, too.

In Malaysia, the standard deviation of borrowing costs for issuing US-dollar-denominated bonds is a very low 0.024 percent, not much different from issuing bonds denominated in Malaysian ringgits. The standard deviations of borrowing cost for issuing Japanese yen-denominated bonds and euro-denominated bonds are 0.651 percent and 0.643 percent, respectively, much higher than for dollar-denominated bonds. These results reflect the US dollar peg that Malaysia adopted in September 1999. For currency-basket-denominated bonds, the standard deviation of borrowing costs is lowest—0.191 percent—for those with shares based on trade-weight II. This is far lower than for Japanese yen- and euro-denominated bonds, but still far higher than for dollar-denominated bonds. This suggests that issuing currency-basket-denominated bonds is not so effective in decreasing the volatility of borrowing costs in Malaysia.

For the Philippines, the standard deviation of borrowing costs is highest for issuing euro-denominated bonds: 0.827 percent. The standard deviation of borrowing costs for Japanese yen-denominated bonds is 0.809 percent and for US dollar-denominated bonds 0.543 percent, the lowest among the three major currencies. For currency-basket-denominated bonds the lowest standard deviation of borrowing cost is for bonds with basket shares based on trade-weight II, 0.560 percent, which is about the same as for dollar-denominated bonds. However, the mean borrowing costs of currency-basket-denominated bonds are all lower than those of US dollar-denominated bonds.

For Indonesia, the standard deviations of borrowing costs are higher than in other East Asian countries for issuing bonds in all three major currencies (1.239 percent for the Japanese yen, 1.290 percent for the euro, and 1.111 percent for the US dollar). For currency-basket-denominated bonds, the lowest standard deviation is for bonds with basket shares based on trade-weight II: 1.116 percent. This is almost the same as for dollar-denominated bonds. Comparing the differences in annual volatility between dollar-denominated bonds and currency-basket-denominated bonds, we observe that currency-basket-denominated-bonds made a greater contribution in decreasing volatility in 2004. This suggests that issuing the currency-basket-denominated bonds becomes more useful to decrease the volatilities of daily rate of foreign borrowing costs in Indonesia.

For Taiwan, the standard deviation of borrowing costs for Japanese yen-denominated bonds is 0.700 percent, the most volatile of the three major currencies. For euro-denominated bonds, the standard deviation of borrowing costs is 0.672 percent, making it the second most volatile of the three major currencies. For dollar-denominated bonds the figure is 0.311 percent, far less risky than the euro or the Japanese yen. Among currency-basket-denominated bonds, the lowest standard deviation of borrowing cost is for bonds with basket shares based on trade-weight II, 0.346 percent. While the standard deviations of currency-basket bonds are far lower than the euro- and Japanese yen-denominated bonds, they are still higher than for dollar-denominated bonds.

For Korea, the standard deviation of borrowing costs is 0.809 percent for euro-denominated bonds, making these the most volatile among the three major currencies. The standard deviation of borrowing costs is 0.733 percent for Japanese yen-denominated bonds. For dollar-denominated bonds, the figure is 0.512 percent, the lowest among the three major currencies. For currency-basket-denominated bonds, the lowest standard deviation of borrowing costs is for bonds with trade-weight II shares, 0.512 percent. While the standard deviation for these bonds is the same as for dollar-denominated bonds, the mean borrowing cost is lower.

In summary, for all seven East Asian countries, it is obvious that issuing bonds in the home currency entails the least foreign exchange risk.

Issuing currency-basket-denominated bonds could lower foreign-exchange risk for Singapore, Thailand, Indonesia, and Korea. In addition, the mean of borrowing cost is lower for currency-basket-denominated bonds than for dollar-denominated bonds, suggesting that currency-basket-denominated bonds could lower borrowing costs as well as volatility. Regarding the types of currency basket share, in all East Asian countries trade-weight II bonds display the lowest volatility. Moreover, the issuance of currency-basket-denominated bonds made a larger contribution to decreased volatility in Singapore, Thailand, Indonesia, and Korea in 2004.

3.3.   Results—Investment returns for investors in the united states, the euro area, and Japan

Table 7.12 shows the means and standard deviations of daily rates of investment return that international investors obtain by investing in bonds issued in the seven East Asian countries, denominated in the home currencies, the US dollar, the euro, the Japanese yen, and the several types of currency baskets with shares based on trade-weights, as discussed in the previous section. International investors in the United States, the euro area, and Japan presumably evaluate their investment returns in terms of the US dollar, the euro, and the Japanese yen, respectively.

Figures 7.9–7.11 show the relationships among means and standard deviations of daily rates of investment returns for international investors in the United States, the euro area, and Japan. For each international investor, we can compare the means and standard deviations of investment returns for bonds denominated in the seven East Asian currencies, the three major currencies, and currency baskets with shares based on trade-weight I, trade-weight II, and trade-intensity for each East Asian country.

For investors in the United States, bonds denominated in terms of the Indonesian rupiah have the highest risk and highest return. Malaysian ringgit bonds have the lowest foreign exchange risk among the currencies in the sample (excluding dollar-denominated bonds), reflecting the fact that Malaysia adopted a dollar peg for its currency in September 1999. The standard deviation of investment returns is second-lowest (0.117) for currency-basket-denominated bonds with shares based on trade-weight II (US dollar 63.4 percent, Japanese yen 23.3 percent, and euro 13.3 percent), and third-lowest (0.267) for currency-basket-denominated bonds with shares based on trade-weight I (US dollar 42.4 percnet, Japanese yen 34.7 percent, and euro 22.9 percent). Currency-basket-denominated bonds showed lower standard deviations of investment returns than those denominated in any single currency. For investors in bonds issued in Indonesia, the standard deviation of investment returns for currency-basket-denominated bonds with shares corresponding to trade-intensity (US dollar 17.9 percent, Japanese yen 73.9 percent, and euro 8.2 percent), 0.471, is far lower than for bonds denominated in the Indonesian rupiah. Similar results were obtained for bonds issued in the Philippines, Korea, and Thailand. For bonds issued in these countries currency-basket denomination may be more attractive to US investors than bonds denominated in the home currencies.

Table 7.12 Investment returns into East Asian Countries (%)

Invest into		For US Investor (US dollar)	For Euro Area Investor (Euro)	For Japan Investor (Yen)
Singaporian Dollar	Max	1.629	2.173	3.486
	Min	−1.524	−3.370	−3.025
	Mean	0.003	0.001	0.003
	Std Dev.	0.278	0.618	0.565
Thai Baht	Max	3.401	3.575	4.470
	Min	−3.151	−4.465	4.881
	Mean	0.000	−0.002	−0.001
	Std Dev.	0.426	0.715	0.674
Malaysian Ringgit	Max	0.351	2.300	4.050
	Min	−0.202	−3.257	−2.800
	Mean	0.009	0.008	0.009
	Std Dev.	0.024	0.633	0.651
Philippine Peso	Max	11.768	12.891	10.802
	Min	−3.515	−3.821	−4.222
	Mean	0.000	−0.001	0.001
	Std Dev.	0.561	0.842	0.819
Indonesian Rupiah	Max	9.440	10.057	10.676
	Min	−6.841	−8.121	−6.384
	Mean	0.031	0.030	0.031
	Std Dev.	1.116	1.294	1.244
New Taiwanese Dollar	Max	3.321	3.502	4.475
	Min	−3.204	−3.253	−5.100
	Mean	0.005	0.004	0.006
	Std Dev.	0.311	0.672	0.700
Korean Won	Max	4.178	4.274	4.052
	Min	−4.223	−4.145	−4.170
	Mean	0.019	0.018	0.020
	Std Dev.	0.511	0.807	0.733
US Dollar	Max	0.018	2.301	2.891
	Min	0.002	−3.253	−3.876
	Mean	0.009	0.008	0.004
	Std Dev.	0.006	0.632	0.649
Japanese Yen	Max	4.047	4.708	0.003
	Min	−2.795	−3.534	0.000
	Mean	0.010	0.014	0.001
	Std Dev.	0.650	0.802	0.001
Euro	Max	3.394	0.014	3.674
	Min	−2.236	0.005	−4.483
	Mean	0.014	0.009	0.002
	Std Dev.	0.633	0.003	0.801

Daily returns are calculated by authors. Sample period is 1/1/1999-9/30/2004. All data of exchange rate and interest rate are from Data stream.

continued

Table 7.12—Continued

Invest into		For US Investor (US dollar)	For Euro Area Investor (Euro)	For Japan Investor (Yen)
Basket (Trade-Weight T)	Max	1.226	0.978	2.521
	Min	−1.498	−1.290	−2.106
	Mean	0.007	0.008	0.008
	Std Dev.	0.267	0.216	0.438
Basket (Trade-weight U)	Max	0.785	1.127	3.033
	Min	−0.826	−1.114	−2.235
	Mean	0.008	0.011	0.008
	Std Dev.	0.156	0.323	0.487
Basket (Trade-intensity Singapore)	Max	1.748	1.878	1.662
	Min	−2.167	−2.102	−1.265
	Mean	0.006	0.007	0.005
	Std Dev.	0.364	0.373	0.270
Basket (Trade-intensity Thailand)	Max	1.854	2.055	1.495
	Min	−2.357	−2.246	−1.118
	Mean	0.006	0.006	0.004
	Std Dev.	0.394	0.409	0.241
Basket (Trade-intensity Malaysia)	Max	1.880	2.095	1.459
	Min	−2.392	−2.272	−1.093
	Mean	0.006	0.006	0.004
	Std Dev.	0.400	0.417	0.235
Basket (Trade-intensity Philippines)	Max	1.702	1.820	1.710
	Min	−2.151	−2.093	−1.265
	Mean	0.006	0.007	0.005
	Std Dev.	0.360	0.363	0.275
Basket (Trade-intensity Indonesia)	Max	2.196	2.582	1.013
	Min	−2.819	−2.704	−0.788
	Mean	0.005	0.005	0.003
	Std Dev.	0.471	0.530	0.166
Basket (Trade-intensity Taiwan)	Max	2.031	2.326	1.247
	Min	−2.593	−2.422	−0.950
	Mean	0.005	0.005	0.004
	Std Dev.	0.434	0.469	0.202
Basket (Trade-intensity Korea)	Max	1.757	1.905	1.633
	Min	−2.225	−2.148	−1.213
	Mean	0.006	0.007	0.005
	Std Dev.	0.373	0.379	0.263

Daily returns are calculated by authors. Sample period is 1/1/1999t-12/31/2002. All data of exchange rate and interest rate are from Data stream.
For Basket investment, we apply the basket share of Trade-weight T and Trade-weight U as a common basket ratio. Their basket shares are US JapanEuro=42.4% 34.7% 22.9% and 63.4% 23.3, respectively.

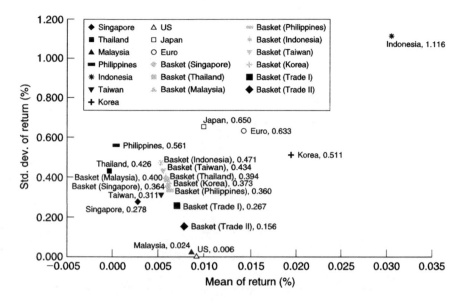

Figure 7.9 Mean and standard deviation of investment return for US investor (%).

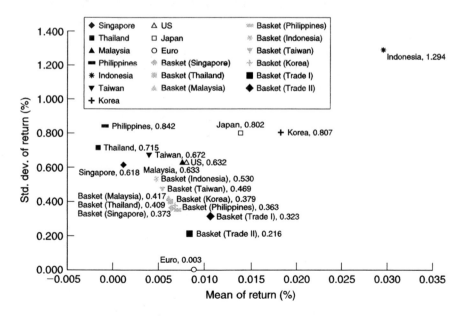

Figure 7.10 Mean and standard deviation of investment return for Euro Area investor (%).

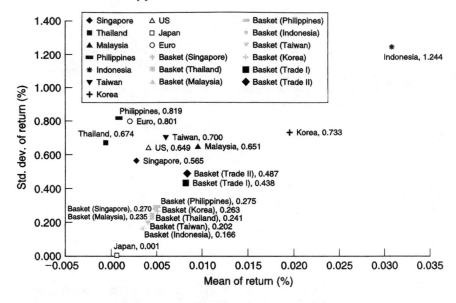

Figure 7.11 Mean and standard deviation of investment return for Japanese investor (%).

For investors in the euro area as well, bonds denominated in terms of the Indonesian rupiah exhibit both the highest risk and the highest return. The standard deviations of investment returns for bonds denominated in the Philippine peso, Korean won, and Japanese yen are all above 0.8 percent, tightly clumped for second-highest. Investing in currency-basket-denominated bonds of any share-weighting has lower volatility of investment return than investing in bonds denominated in local currencies, showing that none of the seven East Asian currencies is closely tied to the euro. Bond issuers in the seven East Asian countries could lower the standard deviation of returns for euro area investors by issuing currency-basket-denominated bonds rather than bonds denominated in their home currencies.

For Japanese investors, as for other international investors, bonds denominated in terms of the Indonesian rupiah had the highest risk and the highest returns. Bonds denominated in the Philippine peso and the euro are the second-riskiest. The standard deviations of investment returns for currency-basket-denominated bonds with shares corresponding to trade-weight I and trade-weight II are 0.438 percent and 0.487 percent, respectively. The standard deviation of investment returns for currency-basket-denominated bonds with shares corresponding to trade-intensity are around 0.2–0.3 percent, lower than those of other currency-basket-denominated bonds, and lower than bonds in every local currency. This suggests that bonds issued in terms of currency baskets, especially those with shares based on trade-intensity, should be more attractive to Japanese investors.

In summary, it is natural that for investors in the United States, the euro area, and Japan, bonds denominated in the investor's home currency offer the lowest level of foreign exchange risk, followed by currency-basket-denominated bonds. In this chapter, three types of currency basket share are examined, and their effectiveness in reducing foreign-exchange risk compared. It is interesting to discover that the most effective type of basket share, in terms of risk reduction, is different for different classes of international investors. For investors in the United States, currency basket shares based on trade-weight II are the most effective in reducing foreign-exchange risks, while for investors in the euro area trade-weight I is the most effective, and for Japanese investors shares based on trade-intensity are the most effective. Clearly, though, currency-basket-denominated bonds can decrease foreign exchange risk in many cases.

4.   Liquidity

Next, we compare liquidity among bonds denominated in terms of each of the three major currencies, focusing especially on differences in liquidity between dollar-denominated bonds on the one hand and euro- and yen-denominated bonds on the other.

As our key indicator of liquidity we use bid-ask spreads in foreign exchange markets. Bid-ask spreads are determined by three factors: (1) order processing costs, (2) inventory holding costs, and (3) information costs for market-making (Hartmann 1998). As a result, bid-ask spreads tend to be lower in liquid markets due to the large volume of trading. In order processing costs, economies of scale are at work because costs of purchasing electric market information are fixed. In inventory holding costs, the law of large numbers tends to lessen the average cost of holding inventory as statistically independent orders increase. Economies of scale are also operative because of the substantial fixed costs for information used in market-making.

Bid-ask spreads are basically very narrow and virtually costless for the major currencies vis-à-vis the US dollar and for frequently quoted major cross currencies, such as euro/yen, sterling/yen, Swiss franc/yen, and Sterling/euro. For so-called exotic currencies, however, such as other East Asian currencies, some degree of inconvenience and higher transaction costs are involved in direct exchanges with currencies other than the US dollar, especially in forward outright trading.

East Asian currencies are generally quoted against the US dollar and not against the euro or the Japanese yen. The cross rates must be calculated using the dollar/yen rate and the exchange rates for the dollar vis-à-vis the East Asian currencies. Calculation of cross rates for East Asian currencies vis-à-vis the euro requires a similar procedure. Quoting forward outright rates involves similar procedures for calculating cross swap rates. One consequence of this is that bid-ask spreads for forward outright rates for East Asian currencies vis-à-vis the euro or the Japanese yen are wider than for major currencies. This may be one reason why borrowers in East Asian countries did not generally use swap transactions to hedge their borrowings of foreign currencies, especially before the Asian currency crises of 1997.

We compare bid-ask spreads in forward swap rates for the seven East Asian currencies against the three major currencies, and for the euro and the Japanese yen vis-à-vis the US dollar. We try to express the bid-ask spreads as a percentage of transaction cost and as a percentage of daily cost. Transaction cost refers to the total customer cost for one forward outright transaction, while daily cost refers to the cost per day of one forward outright transaction. We calculated bid-ask spreads for the seven East Asian currencies against the US dollar, the euro, and the Japanese yen for terms of 1, 3, and 6 months. For comparison with bid-ask spreads for major traded currencies, we calculated spreads for the euro and the yen vis-à-vis the dollar and for the yen *vs.* the euro. We used spot rates and forward rates from the Bloomberg Currency Composite pages and from the Prebon Yamane Asia Region broker's page on Bloomberg dated 13 September 2002 and 6 February 2003.

Table 7.13 shows the transaction-based bid-ask spreads. The bid-ask spreads for all East Asian currencies are lowest vis-à-vis the dollar for all terms, while they are highest vis-à-vis the euro for terms of 1 and 3 months. In addition, the bid-ask spreads for all East Asian currencies *vs.* the dollar are far higher than for the euro and the Japanese yen vis-à-vis the US dollar. Bid-ask spreads for the euro and the Japanese yen vis-à-vis the US dollar are 3 to 4 percent per transaction, while similar spreads for East Asian currencies range from 5 percent for the Taiwan dollar to nearly 50 percent for the Philippine peso and the Indonesian rupiah vis-à-vis the US dollar, and more than 50 percent vis-à-vis the euro. Bid-ask spreads for all East Asian currencies vis-à-vis the euro and the Japanese yen are 3–4 percent higher than vis-à-vis the US dollar, and they are also higher than spreads for the Japanese yen vis-à-vis the euro. With regard to terms, differences are minimal in bid-ask spreads for 1, 3, and 6 months for the Singapore dollar, the Thai baht, and the Korean won, and for the euro and the Japanese yen. In contrast, bid-ask spreads for other East Asian currencies grow wider as terms grow longer.

Table 7.14 shows bid-ask spreads on a daily percentage basis. Expressing these spreads as a daily percentage enables us to compare them to foreign exchange risk expressed in terms of the standard deviation of borrowing costs and investment returns, also as a daily percentage. As the daily bid-ask spreads are equivalent to the transaction-based bid-ask spreads divided by the number of days in the transaction term, they tend to shrink as terms become longer. The differences in daily bid-ask spreads between East Asian currencies and the major trading currencies become more trivial as the terms are longer. Comparing the differences in bid-ask spreads for East Asian currencies vis-à-vis the US dollar and vis-à-vis the euro or the Japanese yen, the differences between the lowest and the highest are 0.0006–0.0015 percent for 1 month swap transactions, 0.0002–0.0006 percent for 3 month swap transactions, and 0.0001–0.0003 percent for 6 month swap transactions. Comparing the differences in bid-ask spreads for the East Asian currencies vis-à-vis the euro or the Japanese yen and those of the Japanese yen vis-à-vis the euro, the differences between the lowest and the highest are 0.0001–0.0084 percent for 1 month swap transactions, 0.0001–0.0040 percent for 3 month swap transactions, and 0–0.0028 percent for 6 month swap transaction.

Of the seven East Asian currencies, the Taiwan dollar has the lowest bid-ask spreads. The Singapore dollar, Thai baht, and the Korean won form a tight group as the next lowest. Spreads for the Malaysian ringgit, Philippine peso, and Indonesian

Table 7.13 Investment returns into East Asian Countries (%)

Currency		Spreads (daily, %) (sample day: Sept 13, 2002)			Spreads (daily, %) (sample day: Feb 6, 2003)			Spreads (daily, %) (average)		
		1m	3m	6m	1m	3m	6m	1m	3m	6m
Singaporian Dollar	Agst. US dollar	0.00302	0.00112	0.00056	0.00115	0.00238	0.00019	0.00208	0.00075	0.00038
	Agst. Euro	0.00438	0.00156	0.00076	0.00038	0.00089	0.00038	0.00338	0.00122	0.00057
	Agst. JPYen	0.00361	0.00132	0.00069	0.00258	0.00086	0.00046	0.00310	0.00109	0.00057
	average	0.00367	0.00133	0.00067	0.00204	0.00071	0.00034	0.00285	0.00102	0.00051
Thai Baht	Agst. US dollar	0.00398	0.00154	0.00065	0.00078	0.00045	0.00013	0.00238	0.00100	0.00039
	Agst. Euro	0.00534	0.00198	0.00084	0.00201	0.00096	0.00032	0.00368	0.00147	0.00058
	Agst. JPYen	0.00456	0.00172	0.00076	0.00221	0.00093	0.00039	0.00338	0.00133	0.00057
	average	0.00462	0.00175	0.00075	0.00167	0.00078	0.00028	0.00315	0.00126	0.00052
Malaysian Ringgit	Agst. US dollar	0.00921	0.00318	0.00174	0.00079	0.00040	0.00035	0.00500	0.00179	0.00105
	Agst. Euro	0.01056	0.00361	0.00193	0.00203	0.00091	0.00054	0.00629	0.00226	0.00124
	Agst. JPYen	0.00978	0.00335	0.00183	0.00222	0.00088	0.00060	0.00600	0.00212	0.00122
	average	0.00985	0.00338	0.00184	0.00168	0.00073	0.00050	0.00576	0.00206	0.00117
Philippine Peso	Agst. US dollar	0.00638	0.00210	0.00211	0.00618	0.00407	0.00307	0.00628	0.00309	0.00259
	Agst. Euro	0.00774	0.00254	0.00231	0.00742	0.00458	0.00326	0.00758	0.00356	0.00278
	Agst. JPYen	0.00691	0.00223	0.00210	0.00744	0.00428	0.00297	0.00718	0.00326	0.00253
	average	0.00701	0.00229	0.00217	0.00701	0.00431	0.00310	0.00701	0.00330	0.00264
Indonesian Rupiah	Agst. US dollar	0.00743	0.00429	0.00277	0.00527	0.00310	0.00249	0.00635	0.00369	0.00263
	Agst. Euro	0.00880	0.00473	0.00296	0.00651	0.00361	0.00268	0.00765	0.00417	0.00282
	Agst. JPYen	0.00787	0.00422	0.00257	0.00658	0.00340	0.00248	0.00723	0.00381	0.00252
	average	0.00803	0.00441	0.00277	0.00612	0.00337	0.00255	0.00708	0.00389	0.00266

continued

Table 7.13—Continued

Currency		Spreads (daily, %) (sample day: Sept 13, 2002)			Spreads (daily, %) (sample day: Feb 6, 2003)			Spreads (daily, %) (average)		
		1m	3m	6m	1m	3m	6m	1m	3m	6m
New Taiwanese Dollar	Agst. US dollar	0.00174	0.00089	0.00077	0.00153	0.00082	0.00057	0.00164	0.00086	0.00067
	Agst. Euro	0.00310	0.00133	0.00096	0.00277	0.00133	0.00076	0.00293	0.00133	0.00086
	Agst. JPYen	0.00234	0.00109	0.00089	0.00297	0.00131	0.00084	0.00265	0.00120	0.00087
	average	0.00239	0.00111	0.00088	0.00242	0.00115	0.00072	0.00241	0.00113	0.00080
Korean Won	Agst. US dollar	0.00305	0.00100	0.00069	0.00255	0.00084	0.00042	0.00280	0.00092	0.00056
	Agst. Euro	0.00441	0.00144	0.00089	0.00378	0.00135	0.00062	0.00409	0.00140	0.00075
	Agst. JPYen	0.00362	0.00118	0.00079	0.00396	0.00131	0.00067	0.00379	0.00124	0.00073
	average	0.00369	0.00121	0.00079	0.00343	0.00117	0.00057	0.00356	0.00119	0.00068
Hong Kong Dollar	Agst. US dollar	0.00094	0.00031	0.00018	0.00228	0.00047	0.00038	0.00161	0.00039	0.00028
	Agst. Euro	0.00230	0.00075	0.00038	0.00351	0.00098	0.00057	0.00291	0.00086	0.00047
	Agst. JPYen	0.00181	0.00060	0.00035	0.00370	0.00095	0.00064	0.00275	0.00077	0.00049
	average	0.00168	0.00055	0.00030	0.00316	0.00080	0.00053	0.00242	0.00067	0.00041
Euro	Agst. US dollar	0.00136	0.00044	0.00020	0.00124	0.00051	0.00019	0.00130	0.00048	0.00020
Japanese Yen	Agst. US dollar	0.00087	0.00029	0.00017	0.00143	0.00049	0.00026	0.00115	0.00039	0.00022
Japanese Yen	Agst. Euro	0.00223	0.00073	0.00037	0.00266	0.00099	0.00046	0.00245	0.00086	0.00041

Calculated by authors.

Souces: All spot rates and forward rates are collected from Bloomberg currency com posit pages and Prebon Yamane ASIA Region pages on 13 Sept, 2002. Forward swap spreads are calculated by bid and ask spreads on both spot and forward rates.

Table 7.14 Forward swap bid-ask spread (% in daily basis) of 7 East Asian currencies against 3 Major currencies

Currency		Spreads (daily, %) (sample day: Sept 13, 2002)			Spreads (daily, %) (sample day:Feb 6,2003)			Spreads (daily, %) (average)		
		1m	3m	6m	1m	3m	6m	1m	3m	6m
Singaporian Dollar	Agst. US dollar	0.0907	0.1020	0.1020	0.0344	0.0344	0.0344	0.0625	0.0682	0.0682
	Agst. Euro	0.1313	0.1417	0.1373	0.0714	0.0806	0.0693	0.1014	0.1111	0.1033
	Agst. JPYen	0.1168	0.1281	0.1327	0.0774	0.0787	0.0825	0.0971	0.1034	0.1076
	average	0.1129	0.1239	0.1240	0.0611	0.0646	0.0621	0.0870	0.0943	0.0930
Thai Baht	Agst. US dollar	0.1194	0.1405	0.1171	0.0234	0.0409	0.0234	0.0714	0.0907	0.0702
	Agst. Euro	0.1601	0.1803	0.1526	0.0604	0.0872	0.0586	0.1103	0.1337	0.1056
	Agst. JPYen	0.1450	0.1652	0.1455	0.0662	0.0848	0.0708	0.1056	0.1250	0.1082
	average	0.1415	0.1620	0.1384	0.0500	0.0710	0.0509	0.0958	0.1165	0.0947
Malaysian Ringgit	Agst. US dollar	0.2763	0.2895	0.3158	0.0237	0.0368	0.0632	0.1500	0.1632	0.1895
	Agst. Euro	0.3168	0.3287	0.3499	0.0608	0.0832	0.0982	0.1888	0.2059	0.2241
	Agst. JPYen	0.3016	0.3129	0.3404	0.0665	0.0805	0.1094	0.1840	0.1967	0.2249
	average	0.2982	0.3103	0.3354	0.0503	0.0668	0.0903	0.1743	0.1886	0.2128
Philippine Peso	Agst. US dollar	0.1914	0.1914	0.3827	0.1853	0.3706	0.5559	0.1883	0.2810	0.4693
	Agst. Euro	0.2321	0.2314	0.4172	0.2226	0.4170	0.5894	0.2273	0.3242	0.5033
	Agst. JPYen	0.2157	0.2115	0.3885	0.2233	0.3896	0.5368	0.2195	0.3006	0.4627
	average	0.2130	0.2114	0.3962	0.2104	0.3924	0.5607	0.2117	0.3019	0.4784
Indonesian Rupiah	Agst. US dollar	0.2230	0.3903	0.5018	0.1580	0.2821	0.4514	0.1905	0.3362	0.4766
	Agst. Euro	0.2639	0.4302	0.5365	0.1952	0.3287	0.4855	0.2296	0.3795	0.5110
	Agst. JPYen	0.2443	0.3918	0.4729	0.1975	0.3094	0.4486	0.2209	0.3506	0.4607
	average	0.2437	0.4041	0.5037	0.1836	0.3067	0.4618	0.2137	0.3554	0.4828

continued

Table 7.14—Continued

Currency		Spreads (daily, %) (sample day: Sept 13, 2002)			Spreads (daily, %) (sample day:Feb 6,2003)			Spreads (daily, %) (average)		
		1m	3m	6m	1m	3m	6m	1m	3m	6m
New Taiwanese Dollar	Agst. US dollar	0.0581	0.0872	0.1453	0.0460	0.0748	0.1035	0.0521	0.0810	0.1244
	Agst. Euro	0.0988	0.1270	0.1804	0.0830	0.1207	0.1379	0.0909	0.1239	0.1591
	Agst. JPYen	0.0843	0.1134	0.1759	0.0890	0.1190	0.1516	0.0866	0.1162	0.1638
	average	0.0804	0.1092	0.1672	0.0727	0.1049	0.1310	0.0765	0.1070	0.1491
Korean Won	Agst. US dollar	0.0914	0.0914	0.1246	0.0764	0.0764	0.0764	0.0839	0.0839	0.1005
	Agst. Euro	0.1322	0.1315	0.1604	0.1135	0.1229	0.1117	0.1228	0.1272	0.1360
	Agst. JPYen	0.1169	0.1158	0.1505	0.1188	0.1189	0.1210	0.1178	0.1174	0.1357
	average	0.1135	0.1129	0.1452	0.1029	0.1061	0.1030	0.1082	0.1095	0.1241
Hong Kong Dolalr	Agst. US dollar	0.0282	0.0282	0.0321	0.0683	0.0425	0.0683	0.0483	0.0354	0.0502
	Agst. Euro	0.0690	0.0683	0.0680	0.1053	0.0888	0.1032	0.0872	0.0785	0.0856
	Agst. JPYen	0.0543	0.0543	0.0625	0.1110	0.0864	0.1151	0.0826	0.0703	0.0888
	average	0.0505	0.0503	0.0542	0.0949	0.0726	0.0955	0.0727	0.0614	0.0749
Euro	Agst. US dollar	0.0408	0.0402	0.0362	0.0371	0.0463	0.0352	0.0389	0.0433	0.0357
Japanese Yen	Agst. US dollar	0.0261	0.0262	0.0308	0.0429	0.0442	0.0479	0.0345	0.0352	0.0394
Japanese Yen	Agst. Euro	0.0668	0.0661	0.0664	0.0799	0.0902	0.0826	0.0734	0.0781	0.0745

Calculated by authors.
Souces: All spot rates and forward rates are collected from Bloomberg currency com posit pages and Prebon Yamane Asia Region pages on 13 Sept, 2002.
Forward swap spreads are calculated by bid and ask spreads on both spot and forward rates.

rupiah, on the other hand, are much higher. It is interesting to note that among the seven East Asian countries the spread for the Malaysian ringgit was the highest on the sample date, September 13, 2002. This seems to be because Malaysia has chosen to peg the spot rate of the Malaysian ringgit to the US dollar, so there is not much demand to trade forward swaps in the Malaysian ringgit.

Thus, we compared liquidity among the three major currencies and the currency basket using data on bid-ask spreads for swap transactions. This proved that the US dollar has a higher degree of liquidity than any of the seven East Asian currencies. The differences between the US dollar and the currency basket were large for 1 month swap transactions, but they were not so large for 3 and 6 month swap transactions.

Next, we examine the Singapore dollar and the Thai baht, which are among the more actively traded East Asian currencies, and we calculate forward bid-ask spreads vis-à-vis the US dollar, the euro, and the Japanese yen from 1999 to 2003, to see how market conditions improved after the Asian currency crises. Table 7.15 shows the changes in transactions based on forward bid-ask spreads from 1999 to 2003.

Comparing the same calculations for the euro and the Japanese yen vis-à-vis the US dollar and for the the Japanese yen vis-à-vis the euro, it is clear that the bid-ask spreads of the two East Asian currencies narrowed. For example, the six-month bid-ask spread for the Singapore dollar vis-à-vis the Japanese yen was 0.16 percent on June 20, 1999, and narrowed to 0.08 percent on February 6, 2003, which was almost the same level as the bid-ask spread for the Japanese yen vis-à-vis the euro. Similarly, the 6 month bid-ask spread for the Thai baht vis-à-vis the Japanese yen was 0.36 percent on June 20, 1999, and narrowed to 0.07 percent on February 6, 2003, which was slightly better than the bid-ask spread for the Japanese yen vis-à-vis the euro. This means conditions in foreign exchange markets in East Asia had improved, and forward outright deals in major East Asian currencies have recently been less expensive.

5.   Conclusion

This chapter investigates the foreign exchange risks and liquidity advantages and disadvantages of choosing a regional currency over an international currency when issuing or investing in bonds. The performance of currency-basket-denominated bonds was compared with that of bonds denominated in three major currencies: the US dollar, the euro, and the Japanese yen.

Issuing currency-basket-denominated bonds has the second-lowest foreign exchange risk for borrowers in Singapore, Thailand, Indonesia, and Korea. The foreign-exchange risks are smaller than those associated with issuing US-dollar-denominated bonds. Issuing currency-basket-denominated bonds could help lower foreign exchange risks for borrowers. Currency-basket-denominated bonds also have the second-lowest foreign exchange risks for all international investors. Bond issuers in the seven East Asian countries could lower the standard deviation of returns for international investors by issuing currency-basket-denominated bonds

Table 7.15 The change of forward swap bid-ask spreads (% in transaction basis) in 2 East Asian currencies against 3 major currencies

Currency	Against	Spreads (%) (sample day : June 30, 1999)			Spreads (%) (sample day : June 30, 2000)			Spreads (%) (sample day : July 1, 2001)			Spreads (%) (sample day : July 2, 2002)			Spreads (%) (sample day : Feb 6, 2003)		
		1m	3m	6m	1m	3m	6m	1m	3m	6m	1m	3m	6m	1m	3m	6m
Singaporian Dollar	US dollar	0.0706	0.0882	0.1176	0.0608	0.0926	0.0984	0.0329	0.0604	0.0659	0.0240	0.0282	0.0395	0.0344	0.0344	0.0344
	Euro	0.0948	0.1128	0.1478	0.1139	0.1658	0.1817	0.0901	0.1461	0.1371	0.0847	0.0837	0.0997	0.0714	0.0806	0.0693
	JPyen	0.1121	0.1177	0.1603	0.0992	0.1453	0.1569	0.0684	0.0998	0.1224	0.0591	0.0701	0.0899	0.0774	0.0787	0.0825
	average	0.0925	0.1062	0.1419	0.0913	0.1346	0.1457	0.0638	0.1021	0.1084	0.0559	0.0607	0.0764	0.0611	0.0646	0.0621
Thai Baht	US dollar	0.2171	0.2443	0.3257	0.1532	0.2042	0.2553	0.2869	0.3311	0.4414	0.1445	0.1686	0.1927	0.0234	0.0409	0.0234
	Euro	0.2417	0.2700	0.3591	0.2064	0.2787	0.3416	0.3443	0.4176	0.5138	0.2051	0.2237	0.2520	0.0604	0.0872	0.0586
	JPyen	0.2582	0.2716	0.3606	0.1912	0.2539	0.3062	0.3195	0.3596	0.4706	0.1793	0.2092	0.2402	0.0662	0.0848	0.0708
	average	0.2390	0.2620	0.3485	0.1836	0.2456	0.3010	0.3169	0.3694	0.4753	0.1763	0.2005	0.2283	0.0500	0.0710	0.0509
Euro	US dollar	0.0242	0.0242	0.0290	0.0530	0.0735	0.0840	0.0572	0.0861	0.0720	0.0608	0.0557	0.0608	0.0371	0.0463	0.0352
JPyen	US dollar	0.0413	0.0289	0.0413	0.0386	0.0518	0.0565	0.0354	0.0395	0.0564	0.0350	0.0417	0.0501	0.0429	0.0442	0.0479
JPyen	Euro	0.0654	0.0529	0.0701	0.0914	0.1244	0.1384	0.0925	0.1247	0.1268	0.0957	0.0970	0.1099	0.0799	0.0902	0.0826

Calculated by authors.
Sources: All spot rates and forward rates are collected from Bloomberg Currency Composite pages. Forward swap bid-ask spreads are calculated by and forward rates.

	China	Hong Kong	Indonesia	Japan	Korea	Malaysia	Philippines	Singapore	Taiwan	Thailand	US	EU
China	–											
Hong Kong	8.26	–										
Indonesia	1.06	1.03	–									
Japan	2.12	1.75	3.60	–								
Korea	2.00	1.88	3.41	2.40	–							
Malaysia	0.74	1.94	2.84	2.54	1.53	–						
Philippines	0.43	2.33	1.61	2.54	2.01	2.30	–					
Singapore	0.97	2.74	1.79	1.88	1.43	11.21	3.43	–				
Taiwan	2.21	3.75	1.60	2.80	1.74	1.82	2.28	2.70	–			
Thailand	1.00	1.73	2.59	2.97	1.05	3.00	2.31	4.00	n.a.	–		
US	1.29	0.68	0.87	1.62	1.36	1.17	1.58	1.03	1.43	1.15	–	
EU	0.38	0.41	0.40	0.41	0.33	0.33	0.36	0.36	0.39	0.39	0.56	–

Source: IMF, Direction of Trade Statistics. Index of Trade-Intensity are calculated by authors.

rather than bonds denominated in terms of local currencies. Thus, currency-basket-denominated bonds could decrease foreign exchange risks for investors as well as issuers.

Next, viewing bid-ask spreads in swap transactions as a proxy for liquidity, we compared these spreads for seven East Asian currencies and three major currencies. Our results showed the US dollar has a higher degree of liquidity than any of the seven East Asian currencies. However, while the differences between the US dollar and the currency basket were large for 1 month swap transactions, they were not so large for 3 or 6 month swaps.

Investors and issuers in regional bonds in East Asia face trade-offs between foreign exchange risks and liquidity. Although currency-basket-denominated bonds can decrease foreign-exchange risks, investors and bond issuers prefer US-dollar-denominated bonds because they attach greater importance to liquidity. From a liquidity standpoint, the establishment of markets for regional bonds denominated in regional currencies or a currency basket might help invigorate financial markets in East Asia.

Appendix

Trade-intensity index of East Asian countries against US, EU, and Japan (year of 2000).

Notes

1 This study was based on the article 'Roles of regional currency in bond markets in East Asia' prepared for the JSEPA Workshop on Development of Bond Markets in Asia, which the Monetary Authority of Singapore and the Japanese Ministry of Finance held in Singapore on 17–18 October 2002.

2 ABF2, as announced by EMEAP in April 2004, includes two components: a Pan-Asian Bond Index Fund (PAIF) and a Fund of Bond Funds (FoBF). The PAIF is a single bond fund investing in sovereign and quasi-sovereign domestic-currency-denominated bonds issued in the eight EMEAP markets. The FoBF is a two-layered structure with a parent fund investing in eight sub-funds, each of which will invest in sovereign and quasi-sovereign domestic-currency-denominated bonds issued in the respective markets of the eight EMEAP economies.
3 Kawai and Akiyama (1998) calculated the trade-intensity in 1990.
4 Note that $I_{j,k}$ is defined symmetrically, such that $I_{j,k} = I_{k,j}$. It can be found that intensity is extremely high for many trading pairs in East Asia, frequently exceeding the corresponding figures for European pairs.
5 Appendix 1 shows the results for each East Asian country's trade-intensity.
6 All data were obtained from Datastream. Exchange rates are daily closing rates, and interest rates are the middle of the three month money market rate, except for Indonesia, the Philippines, and Thailand. Details of the data are as follows: US three-month TB, Japan three-month interbank rate, Euro three month interbank rate, Singapore three-month interbank rate (MAS), Malaysia three-month interbank rate, Taiwan Money Market 90 days, and Korea Commercial Paper 91 days. For Indonesia, the Philippines and Thailand, we used interbank call loan rates, since three month money market rates in these countries are officially set and not so active.
7 Investment into the currency basket denominated bonds means a portfolio investment into the bonds denominated in terms of the US dollar, the euro, and the Japanese yen.

References

Bénassy-Quéré, A. (1999). Optimal pegs for East Asian currencies. *Journal of the Japanese and International Economies*, **13**(1), 44–60.

Hartmann, P. (1998). *Currency Competition and Foreign Exchange Markets: The Dollar, the Yen and the Euro*. New York: Cambridge University Press.

Ito, T., Ogawa, E., and Yuri Sasaki, N. (1998). How did the dollar peg fail in Asia? *Journal of the Japanese and International Economies*, **12**(4), 256–304.

Kawai, M. and Akiyama, S. (1998). Roles of the world's major currencies in exchange rate arrangements. *Journal of the Japanese and International Economies*, **13**(4), 334–387.

Ogawa, E. (2001). The Japanese yen as an international currency. In Y. H. Kim and Y. Wang, eds., *Regional Financial Arrangements in East Asia*. Seoul, Korea: Korea Institute for International Economic Policy, pp. 25–51.

Ogawa, E. and Ito, T. (2002). On the desirability of a regional basket currency arrangement. *Journal of the Japanese and International Economies*, **16**(3), 317–334.

Ogawa, E., Ito, T., and Sasaki, N. Y. (2004). *Costs, Benefits, and Constraints of the Basket Currency Regime*. In: Asian Development Bank ed., Monetary and Financial Integration in East Asia: The Way Ahead, Volume 2, Palgrave Macmillan, Basingstoke, pp. 209–239.

Petri, P. A. (1993). The East Asian trading bloc: an analytical history. In J. Frankel and M. Kohler, eds., *Regionalism and Rivalry: Japan and the United State in Pacific Asia*, Chicago: University of Chicago Press, pp. 21–52.

Williamson, J. (2000). *Exchange Rate Regimes of Emerging Markets: Reviving the Intermediate Option*. Washington, DC: Institute for International Economics.

8 Possibilities for the introduction of a currency basket in East Asia, from an OCA standpoint[1]

Eiji Ogawa and Kentaro Kawasaki

1. Introduction

Ever since the East Asian currency crisis, various observers have advocated the view that regional financial cooperation is necessary to prevent another similar crisis. The Chiang Mai Initiatives, a network of bilateral currency swap arrangements among the ASEAN nations plus China, Japan, and Korea (ASEAN +3) are one form of regional financial cooperation. Various developments have given momentum to policy dialogues in the area of international monetary arrangements among East Asian nations. This chapter aims to consider what regional currency arrangement would be most desirable in East Asia.

The experience of the Asian currency crisis is a reminder that the de facto dollar peg was inadequate for East Asian countries, which have close economic relationships with the United States, Japan, and European countries, as well as with other countries in their own region. It follows that if a regional currency arrangement is established in East Asia, regional currencies would have stable linkages with each other and would be stable against a currency basket rather than against a single major currency. The EU created a single common currency, the euro, which was based on its predecessor, the European Currency Unit (ECU). Member countries' currencies were linked with the ECU, a weighted composite and the ECU floated against the US dollar and the Japanese yen. It is likely that a common currency in East Asia would be structured differently from the ECU.

In this chapter, we investigate the possibility of creating a currency basket in East Asia under the optimal currency area (OCA) theory. Bayoumi, *et al.* (2000) used a structural VAR model to make an empirical analysis of an optimal currency area in East Asia. We use a Generalized Purchasing Power Parity (G-PPP) model to analyze the same issue. We investigate which East Asian countries might be able to create a common currency area. Our analytical results suggest that the ASEAN5 countries, plus Korea and China, might be able to form a common currency area, and that if these countries form a common currency area, such a currency basket might be a better anchor currency than the US dollar.

This chapter consists of five sections. Section 2 examines how the creation of a currency basket for East Asia might help resolve coordination failure in exchange rate policies among East Asian countries. In Section 3, we consider the possibilities for creating a currency basket in East Asia by analyzing empirically whether a part of East Asia might be able to form a common currency area with a currency basket as an anchor currency. We use a G-PPP model to investigate which East Asian countries might create such a common currency area. In Section 4, we report our empirical results. In Section 5, based on these empirical results, we discuss policy implications for a common currency area in East Asia. In conclusion, we summarize our considerations for the possibility of creating a currency basket for East Asia.

2.   A currency basket for East Asian countries

Some empirical studies have found that a currency basket system might contribute to stabilizing trade balances and capital flows in East Asian countries. Ito *et al.* (1998, 1999) estimated optimal weights for the US dollar and Japanese yen in a currency basket that would have stabilized trade balances in East Asian countries before the Asian currency crisis. In this estimation, the optimal weight of the US dollar was smaller than the weights estimated by Frankel and Wei (1994) and Kawai and Akiyama (1998). This implies that the better system for stabilizing trade balances would be a currency basket peg system rather than a de facto dollar peg system.

Ogawa and Sun (2001) simulated capital inflows to the three countries hit by the crisis—Thailand, Indonesia, and Korea—if their currencies were pegged to a basket divided 50:50 between the dollar and the yen. The results of their simulation indicated that prior to the Asian currency crisis the *de facto* dollar peg system stimulated capital inflows to the crisis countries.

We should consider why East Asian monetary authorities chose a *de facto* dollar peg system rather than a currency basket peg system. In fact, as McKinnon (2000) and Ogawa (2002a) pointed out, linkages between East Asian currencies and the US dollar have recently returned to high levels, similar to pre-crisis levels. One reason why monetary authorities are reluctant to adopt a currency basket peg system is the prospect of coordination failure in choosing an exchange rate system. As is well known from the prisoner's dilemma in game theory, the first country to adopt a currency basket peg system might temporarily destabilize its currency relations with neighbor countries that still peg their currencies to the dollar.[2]

Ogawa and Ito (2002) used a theoretical two-country model to examine, in an environment where the yen–dollar exchange rate fluctuates, an optimal exchange rate system to minimize trade-balance fluctuation for East Asian countries that export goods to the United States, Japan, and neighboring countries. Their study shows how an East Asian country's best choice of an exchange rate system (or weights in a currency basket) depends on the neighbor country's choice. In a currency basket for the two countries, the dollar's weight is a Nash equilibrium. There may be multiple equilibriums, and a "coordination failure" may result.[3]

Uncertainty about the future dollar–yen exchange rate heightens the possibility of coordination failure when monetary authorities choose an exchange rate system. Suppose the monetary authorities of one country unilaterally switch to a currency basket peg system while a neighbor country keeps the dollar peg system. If the dollar then depreciates against the yen, the country that chose the currency basket peg system might be forced to watch helplessly as its currency appreciates against the currencies of neighbor countries. Given this kind of uncertainty, risk-averse monetary authorities tend to favor a "wait-and-see" strategy.

All risk-averse monetary authorities are likely to take a "wait-and-see" strategy. In game theory this is known as the prisoner's dilemma. Even though monetary authorities know that there is a better cooperative solution, none can help but choose to keep the dollar peg system, which leaves them in a Nash equilibrium. If East Asian countries are ever to shift from a Nash equilibrium to a cooperative solution, coordination among at least some monetary authorities will be necessary.

One possible solution would be international policy coordination aimed at constructing a regional monetary system. For example, all monetary authorities in the region might agree to create a currency basket. Alternatively, they might use a virtual common currency as a benchmark reference in conducting exchange rate policy. A rigid arrangement would be for all monetary authorities in the region to peg their home currencies to a currency basket. A more flexible arrangement would be for them to manage their home currencies in a wider band against a currency basket.

Either case would require the creation of a currency basket that monetary authorities could refer to in formulating an exchange rate policy. This kind of regional currency arrangement could help prevent competitive devaluations among the linked currencies within the region. If the monetary authorities of one country devalue their currency, this devaluation hurts the price competitiveness of products made in neighbor countries. This gives monetary authorities in the neighbor countries an incentive to devalue *their* currencies, creating a possible spiral. A regional currency arrangement might ensure that monetary authorities in the region make a commitment to coordinate exchange rate policies by benchmarking to a currency basket, which could help prevent such competitive devaluation.

Under what circumstances might a group of countries in East Asia use a currency basket? It is clear that the optimal weights for the various currencies in the basket should be the same or nearly so for all participating countries. Thus, the idea of a common currency basket is closely related to the concept of an optimum currency area.

According to the theory of an optimal currency area, the possibility of establishing a common currency area in a region depends on whether the region is an optimal currency area. The literature describes differing views on the characteristics that define an optimal currency area. Mundell (1961) regarded mobility of labor as a necessity for a common currency area, while McKinnon (1963) regarded open economies as a necessity. Symmetry of shocks has also been pointed out as a factor for an optimal currency area (Bayoumi and Eichengreen 1993). In a region where symmetric shocks happen, it is unnecessary to make intra-regional adjustments, and so it is possible to form an optimal currency area. We focus on symmetry of supply shocks because, as long as the natural unemployment hypothesis holds, supply shocks such as productivity shocks and oil price shocks have long-term effects on GDP, while demand shocks have no long-term effects on GDP.

Bayoumi *et al.* (2000) made an empirical analysis of an optimal currency area in East Asia.[4] Their results show that correlations are relatively high among Malaysia, Indonesia, and Singapore. There is also a high correlation between Singapore and Thailand. We may conclude, therefore, that these four ASEAN countries might be able to form an optimal currency area. Moreover, supply shocks in Japan, while having a low correlation with those in ASEAN countries (except Thailand), have a positive correlation with those in Taiwan, Korea, and Australia.

3.   An empirical analysis of an optimal currency area in East Asia

3.1.   G-PPP approach

To empirically analyze an optimum currency area for East Asia, we further extend earlier works of Kawasaki (2000) and Ogawa and Kawasaki (2004). As in earlier works, in this chapter we again use a G-PPP model to conduct our empirical analysis.

The G-PPP model is extended from a simple PPP model by taking into account the difficulties caused in holding PPP by frequent nominal and real shocks, which have ongoing effects on macroeconomic fundamentals. In the long run, changes in the bilateral exchange rates depend on changes in relative prices between the two countries, and also on changes in relative prices between those two countries and other countries. Price levels in other countries may affect domestic prices, because prices of imported intermediate goods may affect prices of domestic products. Therefore, the G-PPP model assumes there are common factors among bilateral real exchange rates of the home currency *vs.* currencies of foreign countries with which the home country has strong economic ties. If countries have strong economic relationships with each other, the real exchange rates between their currencies will exhibit a stable equilibrium in the long run.

The G-PPP model explains that PPP holds if a linear combination of some bilateral real exchange rate series shows long-term equilibrium, even if each individual bilateral rate series is non-stationary.

3.2.   Real effective exchange rates and G-PPP

Now suppose there are m countries expected to adopt a currency basket as an anchor currency. Country j has n trade partners. It has strong trade relationships with m countries, which adopt the same currency basket as Country j, and it has also trade relationships with other countries. Here, the real effective exchange rates of Country j can be defined as follows (Countries $1, 2, \ldots, j, \ldots, m + 1$ have a common currency basket, while countries $m + 2, \ldots, n$ do not share

Table 8.1.1 Summary of empirical analysis : currency basket

Number of countries in the currency area	Korea (Won)	Singapore ($SG)	Indonesia (Rupiah)	Malaysia (Ringgit)	The Philippines (Peso)	Thailand (Baht)	China (Yuan)
3	○	○	○				
		○			○	○	
	○	○				○	
		○		○		○	
			○	○	○		
		○	○		○		○
	○	○					○
4	○		○	○	○	○	
	○	○	○	○			○
	○		○			○	○
	○	○	○			○	○

Table 8.1.2 Summary of empirical analysis : US dollar

Number of countries in the currency area	Korea (Won)	Singapore ($SG)	Indonesia (Rupiah)	Malaysia (Ringgit)	The Philippines (Peso)	Thailand (Baht)	China (Yuan)
4		○	○	○		○	

the common currency basket):

$$ree_j = \xi_j \cdot (\omega_{j,1} re_{j,1} + \omega_{j,2} re_{j,2} + \cdots + \omega_{j,m+1} re_{j,m+1})$$

$$+ (1 - \xi_j) \cdot (\omega_{j,m+2} re_{j,m+2} + \cdots + \omega_{j,n} re_{j,n}), \tag{1}$$

where $\omega_{j,i}$ $\left(\sum_{i=1}^{m+1} \omega_{j,i} = 1,\ \sum_{i=m+2}^{n} \omega_{j,i} = 1\right)$ is Country j's trade weighting with Country i and ξ is the trade weighting among the group of countries that share the currency basket. Here, we assume that the shocks on the second term in the right-hand side of Equation (1) affect the real effective rate of Country j temporarily; even if these shocks are permanent, they affect $m + 1$ real effective rates symmetrically. If only Country j is permanently affected by countries that do not adopt the currency basket as an anchor currency, it is difficult to maintain a common currency in the region, as there would be no reason for Country j to stay in the common currency area. Here, we define the real effective exchange rate in terms of a currency of Country $m + 1$, which is omitted temporary shocks Country j in the long run.

Table 8.2 Maximum number of ranks, 2 information criteria, and residual analysis: P-value

Combination	†1	lags2	lags3	lags4	lags5	lags6	lags7	lags8	lags9	lags10	lags11	lags12 †2
CB301	Rank(s)	0	1	1	0	1	0	0	2	1	1	1
	SBC	-26.22085	-25.9294	-25.49669	-25.17767	-25.00329	-24.75879	-24.50142	-22.00857	-21.62028	-21.34345	-21.19791
	HQC	-26.52551	-26.35722	-26.04362	-25.83986	-25.77714	-25.64088	-25.48852	-23.09762	-22.80837	-22.62783	-22.57596
	LB	199.094 0.89*	189.365 0.96*	191.876 0.95*	183.16 0.98	192.827 0.87*	202.961 0.73*	229.026 0.26*	204.552 0.70*	196.343 0.69*	204.07 0.54*	217.734 0.29*
	LM(1)	10.503 0.31*	7.92 0.54*	12.526 0.19*	15.883 0.07*	4.974 0.84*	4.654 0.86*	17.631 0.04*	24.052 0.00	15.532 0.08*	7.54 0.58*	5.24 0.81*
	LM(4)	7.324 0.60*	6.892 0.65*	7.073 0.63*	5.294 0.81*	6.247 0.72*	2.676 0.98	3.868 0.92*	15.687 0.07*	14.058 0.12*	12.538 0.18*	11.35 0.25*
CB309	Rank(s)	0	0	0	0	0	0	1	3	3	1	1
	SBC	-24.10488	-23.81919	-23.541	-23.32598	-23.10799	-22.90554	-22.75626	-22.64087	-22.37668	-21.97816	-21.73619
	HQC	-24.40954	-24.24702	-24.08792	-23.98817	-23.88184	-23.78763	-23.74336	-23.72992	-23.56478	-23.26254	-23.11423
	LB	219.076 0.60*	229.702 0.40*	237.113 0.28*	231.397 0.37*	235.05 0.18*	246.093 0.08*	250.795 0.05*	242.167 0.11*	237.813 0.07*	244.402 0.04*	253.936 0.01
	LM(1)	2.807 0.97*	4.924 0.84*	11.477 0.24*	8.845 0.45*	7.499 0.59*	6.418 0.70*	16.642 0.05*	8.277 0.51*	8.594 0.48*	6.99 0.64*	4.111 0.90*
	LM(4)	12.711 0.18*	11.034 0.27*	8.72 0.46*	14.009 0.12*	7.321 0.60*	12.054 0.21*	13.41 0.14*	11.815 0.22*	13.678 0.13*	5.506 0.79*	9.108 0.43*
CB311	Rank(s)	0	1	0	0	1	1	1	3	2	2	3
	SBC	-26.76103	-26.51302	-26.13444	-25.83892	-25.72018	-25.5039	-25.28542	-25.12862	-24.78497	-24.50067	-24.26096
	HQC	-27.06569	-26.94084	-26.68137	-26.50112	-26.49403	-26.38599	-26.27252	-26.21767	-25.97307	-25.78505	-25.63901
	LB	235.204 0.31*	239.556 0.24*	230.204 0.39*	234.394 0.32*	220.597 0.40*	234.775 0.18*	243.663 0.10*	241.182 0.12*	234.102 0.10*	234.651 0.09*	243.636 0.04*
	LM(1)	5.491 0.79*	6.112 0.73*	6.648 0.67*	16.228 0.06*	11.35 0.25*	5.672 0.77*	11.678 0.23*	5.921 0.75*	13.731 0.13*	16.939 0.05*	8.186 0.52*
	LM(4)	8.936 0.44*	6.987 0.64*	6.006 0.74*	6.075 0.73*	9.57 0.39*	5.044 0.83*	4.564 0.87*	7.87 0.55*	8.037 0.53*	10.535 0.31*	19.888 0.02
CB315	Rank(s)	0	0	0	0	0	0	0	1	1	1	1
	SBC	-26.40175	-26.22234	-25.92977	-25.68235	-25.55191	-25.31426	-25.11143	-24.92178	-24.59561	-24.3953	-24.0144
	HQC	-26.70641	-26.65016	-26.4767	-26.34454	-26.32576	-26.19635	-26.09853	-26.01083	-25.7837	-25.67968	-25.39244
	LB	243.391 0.19*	228.338 0.43*	225.717 0.47*	233.758 0.33*	226.055 0.31*	228.627 0.27*	236.705 0.16*	239.59 0.13*	234.684 0.09*	241.327 0.05*	248.266 0.03*
	LM(1)	7.697 0.56*	6.507 0.69*	10.717 0.30*	17.261 0.04*	10.003 0.35*	11.923 0.22*	3.953 0.91*	8.189 0.52*	21.378 0.01	8.377 0.50*	11.295 0.26*
	LM(4)	15.676 0.07*	10.742 0.29*	10.876 0.28*	9.634 0.38*	5.087 0.83*	11.129 0.27*	13.078 0.16*	4.584 0.87*	9.627 0.38*	11.25 0.26*	19.676 0.02
CB316	Rank(s)	0	0	0	0	0	0	2	1	1	1	2
	SBC	-26.40772	-26.21989	-25.94439	-25.66839	-25.61743	-25.35435	-25.05906	-22.48445	-22.11876	-21.84019	-21.59274
	HQC	-26.71238	-26.64772	-26.49131	-26.33058	-26.39128	-26.23644	-26.04616	-23.5735	-23.30685	-23.12457	-22.97078
	LB	252.489 0.10*	249.142 0.13*	246.533 0.15*	245.72 0.16*	241.156 0.12*	231.852 0.22*	257.461 0.03*	220.102 0.41*	219.389 0.26*	189.68 0.80*	200.097 0.62*
	LM(1)	14.265 0.11*	11.251 0.26*	11.88 0.22*	24.153 0.00	17.941 0.04*	11.495 0.24*	11.059 0.27*	12.731 0.18*	16.435 0.06*	4.493 0.88*	7.089 0.63*
	LM(4)	11.643 0.23*	9.142 0.42*	7.642 0.57*	6.781 0.66*	12.114 0.21*	12.706 0.18*	16.328 0.06*	24.006 0.00	24.259 0.00	10.916 0.28*	10.098 0.34*
CB324	Rank(s)	0	0	0	0	0	0	0	0	0	0	1
	SBC	-24.46436	-24.22016	-23.87264	-23.61598	-23.44372	-23.20386	-23.04552	-22.76998	-22.38956	-22.23101	-21.88913
	HQC	-24.76902	-24.64799	-24.41956	-24.27817	-24.21757	-24.08595	-24.03262	-23.85903	-23.57765	-23.51539	-23.26718
	LB	192.243 0.94*	196.347 0.92*	193.318 0.94*	205.251 0.82*	197.796 0.81*	199.855 0.78*	202.638 0.73*	218.801 0.43*	215.6 0.33*	225.89 0.18*	244.467 0.04*
	LM(1)	7.4 0.60*	4.025 0.91*	8.907 0.45*	8.878 0.45*	5.436 0.79*	13.616 0.14*	7.75 0.56*	5.34 0.80*	20.908 0.01	6.975 0.64*	12.085 0.21*
	LM(4)	10.05 0.35*	10.16 0.34*	7.992 0.53*	3.321 0.95*	6.595 0.68*	12.72 0.18*	10.064 0.35*	14.385 0.11*	14.282 0.11*	11.976 0.21*	17.229 0.05*

CB335 Rank(s)	0	1	0	0	1	1	0	2	2	2	2
SBC	-23.51983	-23.24617	-22.8484	-22.5376	-22.35517	-22.10509	-21.90234	-21.65465	-21.38037	-21.19254	-20.97901
HQC	-23.8245	-23.67399	-23.39532	-23.19979	-23.12902	-22.98718	-22.88944	-22.7437	-22.56847	-22.47692	-22.35706
LB	208.317 0.78*	199.966 0.88*	216.458 0.65*	217.007 0.64*	211.349 0.58*	217.618 0.46*	225.313 0.32*	210.932 0.58*	212.575 0.38*	237.893 0.07*	252.006 0.02
LM(1)	3.645 0.93*	2.9 0.97*	10.207 0.33*	10.114 0.34*	5.045 0.83*	10.427 0.32*	9.009 0.44*	4.478 0.88*	13.49 0.14*	5.662 0.77*	4.088 0.91*
LM(4)	6.256 0.71*	5.559 0.78*	6.854 0.65*	12.517 0.19*	7.276 0.61*	13.38 0.15*	11.564 0.24*	12.998 0.16*	12.147 0.21*	10.702 0.30*	16.405 0.06*
CB404 Rank(s)	0	0	0	1	1	1	1	1	2	1	2
SBC	-32.51001	-32.22187	-31.81156	-31.37777	-30.93469	-30.62089	-30.25674	-29.7509	-27.3851	-26.60694	-26.35307
HQC	-33.06478	-33.00361	-32.80967	-32.5825	-32.33705	-32.21259	-32.0301	-31.69877	-29.50085	-28.88436	-28.78637
LB	388.281 0.22*	398.022 0.14*	415.058 0.05*	413.7 0.05*	433.99 0.01	417.817 0.04*	437.315 0.01	461.483 0.00	476.589 0.00	391.433 0.19*	417.9 0.04*
LM(1)	26.237 0.05*	16.498 0.42*	19.196 0.26*	17.526 0.35*	23.044 0.11*	13.822 0.61*	13.402 0.64*	27.373 0.04*	23.567 0.10*	26.176 0.05*	18.801 0.28*
LM(4)	13.731 0.62*	9.515 0.89*	10.349 0.85*	10.189 0.86*	12.809 0.69*	20.965 0.18*	18.934 0.27*	30.895 0.01	57.934 0.00	11.012 0.81*	22.356 0.13*
CB406 Rank(s)	0	0	1	2	1	1	1	1	2	1	1
SBC	-36.03677	-35.54797	-35.11143	-34.62372	-34.27158	-33.95367	-33.44468	-33.12949	-30.17651	-29.57632	-29.13976
HQC	-36.59154	-36.32972	-36.10954	-35.82844	-35.67395	-35.54538	-35.21805	-35.07737	-32.29226	-31.85374	-31.57306
LB	393.878 0.17*	386.792 0.24*	377.151 0.36*	382.389 0.29*	395.247 0.16*	417.277 0.04*	431.68 0.01	466.06 0.00	411.765 0.06*	418.594 0.04*	408.983 0.07*
LM(1)	11.058 0.81*	17.206 0.37*	11.442 0.78*	21.019 0.18*	20.167 0.21*	5.766 0.99	25.131 0.07*	16.505 0.42*	17.521 0.35*	10.426 0.84*	19.774 0.23*
LM(4)	12.037 0.74*	6.683 0.98	9.977 0.87*	12.546 0.71*	24.746 0.07*	13.105 0.67*	17.817 0.33*	5.888 0.99	26.113 0.05*	25.411 0.06*	30.958 0.01
CB418 Rank(s)	0	0	0	0	1	0	0	1	2	2	2
SBC	-31.92534	-31.5471	-31.12505	-30.65164	-30.25719	-29.85706	-29.44158	-28.92974	-26.26923	-25.85227	-25.58508
HQC	-32.48012	-32.32884	-32.12316	-31.85637	-31.65955	-31.44877	-31.21494	-30.87762	-28.38498	-28.12969	-28.01838
LB	358.433 0.63*	371.943 0.43*	379.408 0.33*	396.615 0.15*	389.363 0.21*	397.603 0.14*	418.941 0.03*	437.971 0.01	375.113 0.39*	394.744 0.16*	405.687 0.09*
LM(1)	19.262 0.26*	18.302 0.31*	14.75 0.54*	27.895 0.03*	6.872 0.98	7.636 0.96	13.442 0.64*	24.497 0.08*	21.953 0.14*	9.127 0.91*	9.821 0.88*
LM(4)	15.764 0.47*	12.445 0.71*	12.722 0.69*	8.751 0.92*	10.977 0.81*	13.182 0.66*	14.963 0.53*	24.621 0.08*	42.841 0.00	14.349 0.57*	15.763 0.47*
CB426 Rank(s)	0	0	0	0	1	1	2	2	1	1	1
SBC	-33.11203	-32.62422	-32.1471	-31.70395	-31.28518	-30.9883	-30.72947	-30.43824	-29.98484	-29.66688	-29.0521
HQC	-33.6668	-33.40596	-33.14521	-32.90868	-32.68755	-32.58001	-32.50283	-32.38612	-32.10059	-31.9443	-31.4854
LB	347.686 0.77*	360.157 0.61*	351.86 0.72*	365.732 0.52*	369.02 0.48*	378.127 0.35*	399.916 0.12*	414.104 0.05*	412.402 0.05*	440.608 0.01	455.948 0.00
LM(1)	9.592 0.89*	11.035 0.81*	13.419 0.64*	17.829 0.33*	18.029 0.32*	17.055 0.38*	9.248 0.90*	9.089 0.91*	16.788 0.40*	4.651 1.00	11.265 0.79*
LM(4)	13.281 0.65*	7.931 0.95*	11.205 0.80*	6.879 0.98	14.147 0.59*	7.658 0.96*	4.813 1.00	7.85 0.95*	18.862 0.28*	17.846 0.33*	21.139 0.17*
CB428 Rank(s)	0	1	1	0	0	0	1	0	0	0	1
SBC	-33.60422	-33.16457	-32.72377	-32.29825	-32.02852	-31.68507	-31.30122	-30.7452	-27.78329	-27.27472	-26.8223
HQC	-34.15899	-33.94631	-33.72187	-33.50297	-33.43089	-33.27678	-33.07458	-32.69307	-29.89904	-29.55215	-29.2556
LB	390.143 0.20*	396.407 0.15*	388.234 0.22*	391.558 0.19*	373.738 0.41*	377.589 0.35*	399.653 0.12*	477.017 0.00	388.266 0.22*	377.983 0.35*	393.898 0.17*
LM(1)	11.249 0.79*	18.926 0.27*	14.797 0.54*	25.65 0.06*	11.185 0.80*	13.059 0.67*	12.13 0.73*	21.214 0.17*	23.916 0.09*	9.153 0.91*	21.119 0.17*
LM(4)	18.147 0.32*	11.664 0.77*	11.007 0.81*	11.494 0.78*	11.284 0.79*	16.213 0.44*	10.034 0.86*	12.701 0.69*	17.175 0.37*	15.145 0.51*	24.463 0.08*

continued

Table 8.2—Continued

US409 Rank(s)	0	1	2	2	4	2	2	2	2	2	2
SBC	-37.25164	-36.84674	-36.54893	-36.19019	-35.69787	-35.42508	-35.02053	-34.74097	-31.33879	-30.87997	-30.44614
HQC	-37.80641	-37.62848	-37.54704	-37.39492	-37.10023	-37.01678	-36.79389	-36.68884	-33.45454	-33.1574	-32.87944
LB	446.074 0.00	447.708 0.00	414.458 0.05*	418.45 0.04*	413.542 0.05*	425.809 0.02	446.847 0.00	483.86 0.00	475.517 0.00	480.122 0.00	494.301 0.00
LM(1)	15.999 0.45*	25.992 0.05*	25.731 0.06*	22.083 0.14*	19.258 0.26*	13.431 0.64*	18.805 0.28*	19.634 0.24*	27.033 0.04*	15.24 0.51*	16.588 0.41*
LM(4)	26.658 0.05*	24.256 0.08*	24.091 0.09*	11.401 0.78*	4.84 1.00	16.479 0.42*	18.936 0.27*	8.296 0.94*	35.223 0.00	23.802 0.09*	29.056 0.02

*5% of upper and lower tail.

†1: Combination

CB/US301 : Korea + Singapore + Indonesia
CB/US302 : Korea + Singapore + Malaysia
CB/US303 : Korea + Indonesia + Malaysia
CB/US304 : Singapore + Indonesia + Malaysia
CB/US305 : Korea + Singapore + The Philippines
CB/US306 : Korea + Indonesia + The Philippines
CB/US307 : Singapore + Indonesia + The Philippines
CB/US308 : Korea + Malaysia + The Philippines
CB/US309 : Singapore + Malaysia + The Philippines
CB/US310 : Indonesia + Malaysia + The Philippines
CB/US311 : Korea + Singapore + Thailand
CB/US312 : Korea + Indonesia + Thailand
CB/US313 : Singapore + Indonesia + Thailand
CB/US314 : Korea + Malaysia + Thailand
CB/US315 : Singapore + Malaysia + Thailand
CB/US316 : Indonesia + Malaysia + Thailand
CB/US317 : Korea + The Philippines + Thailand
CB/US318 : Singapore + The Philippines + Thailand
CB/US319 : Indonesia + The Philippines + Thailand
CB/US320 : Malaysia + The Philippines + Thailand
CB/US321 : The Philippines + Thailand + China
CB/US322 : Malaysia + Thailand + China
CB/US323 : Indonesia + Thailand + China
CB/US324 : Singapore + Thailand + China
CB/US325 : Korea + Thailand + China
CB/US326 : Malaysia + The Philippines + China
CB/US327 : Indonesia + The Philippines + China
CB/US328 : Singapore + The Philippines + China
CB/US329 : Korea + The Philippines + China
CB/US330 : Indonesia + Malaysia + China
CB/US331 : Singapore + Malaysia + China
CB/US332 : Korea + Malaysia + China
CB/US333 : Singapore + Indonesia + China
CB/US334 : Korea + Indonesia + China
CB/US335 : Korea + Singapore + China

CB/US401 : Korea + Singapore + Indonesia + Malaysia
CB/US402 : Korea + Singapore + Indonesia + The Philippines
CB/US403 : Korea + Singapore + Malaysia + The Philippines
CB/US404 : Korea + Indonesia + Malaysia + The Philippines
CB/US405 : Singapore + Indonesia + Malaysia + The Philippines
CB/US406 : Korea + Singapore + Indonesia + Thailand
CB/US407 : Korea + Singapore + Malaysia + Thailand
CB/US408 : Korea + Indonesia + Malaysia + Thailand
CB/US409 : Singapore + Indonesia + Malaysia + Thailand
CB/US410 : Korea + Singapore + The Philippines + Thailand
CB/US411 : Korea + Indonesia + The Philippines + Thailand
CB/US412 : Singapore + Indonesia + The Philippines + Thailand
CB/US413 : Korea + Malaysia + The Philippines + Thailand
CB/US414 : Singapore + Malaysia + The Philippines + Thailand
CB/US415 : Indonesia + Malaysia + The Philippines + Thailand
CB/US416 : Korea + Singapore + Indonesia + China
CB/US417 : Korea + Singapore + Malaysia + China
CB/US418 : Korea + Indonesia + Malaysia + China
CB/US419 : Singapore + Indonesia + Malaysia + China
CB/US420 : Korea + Singapore + The Philippines + China
CB/US421 : Korea + Indonesia + The Philippines + China
CB/US422 : Singapore + Indonesia + The Philippines + China
CB/US423 : Korea + Malaysia + The Philippines + China
CB/US424 : Singapore + Malaysia + The Philippines + China
CB/US425 : Indonesia + Malaysia + The Philippines + China
CB/US426 : Korea + Singapore + Thailand + China
CB/US427 : Korea + Indonesia + Thailand + China
CB/US428 : Singapore + Indonesia + Thailand + China
CB/US429 : Korea + Malaysia + Thailand + China
CB/US430 : Singapore + Malaysia + Thailand + China
CB/US431 : Indonesia + Malaysia + Thailand + China
CB/US432 : Korea + The Philippines + Thailand + China
CB/US433 : Singapore + The Philippines + Thailand + China
CB/US434 : Indonesia + The Philippines + Thailand + China
CB/US435 : Malaysia + The Philippines + Thailand + China

CB/US501 : Korea + Singapore + Indonesia + Malaysia + The Philippines
CB/US502 : Korea + Singapore + Indonesia + Malaysia + Thailand
CB/US503 : Korea + Singapore + Indonesia + Malaysia + Thailand
CB/US504 : Korea + Singapore + Malaysia + The Philippines + Thailand
CB/US505 : Korea + Indonesia + Malaysia + The Philippines + Thailand
CB/US506 : Singapore + Indonesia + Malaysia + The Philippines + Thailand
CB/US507 : Korea + Singapore + Indonesia + Malaysia + China
CB/US508 : Korea + Singapore + Indonesia + The Philippines + China
CB/US509 : Korea + Singapore + Malaysia + The Philippines + China
CB/US510 : Korea + Indonesia + Malaysia + The Philippines + China
CB/US511 : Singapore + Indonesia + Malaysia + The Philippines + China
CB/US512 : Korea + Singapore + Indonesia + Thailand + China
CB/US513 : Korea + Singapore + Malaysia + Thailand + China
CB/US514 : Korea + Indonesia + Malaysia + Thailand + China
CB/US515 : Singapore + Indonesia + Malaysia + Thailand + China
CB/US516 : Korea + Singapore + The Philippines + Thailand + China
CB/US517 : Korea + Indonesia + The Philippines + Thailand + China
CB/US518 : Singapore + Indonesia + The Philippines + Thailand + China
CB/US519 : Korea + Malaysia + The Philippines + Thailand + China
CB/US520 : Singapore + Malaysia + The Philippines + Thailand + China
CB/US521 : Indonesia + Malaysia + The Philippines + Thailand + China :
CB/US601 : Korea + Singapore + Indonesia + Malaysia + The Philippines + Thailand +
CB/US602 : Korea + Singapore + Indonesia + Malaysia + The Philippines + China
CB/US603 : Korea + Singapore + Indonesia + Malaysia + Thailand + China
CB/US604 : Korea + Singapore + Indonesia + The Philippines + Thailand + China
CB/US605 : Korea + Singapore + Malaysia + The Philippines + Thailand + China
CB/US606 : Korea + Indonesia + Malaysia + The Philippines + Thailand + China
CB/US607 : Singapore + Indonesia + Malaysia + The Philippines + Thailand + China
CB/US701 : Korea + Singapore + Indonesia + Malaysia + The Philippines + Thailand + China

†2 Since we set that DGF are equalized from lags 2 to lags12, the starting point of the sample period for all estimations are valid.
CB/US301-335; DGF = 105, Lags2 = 1988:04, Lags3 = 1988:01, Lags4 = 1987:10, Lags5 = 1987:07, Lags6 = 1987:04, Lags7 = 1987:01, Lags8 = 1986:10, Lags9 = 1986:07, Lags10 = 1986:04, Lags11 = 1986:01, Lags 12 = 1985:10.
CB/US401-435; DGF = 93, Lags2 = 1989:02, Lags3 = 1988:10, Lags4 = 1988:07, Lags5 = 1988:02, Lags6 = 1987:06, Lags7 = 1987:02, Lags8 = 1987:02, Lags9 = 1986:10, Lags10 = 1986:06, Lags11 = 1986:02, Lags12 = 1985:10.
CB/US501-521; DGF = 81, Lags2 = 1989:12, Lags3 = 1989:07, Lags4 = 1989:02, Lags5 = 1988:09, Lags6 = 1988:04, Lags7 = 1987:11, Lags8 = 1987:06, Lags9 = 1987:01, Lags10 = 1986:08, Lags11 = 1986:03, Lags 12 = 1985:10.
CB/US601-607; DGF = 69, Lags2 = 1991:10, Lags3 = 1990:04, Lags4 = 1989:10, Lags5 = 1989:04, Lags6 = 1988:10, Lags7 = 1988:04, Lags8 = 1987:10, Lags9 = 1987:04, Lags10 = 1986:10, Lags11 = 1986:04, Lags 12 = 1985:10.
CB/US701; DGF = 57, Lags2 = 1991:08, Lags3 = 1991:01, Lags4 = 1990:06, Lags5 = 1989:11, Lags6 = 1989:04, Lags7 = 1988:09, Lags8 = 1988:02, Lags9 = 1987:07, Lags10 = 1986:12, Lags11 = 1986:05, Lags 12 = 1985:10.

$$ree^{\xi}_{j,t} = \omega_{j,1}(re_{j,1,t} - re_{j,m+1,t}) + \cdots + \omega_{j,m-1}(re_{j,m-1,t} - re_{j,m+1,t}) + re_{j,m+1,t}$$

$$= \omega_{j,1}re_{m+1,1,t} + \cdots + \omega_{j,1}re_{m+1,m,t} - re_{m+1,j,t}, \tag{2}$$

where $re_{j,k} = re_{j,n} - re_{k,n} = -re_{n,j} + re_{n,k}$ We can write real effective rates in terms of the currency of Country $m + 1$ in the same way (Tables 8.3, and 8.4),

$$ree^{\xi}_{1,t} = -re_{m+1,j,t} + \omega_{1,2}re_{m+1,2,t} + \cdots + \omega_{1,m}re_{m+1,m,t}$$

$$ree^{\xi}_{2,t} = \omega_{2,1}re_{m+1,1,t} - re_{m+1,2,t} + \cdots + \omega_{2,m}re_{m+1,m,t}$$

$$\vdots$$

$$ree^{\xi}_{m,t} = \omega_{m,1}re_{m+1,1,t} + \cdots + \omega_{m,m-1}re_{m+1,m-1,t} - re_{m+1,m,t}$$

$$ree^{\xi}_{m+1,t} = \omega_{m+1,1}re_{m+1,1,t} + \cdots + \omega_{m+1,m-1}re_{m+1,m-1,t} + \omega_{m+1,m}re_{m+1,m,t}.$$

Table 8.3.1 Johansen tests (currency basket)

Combination		k	H_0	Currency basket		
				Eigen vector	L-max	L-trace
301	Korea + Singapore + Indonesia	11	0	0.197	30.270***	41.280***
			1	0.069	9.890	11.010
			2	0.008	1.120	1.120
309	Singapore + Malaysia + the Philippines	11	0	0.242	38.320***	54.130***
			1	0.069	9.900	15.810*
			2	0.042	5.910**	5.910**
311	Korea + Singapore + Thailand	10	0	0.175	25.990***	44.300***
			1	0.106	15.070***	18.310**
			2	0.024	3.240	3.240
315	Singapore + Malaysia + Thailand	11	0	0.321	53.510***	65.200***
			1	0.060	8.560	11.690
			2	0.022	3.120	3.120
316	Indonesia + Malaysia + Thailand	8	0	0.131	18.040***	34.730**
			1	0.113	15.480***	16.690*
			2	0.009	1.210	1.210
324	Singapore + Thailand + China	11	0	0.220	34.300***	39.260***
			1	0.034	4.760	4.960
			2	0.002	0.200	0.200

continued

Table 8.3.1—Continued

Combination		k	H_0	Currency basket		
				Eigen vector	L-max	L-trace
335	Korea + Singapore + China	9	0	0.171	24.690***	41.910***
			1	0.110	15.380***	17.220*
			2	0.014	1.840	1.840
404	Korea + Indonesia + Malaysia + the Philippines	12	0	0.239	38.530***	77.400***
			1	0.155	23.720***	38.860***
			2	0.087	12.840**	15.140
			3	0.016	2.300	2.300
406	Korea + Singapore + Indonesia + Thailand	4	0	0.204	24.890***	51.090**
			1	0.168	20.060***	26.200
			2	0.055	6.130	6.130
			3	0.000	0.000	0.000
418	Korea + Indonesia + Malaysia + China	11	0	0.219	33.940***	67.740***
			1	0.145	21.470***	33.800**
			2	0.070	9.880	12.330
			3	0.018	2.450	2.450
426	Korea + Singapore + Thailand + China	9	0	0.259	39.850***	68.720***
			1	0.156	22.600***	28.870
			2	0.041	5.490	6.270
			3	0.006	0.780	0.780
428	Singapore + Indonesia + Thailand + China	10	0	0.218	32.730***	47.820*
			1	0.065	8.920	15.090
			2	0.044	5.990	6.1170
			3	0.001	0.170	0.170

Table 8.3.2 Johansen tests (US dollar)

Combination		k	H_0	US dollar		
				Eigen vector	L-max	L-trace
409	Singapore + Indonesia + Malaysia + Thailand	4	0	0.226	27.960***	62.010***
			1	0.188	22.730***	34.050**
			2	0.067	7.530	11.330
			3	0.034	3.800	3.800

k: lag length.
*95%, **97.5%, ***99.0%

Table 8.4 Chi-square-based tests

Combination	CHISQ							Korea (Won)	Singapore ($SG)	Indonesia (Rupiah)	Malaysia (Ringgit)	The Philippines (Peso)	Thailand (Baht)	China (Yuan)
	k	r	DGF	10%	5%	2.5%	1%							
CB301	11	1	1	2.71	3.84	5.02	6.63	10.42****	3.42*	19.92****				
		1	2	4.61	5.99	7.38	9.21	23.27****	25.60****	10.66****				
		1	1	2.71	3.84	5.02	6.63	3.52*	15.93****	7.07****				
CB309	11	1	1	2.71	3.84	5.02	6.63		13.81****		24.57****	13.12****		
		1	2	4.61	5.99	7.38	9.21		24.75****		15.52****	27.47****		
		1	1	2.71	3.84	5.02	6.63		26.23****		15.25****	3.54*		
CB311	11	2	2	4.61	5.99	7.38	9.21	10.07****	11.30****				15.05****	
		2	1	2.71	3.84	5.02	6.63	6.87****	7.00****				7.13****	
		2	2	4.61	5.99	7.38	9.21	8.19***	16.41****				5.41*	
CB315	11	1	1	2.71	3.84	5.02	6.63		12.48****		31.48****		7.90****	
		1	2	4.61	5.99	7.38	9.21		39.22****		12.54****		31.67****	
		1	1	2.71	3.84	5.02	6.63		28.05****		15.12****		5.87***	
CB316	8	2	2	4.61	5.99	7.38	9.21			16.67****	13.82****		10.71****	
		2	1	2.71	3.84	5.02	6.63			10.42****	8.77****		11.77****	
		2	2	4.61	5.99	7.38	9.21			15.12****	12.91****		8.18***	
CB324	11	1	1	2.71	3.84	5.02	6.63		10.79****				3.20*	9.41****
		1	2	4.61	5.99	7.38	9.21		19.13****				10.91****	29.23****
		1	1	2.71	3.84	5.02	6.63		22.01****				6.87****	4.04**
CB335	9	2	2	4.61	5.99	7.38	9.21	18.50****	12.21****					13.71****
		2	1	2.71	3.84	5.02	6.63	7.90****	11.31****					11.58****
		2	2	4.61	5.99	7.38	9.21	13.53****	14.11****					6.78**

continued

Table 8.4—Continued

Combination	k	r	DGF	CHISQ				Korea (Won)	Singapore ($SG)	Indonesia (Rupiah)	Malaysia (Ringgit)	The Philippines (Peso)	Thailand (Baht)	China (Yuan)
				10%	5%	2.5%	1%							
CB404	12	2	2	4.61	5.99	7.38	9.21	18.15*****		22.46****	15.58****	14.94****		
		2	2	4.61	5.99	7.38	9.21	11.33*****			8.02***	7.57***	17.46****	
		2	2	4.61	5.99	7.38	9.21	6.76**		12.70****	14.87****	5.26*		
CB406	4	2	2	4.61	5.99	7.38	9.21	12.15*****	12.74****	15.92****			13.73****	
		2	2	4.61	5.99	7.38	9.21	11.45*****	8.40****	13.89****			15.45*****	
		2	2	4.61	5.99	7.38	9.21	11.99*****	6.34**	15.03****			5.32*	
CB418	11	1	1	2.71	3.84	5.02	6.63	11.28****		10.36****	8.41****			7.22****
		1	3	6.25	7.81	9.35	11.34	26.23****		13.84****	14.49****			19.81*****
		1	1	2.71	3.84	5.02	6.63	4.36**		12.42****	3.66*			11.86*****
CB426	9	2	2	4.61	5.99	7.38	9.21	30.98****	29.00****				14.86****	25.57****
		2	2	4.61	5.99	7.38	9.21	16.43*****	15.55*****				29.09*****	26.05*****
		2	2	4.61	5.99	7.38	9.21	17.00****	32.61****				12.55****	4.85*
CB428	10	1	1	2.71	3.84	5.02	6.63		4.82**	13.57****			5.41***	3.08*
		1	3	6.25	7.81	9.35	11.34		28.57****	6.52*			19.20****	24.46****
US409	4	1	1	2.71	3.84	5.02	6.63		16.51****	17.02****			13.07****	12.49*****
		2	2	4.61	5.99	7.38	9.21		18.10*****	15.29*****	9.83****		13.55*****	
		2	2	4.61	5.99	7.38	9.21		10.91*****	18.37*****	13.22*****		14.41****	
		2	2	4.61	5.99	7.38	9.21		8.21***	9.42****	13.35****		14.61****	

Test statistics indicate for "long-run exclusion" (top), "stationarity" (middle), and "weak exogeneity" (bottom), respectively. k is lag-order of ECM, r is row of matrix beta.

†Significance level: *90%, **95%, ***97.5%, ****99%.

These $m + 1$ real effective rates can be shown as the matrix Ω which defines the trade weights, and the vector **re** which includes m elements of the real exchange rate re_{m+1_i} as below,

$$\textbf{ree}_t = \Omega \cdot \textbf{re}_t, \tag{3}$$

where

$$
\underset{(m+1)\times m}{\Omega} =
\begin{bmatrix}
-1 & \omega_{1,2} & \cdots & \omega_{1,m-1} & \omega_{1,m} \\
\omega_{2,1} & -1 & \cdots & \omega_{2,m-1} & \omega_{2,m} \\
\vdots & \vdots & \cdots & \vdots & \vdots \\
\omega_{m,1} & \omega_{m,2} & \cdots & \omega_{m,m-1} & -1 \\
\omega_{m+1,1} & \omega_{m+1,2} & \cdots & \omega_{m+1,m-1} & \omega_{m+1,m}
\end{bmatrix},
$$

and the vector **ree** includes the $m + 1$ real effective rates (Tables 8.5 and 8.6).

Table 8.5.1 Trade weights of East Asian countries

1981:1–1998:12 Trade Partner	China	Indonesia	Korea	Malaysia
United States	12.38%	15.00 %	25.07 %	16.84%
Japan	20.41%	31.66%	20.12%	20.51%
EU Area	10.20%	11.08%	8.85%	10.41%
East Asia (Common Area)	7.31%	19.42%	9.07%	28.16%
Rest of the World	49.70%	22.84%	36.90%	24.08%

1981:1-1998:12 Trade Partner	The Philippines	Singapore	Thailand
United States	27.26%	17.53%	15.39%
Japan	18.87%	14.41%	22.17%
EU Area	10.38%	9.14%	13.22%
East Asia (Common Area)	13.51%	25.78%	18.18%
Rest of the World	29.98%	33.15%	31.04%

Table 8.5.2 Trade weights of the common currency area

1981:1–1998:12 Trade Partner	Common area	Outside area	Basket weight
United States	18.09%	21.56%	37.18%
Japan	20.59%	24.48%	42.22%
EU Area	10.00%	11.94%	20.60%
East Asia (Common Area)	16.07%		
Rest of the World	35.24%	42.02%	

Table 8.6 Johansen tests (US dollar)

Combination	k	H_0	Exogenous weights		
			Eigen vector	*L-max*	*L-trace*
	2	0	0.376	38.240***	81.720
		1	0.212	19.300	43.480
ASEAN5 + Korea		2	0.134	11.640	24.190
	3	3	0.116	9.980	12.540
		4	0.031	2.540	2.560
		5	0.000	0.020	0.020
	3	0	0.368	39.960***	115.730***
		1	0.304	31.530***	75.770***
ASEAN5 + China		2	0.268	27.100***	44.230**
		3	0.125	11.590	17.140
		4	0.059	5.250	5.550
		5	0.003	0.300	0.300
	2	0	0.476	45.920***	133.740***
		1	0.416	38.150***	87.820**
ASEAN5 + Korea +		2	0.261	21.520***	49.670
China		3	0.203	16.100*	28.150
		4	0.109	8.210	12.050
		5	0.050	3.600	3.840
		6	0.003	0.240	0.240

k: lag lengths, upper is for the currency basket, lower is for the US dollar.
*95%, **97.5%, ***99.0%.

Each of the real effective exchange rates is expected to follow a common stochastic trend, because the countries have strong trade relationships with each other and they seem to share common technologies.[5] We assume that the $m+1$ real effective exchange rates share a common stochastic trend. Using Stock and Watson's (1988) common trend representation for any cointegrated system, we can show that the vector **ree**, which is characterized by m co-integrating relations, can be described as the sum of a stationary component and a non-stationary component (Table 8.7).

$$\mathbf{ree}_t = \bar{\mathbf{ree}}_t + \tilde{\mathbf{ree}}_t \tag{4}$$

In this model, the stationary component $\bar{\mathbf{ree}}_t$ is $E(\bar{\mathbf{ree}}_t) = 0$, since the logarithm of the real effective exchange rate can be expected to converge toward the zero-mean in the long run. Therefore, the vector **ree** can only be described as the non-stationary component $\tilde{\mathbf{ree}}$. By the definition of common trend in Stock and Watson (1988), we obtain the following equation:

$$\mathbf{ree}_t = \Phi \cdot \mathbf{w}_t, \tag{5}$$

where Φ is the matrix $(m+1) \times (m+1)$. The vector $\mathbf{w}_t$ is the non-stationary stochastic trend, which is characterized as a random walk. Substituting Equation (5) into

Table 8.7 Chi-square-based tests

Combination	k	r	DGF	CHISQ				Korea (Won)	Singapore ($SG)	Indonesia (Rupiah)	Malaysia (Ringgit)	The Philippines (Peso)	Thailand (Baht)	China (Yuan)
				10%	5%	2.5%	1%							
ASEAN5 + China	3	3	3	6.25	7.81	9.35	11.34		17.09****	23.39*****	23.67*****	18.63****	18.06****	20.56*****
			3	6.25	7.81	9.35	13.28		19.72****	25.79*****	19.55*****	25.42****	21.72****	17.05****
			3	6.25	7.81	9.35	11.34		8.33**	6.68*	10.8 ***	7.84**	10.54***	20.36*****
ASEAN5 + China + Korea	2	2	2	4.61	5.99	7.38	9.21	14.4****	0.92	5.38*	11.32*****	16.85*****	17.77*****	6.52**
		5		9.24	11.07	12.83	16.81	19.01*****	34.03****	35.29****	32.7****	32.58****	28.18*****	28.97****
		2	2	4.61	5.99	7.38	9.21	18.04*****	14.17****	4.34	11.18*****	8.55***	12.34*****	8.22***

Test statistics indicate for "long-run exclusion" (upper), "stationarity" (middle), and "weak exogeneity" (lower), respectively.

Equation (3), we obtain the following equation:

$$\Phi \cdot \mathbf{w}_t = \Omega \cdot \mathbf{re}_t. \tag{6}$$

Here, we define the non-null matrix Ψ, which is composed of $(m + 1) \times (m + 1)$, and rewrite Equation (6) to obtain the following equation:

$$\Psi \cdot \Phi \cdot \mathbf{w}_t = \Psi \cdot \Omega \cdot \mathbf{re}_t. \tag{7}$$

If there exists a nonzero w for which $\Psi \cdot \Phi \cdot \mathbf{w}_t = 0$, $\Psi \cdot \Phi$ does not have a full rank. The rank condition will be expected as follows:

$$\text{rank}(\Psi \cdot \Phi) = \text{rank}(\Phi) < m.$$

As long as the rank condition holds, there exists a non-null matrix Ψ which satisfies the following equation:

$$\Psi \cdot \Phi = 0. \tag{8}$$

When we set $Z = \Psi \cdot \Omega$ and substitute it into Equation (7), we obtain the following equation:

$$Z \cdot \mathbf{re} = 0. \tag{9}$$

If we can find a matrix Z, which satisfies $\text{rank}(Z) < m$ and Equation (9), it means there exists a non-zero **re** for $Z \cdot \mathbf{re} = 0$, and that the matrix Ψ is not a null matrix. Accordingly, the number of rank Ω must be smaller than m. Here, we assume that $\text{rank}(Z) = 1$. We can rewrite Equation (9) to obtain the following linear combination:

$$\zeta_1 \cdot re_{m+1,1} + \zeta_2 \cdot re_{m+1,2} + \cdots + \zeta_m \cdot re_{m+1,m} = 0. \tag{10}$$

This linear combination is the same as that of Enders and Hurn (1994). Therefore, we can use the Johansen and Juselius (1990) method to estimate the co-integrating vector.

3.3.   *Anchor currencies and common currency areas*

We considered the cases of two possible anchor currencies: one the US dollar and the other a currency basket composed of the US dollar, the German mark, and the Japanese yen. We supposed that each of the three major currencies had the same weight in the currency basket, allowing us to define the real exchange rate between each of the seven East Asian currencies and the currency basket as follows:

$$RE_{CB,i} = (RE_{EU,i})^{\alpha} \cdot (RE_{JP,i})^{\beta} \cdot (RE_{US,i})^{\gamma}, \alpha + \beta + \gamma = 1 \qquad (11)$$

where RE is the real exchange rate and (α, β, γ) are the weights of the three major currencies. Equation (11) is rewritten in terms of the logarithm:

$$re_{CB,i} = \alpha \cdot re_{EU,i} + \beta \cdot re_{JP,i} + \gamma \cdot re_{US,i}. \qquad (12)$$

where re is the logarithm of the bilateral real exchange rate.

3.4. Co-integration analysis

We used the Johansen method (Johansen and Juselius 1990) to test whether a long-term relationship can exist in the vector auto regressive (VAR) model. When we estimate the co-integrating vector, given the weights of the three major currencies in the currency basket, endogenous variables in the m-dimensional vector autoregressive model are defined as

$$X' = [re_{CB,1}, re_{CB,2}, \ldots, re_{CB,m}]'. \qquad (13)$$

In the case where there is at least one co-integration relationship between endogenous variables, the m-dimensional vector autoregressive model can be written according to an Error Correction Model (ECM) as follows:

$$\Delta X_t = \sum_{i=1}^{k-1} \Lambda_i \Delta X_{t-1} + \Pi \cdot X_{t-1} + \varepsilon_t, \qquad (14)$$

We tested a hypothesis that the reduced rank of the Π matrix is

$$H_1(r) : \Pi = \upsilon \cdot \zeta$$

where υ is the loading matrix. The reduced rank r is the number of co-integration relationships. Hence, there is a long-term equilibrium among m bilateral exchange rates if the Π matrix is stable, or in other words, if the rank is non-zero.

We tested whether products of the non-stationary vector R_t and the matrix Π, which contained the co-integration vector, were stationary at a significance level of less than 5 percent.

3.5.   Currency basket with equal weights for the dollar, mark, and yen

3.5.1.   Empirical strategy

We analyzed which of the seven East Asian countries (Korea, Singapore, Malaysia, Thailand, the Philippines, Indonesia, and China) could possibly form a common currency area using either the currency basket or the US dollar as an anchor currency. In this chapter, we focus on cases in which more than two countries are included in the linear combinations; therefore, as possible optimal currency areas we examined combinations of three, four, five, six, or seven countries. We defined a currency basket composed of the US dollar, the German mark, and the Japanese yen. In Equation (12) we have defined the weights of the three currencies as equal: $\alpha = \beta = \gamma$.

3.5.2.   Data

In our empirical tests, we used a G-PPP model, and sample data covering the period from October 1985 to June 1997 in seven East Asian countries: South Korea, Singapore, Malaysia, Thailand, the Philippines, Indonesia, and China. Real exchange rates were based on monthly data for nominal exchange rates and consumer price indices of these countries.[6] Other data are from the IMF, *International Financial Statistics* (CD-ROM).[7]

3.5.3.   Empirical results

We conducted Johansen tests for the 198 possible linear combinations. Since the G-PPP model assumes that all real exchange rates in a common currency area must be nonstationary, we conducted unit root tests: the Augmented Dickey–Fuller (ADF) test, and the Kwiatkowski–Phillips–Schmidt–Shin (KPSS) test for each real exchange rate series. These tests confirmed that all series have a unit root. We carefully chose the optimal error correction model with lags according to our strategy. We had several co-integration relationships: 70 combinations for the US dollar as an anchor currency and 49 combinations for the currency basket as an anchor currency. Here, we focus only on combinations in which all countries in a linear combination have significant results on those three tests, because we need to specify the minimum combination of currency areas for all seven East Asian countries.

Table 8.1 shows linear combinations in which all countries involved have at least one long-term stable relationship and show significant results on the three chi-square-based tests. For the dollar, we could find only one currency-area combination in which all countries showed significant results on the three tests: Singapore, Malaysia, Thailand, and Indonesia. For the currency basket, we found 12 combinations in which all countries concerned showed significant results on the three tests. Seven of the 12 combinations group three East Asian countries as a currency area: Korea, Singapore, and Indonesia; Singapore, Malaysia, and the Philippines; Korea, Singapore, and Thailand; Singapore, Malaysia, and Thailand; Indonesia, Malaysia, and Thailand; Singapore, Thailand, and China; and Korea, Singapore, and China. The remaining five combinations group four East Asian countries as a currency area: Korea, Malaysia, the Philippines, and Indonesia; Korea, Singapore, Thailand, and Indonesia; Korea, Malaysia, Indonesia, and China; Korea, Singapore, Thailand, and China; and Singapore, Thailand, Indonesia, and China.

Due to space constraints, in Tables 8.2–8.4[8] we show the results of the co-integrating analysis only for these combinations. Table 8.2 shows the maximum ranks of co-integrating vectors, two kinds of information criteria, and three tests for residuals from 2 to 12 lags in each of nine combinations. Table 8.3 shows the result of the Johansen tests; λ-trace and λ-max tests after selecting the correct lag-order for all ECMs in each of the nine combinations. Table 8.4 shows the results of three kinds of the chi-square-based tests identified as the optimal models.

In comparing the US dollar with the currency basket as an anchor currency, our empirical results revealed three features. First, using the US dollar as an anchor currency, only one combination formed a viable common currency area, but using the currency basket as an anchor currency several combinations formed viable common currency areas. Second, using the US dollar as an anchor currency the common currency area is limited to four ASEAN countries, but using the currency basket as an anchor currency some ASEAN countries could form a common currency area together with Korea or China. Third, using the currency basket as an anchor currency, we found two non-overlapping groups, including all of the East Asian countries; one group consists of South Korea, Malaysia, the Philippines and Indonesia, and the other consists of Singapore, Thailand, and China. Testing the possibility of using the US dollar as an anchor currency, we could not find any combination of complementary groups. Based on these points, our empirical results suggest that a currency basket would be more appropriate than the US dollar as an anchor currency if and when East Asian countries form a common currency area.

3.6. Currency basket with trade weights for the dollar, ECU, and yen

3.6.1. Empirical strategy

In the previous section, we arrived at the conclusion that a currency basket is desirable as an anchor currency, but the equal basket weights we used might not have been the best possible choice for East Asia. We would also like to test the hypothesis that a trade-weighted currency basket might perform better in the long-term stabilization of trade balances.

Again we define a currency basket composed of three major currencies; the dollar, the ECU (this time not the German mark), and the yen. In this basket, we will use weights based on trade volume (exports and imports) with the United States, Japan, and Europe. We investigate currency basket areas with five or more East Asian countries: ASEAN5, ASEAN5 + Korea, ASEAN5 + China, and ASEAN5 + Korea + China. We conduct the Johansen test for each of the combinations. Our empirical analysis using the Johansen co-integrating frameworks follows the arbitrary strategy in Ogawa and Kawasaki (2003) to improve robustness.[9]

3.6.2.   Data

The sample data for our empirical tests covers the period from January 1981 to June 1997.[10] The ECU data and all other data were obtained from the IMF, *International Financial Statistics* (CD-ROM). The export and import data are from the IMF, *Direction of Trade Statistics* (CD-ROM). The values for trade weights for the three major currencies are shown in Table 8.5s. Table 8.5.1 shows trade weights for each of the East Asian countries with various trade partners: the US, Japan, Europe, intra-regional trade in East Asia, and the rest of the world. Table 8.5.2 shows the aggregate trade weights for the trade partners and trade-based weights for the three major currencies in the currency basket.

3.6.3.   Empirical results

Table 8.6 shows the results of the Johansen tests; λ-trace and λ-max tests after selecting the correct lag-order for all ECMs. The combination of ASEAN5 did not pass the pre-test for the Johansen test, which could not reject the null of auto correlation of the residuals in each VAR model, so we excluded this case from our analysis in this section. While we could not find any co-integration relationships in the combination of ASEAN5 + Korea, we found several co-integrating vectors in the combination of ASEAN5 + China and for ASEAN5 + Korea + China.

Table 8.7 shows the result of three kinds of the chi-square-based tests identified as the optimal models. The first row for each vector shows the test statistics for the null hypothesis of $\zeta_{ij} = 0\,(1 \leq j \leq r)$. The second row shows test statistics for stationarity. This test is to check whether the individual series themselves can be stationary. The null is $\zeta = (H_i, \varphi)$. The third row shows test statistics for weak exogeneity for the long-term equilibrium. The null hypothesis is $\nu_{ij} = 0\,(1 \leq j \leq r)$. Here, we focus only on combinations in which all countries involved have significant results in those three tests, because we need to specify the minimal combination for the currency basket area.

From the results of Table 8.7, we see that the ASEAN5 + China could form an optimum currency area using a currency basket with aggregated trade weights for the three major currencies. On the other hand, the combination of ASEAN + Korea + China includes countries for which chi-square test results were insignificant, e.g., the variable Singapore might be excluded from the co-integration relationship and the variable of Indonesia might be exogenous. This means that it might be difficult for the combination of ASEAN5 + Korea + China to form an optimum currency area using a currency basket with aggregated trade weights for the three major currencies.

4.   Policy implications

Our empirical results indicate that the group that includes all seven countries would not be stable in the long run, but the two non-overlapping combinations should have co-integration relationships. This means that each of the two groups would be able to create a different common currency area by using a currency basket and the identical basket weights simultaneously. While the two groups could share the same basket weights, their speed of adjustment toward long-term equilibrium would likely be different. The equilibrium defined by our G-PPP model could be interpreted as the most sustainable value over the long-term for the balance of payments. In the adjustment process toward long-term equilibrium, the two groups might face a deficit or surplus in the current account. If the two groups have different adjustment speeds toward long-term equilibrium, there is a possibility that one group might show an aggregate current account surplus, while the other might show an aggregate current account deficit.

If this occurs, governments would need to coordinate policy between the two groups. We would suggest that the key feature of such inter-group policy coordination should be to employ macroeconomic policies during the adjustment process, including fiscal spending or transfers to adjust the transitional asymmetry in the balance of payments between the two groups. In addition to inter-group policy coordination, we would suggest that the deepening of financial integration and structural economic integration in East Asia might help to equalize the different adjustment speeds between the two groups.

We also found that the combination of ASEAN5 + China could form a currency area using a currency basket of three major currencies weighted by trade volume. This means that the optimal values for ASEAN5 + China would be larger basket weights for the dollar and yen than for the euro. While optimized currency basket weights could lead these countries to stable equilibrium in the long run, international or inter-group policy coordination would still be needed to enlarge the common currency area to include Korea or other countries.

5.   Conclusion

In this chapter, we suggest that in choosing the most desirable exchange rate system, a currency basket may be the best way for East Asian countries to address the problem of coordination failure. From this perspective, it would be natural for a future regional currency arrangement in East Asia to be connected with the creation of a currency basket. In considering a common currency unit for East Asia, Europe's experience with the ECU provides us with useful information. East Asian countries have international trade relationships with Japan, the United States, and European countries, as well as with other regions, and within a region. One possible currency basket for East Asia might include the US dollar, the yen, and the euro as well as other currencies. This would be in contrast to the ECU, which consisted solely of intra-regional currencies.

We used a G-PPP model to investigate the possibilities for a common currency area for some East Asian countries, by examining long-term stable linear combinations among regional currencies. The results of this analysis imply that the ASEAN5 countries plus China and Korea could be good candidates for a currency area with a currency basket as an anchor currency. We also conclude that in forming a common currency area in the region, a currency basket would be more appropriate than the US dollar as an anchor currency. When we investigated the possibilities of forming a currency basket area with more than five East Asian countries using a trade-weighted basket of three major currencies, we found that the combination of ASEAN5 + China could form such a currency basket area. This means that for a currency basket area of ASEAN5 + China, weights based on trade volumes appear to yield the optimal basket values for the three major currencies.

We do not know whether a currency union could be established in the East Asian region in the near future. The possibilities for regional policy coordination depend on the formation of a consensus of policy objectives among East Asian governments. Needless to say, before creating a common currency area, monetary authorities would have to coordinate policy across the region. This would be difficult without common policy objectives. Common objectives for monetary and exchange rate policies would be particularly important for the creation of a common currency area.

Notes

1   The authors thank Yu Yongding for providing data on China.
2   Bénassy-Quéré (1999) and Ohno (1999) analyzed how coordination failure leads monetary authorities to peg the home currency to the US dollar.
3   Ogawa (2002b) and Nakata and Ogawa (2002) conducted empirical analyses of the possibility of coordination failure in choosing exchange rate systems in East Asia. They found the possibility of coordination failure among the ASEAN nations, China, and Korea.
4   Sato *et al.* (2001) used a similar structural VAR method to investigate an optimal currency area for East Asia.
5   Enders and Hurn (1994) developed the G-PPP model based on the real fundamental macroeconomic variables. They assumed these variables shared common trends within a currency area.
6   Although Enders and Hurn (1994) used the wholesale price index to calculate the real exchange rate, we use the consumer price index because we assume two commodities which include the tradable and the non-tradable goods. See Kawasaki (2002) for details of the theoretical background.
7   The Chinese consumer price index was provided by Yu Yongding of the Chinese Academy of Social Sciences (CASS).
8   Results of empirical tests for all 198 combinations are shown in Ogawa and Kawasaki (2003).
9   To improve the robustness for the Johansen co-integration framework, we should choose a lag length by taking into account whether the equilibrium of that model is adequate for the co-integration relationship or not. See details of our strategy to define the unique model in the Appendix of Ogawa and Kawasaki (2003).
10 We were able to obtain Chinese trade data from January 1981 from DOT.

References

Bayoumi, T. and Eichengreen, B. (1993). Shocking aspects of European monetary integration. In F. Torres and F. Givavazzi, eds., *Adjustment and Growth in the European Monetary Union*. Cambridge: Cambridge University Press, pp. 193–229.

Bayoumi, T., Eichengreen, B., and Mauro, P. (2000). On regional monetary arrangements for ASEAN. CEPR Discussion Paper, No. 2411.

Bénassy-Quéré, A. (1999). Optimal pegs for East Asian currencies. *Journal of the Japanese and International Economies*, 13(1), 44–60.

Enders, W., and Hurn, S. (1994). Theory and tests of generalized purchasing-power parity: common trends and real exchange rates in the Pacific Rim. *Review of International Economics*, 2(2), 179–90.

Frankel, J. A., and Wei, S. (1994). Yen bloc or dollar bloc? exchange rate policies of the East Asian economies. In T. Ito and A. O. Krueger, eds., *Macroeconomic Linkage: Savings. Exchange Rates and Capital Flows*. Chicago: University of Chicago Press, pp. 295–355.

Ito, T., Ogawa, E., and Sasaki, N. Y. (1998). How did the dollar peg fail in Asia? *Journal of the Japanese and International Economies*, 12(4), 256–304.

Ito, T., Ogawa, E., and Sasaki, N. Y. (1999). A regional currency system in East Asia. *Stabilization of Currencies and Financial Systems in East Asia and International Financial Cooperation*. Institute for International Monetary Affairs.

Johansen, S., and Juselius, K. (1990). Maximum likelihood estimation and inference on co-integration; with application to the demand for money. *Oxford Bulletin of Economics and Statistics*, 52(2), 169–210.

Kawai, M., and Akiyama, S. (1998). The role of nominal anchor currencies in exchange arrangements. *Journal of the Japanese and International Economies*, 12(4), 334–87.

Kawasaki, K. (2000). A test of OCA in Asian currency area: empirical analysis based on G-PPP theory. *The Hitotsubashi Review*, 124(6), 127–46 (in Japanese).

Kawasaki, K., (2002). Give a new life to the PPP theory: modifying the generalized PPP model. Mimeo.

Kim, T., Ryou, J., and Wang, Y. (2000). *Regional Arrangements to Borrow: A Scheme for Preventing Future Asian Liquidity Crises*, Korea Institute for International Economic Policy, Seoul.

McKinnon, R. I. (1963). Optimum currency area. *American Economic Review*, 53(4), 717–25.

McKinnon, R. I. (2000). After the crisis, the East Asian dollar standard resurrected: an interpretation of high-frequency exchange rate pegging. August.

Mundell, R. A. (1961). A theory of optimum currency areas. *American Economic Review*, 51(4), 657–65.

Nakata, H., and Ogawa, E. (2002). Necessity and scope of coordination for currency system in East Asia. Hitotsubashi University Faculty of Commerce, Working Paper Series, No. 80 (in Japanese).

Ogawa, E. (2002a). Should East Asian countries return to dollar peg again? In P. Drysdale and K. Ishigaki, eds., *East Asian Trade and Financial Integration: New Issues*. Canberra: Asia Pacific Press, pp. 159–184.

Ogawa, E. (2002b). Economic interdependence and international coordination in East Asia. In Exchange Rate Regimes for Asia (Kobe Research Project). (http://www.mof.go.jp/jouhou/kokkin/tyousa/tyou042.pdf), Ministry of Finance.

Ogawa, E., and Ito, T. (2002). On the desirability of a regional basket currency arrangement. *Journal of the Japanese and International Economies*, 16(3), 317–34.

Ogawa, E., and Kawasaki, K. (2003). Possibility of creating a currency basket for East Asia. JBICI Discussion Paper No.5, Japan Bank for International Cooperation.

Ogawa, E., and Kawasaki, K. (2004). Toward an Asian Currency union. In: Yoon Hyung Kim and Chang Jae Lee, eds, Strengthening Economic Cooperation in Northeast Asia, KIEP, Seoul, pp. 311–347.

Ogawa, E., and Sun, L. (2001). How were capital inflows stimulated under the dollar peg system? In T. Ito and A. O. Krueger, eds., *Regional and Global Capital Flows: Macroeconomic Causes and Consequences*, Chicago: University of Chicago Press, pp. 151–190.

Ohno, K. (1999). Exchange rate management in developing Asia: reassessment of the pre-crisis soft dollar zone. ADB Institute, Working Paper Series, No. 1, January 1999.

Sato, K., Zhang, Z., and Mcaleer, M. (2001). Is East Asian optimum currency area? A paper prepared for 2001 Far Eastern Meeting of the Econometric Society in Kobe.

Stock, J. and Watson, M. (1988). Testing for common trends, *Journal of the American Statistical Association*, **83**(404), 1097–107.

Subject Index

Name Index